Affordable Housing and the Homeless

Editor: Jürgen Friedrichs

Affordable Housing and the Homeless

Editor
Jürgen Friedrichs

Walter de Gruyter · Berlin · New York 1988

Prof. Dr. Jürgen Friedrichs
Lehrstuhl für Allgemeine Soziologie und Stadtforschung,
Institut für Soziologie der Universität Hamburg,
Leiter der Forschungsstelle Vergleichende Stadtforschung Hamburg

Library of Congress Cataloging in Publication Data

Affordable housing and the homeless / editor, Jürgen Friedrichs.
p. cm.
A selection of papers initially presented at a symposium on affordable housing, organized by the Ad Hoc Group of Housing and the Built Environment of the International Sociological Association, held Sept. 16-20, 1987 at the University of Hamburg.
Bibliography: p.
ISBN 0-899925-451-9 (U.S.)
1.Housing--Congresses. 2.Housing policy--Congresses. 3.Homelessness--Congresses. 4. Self-help housing--Congresses.
I. Friedrichs, Jürgen.
HD7286.A34 1988 88-18919
363.5'8--dc 19 CIP

CIP-Titelaufnahme der Deutschen Bibliothek

Affordable housing and the homeless / Ed. Jürgen Friedrichs. – Berlin ; New York : de Gruyter, 1988
ISBN 3-11-011-611-1
NE: Friedrichs, Jürgen [Hrsg.]

 Printing: Gerike GmbH, Berlin. Binding: Dieter Mikolai, Berlin. Cover Design: K. Lothar Hildebrand, Berlin. – Printed in Germany.

CONTENTS

PREFACE

Elizabeth Huttman and Willem van Vliet--

In recent years, a relative decline in national revenue growth rates has prompted many countries worldwide to re-arrange their economic and social priorities. Typically, expenditure cutbacks have affected the provision and maintenance of housing, particularly low-income housing.

Among the results have been homelessness and housing deprivation such as squatter settlements. The ways and the extent in which this situation has been developing vary a great deal from one country to another, depending in part on whether the prevailing ideology views housing primarily as a basic human entitlement or as a consumer good and potentially (private) profit-generating commodity, and whether economic factors such as high interest rates and low return on investment dampen new housing starts. Considering the range of approaches to the existing problems, it is of interest to inquire about their effectiveness, to evaluate the reasons behind their success or failure, and to explore the possibilities for adapting a policy or program that has worked in one country to the conditions specific to other countries.

These and other questions drive the research of a growing international network of housing experts organized under the *Ad Hoc Group of Housing and the Built Environment* of the International Sociological Association. During the past decade this group has held meetings and conferences in Uppsala (Sweden), Mexico City, New Delhi, Amsterdam, and most recently in 1987 in Hamburg, Federal Republic of Germany. At these meetings, researchers (primarily sociologists, but also planners, political scientists, economists, geographers, policy analysts, anthropologists, psychologists and others) as well as practitioners have presented and discussed papers, exchanged information, and laid the groundwork for collaborative work.

At the next conference, to be held in June 1988 in Amsterdam, more than 400 participants from around the world are expected. Future meetings are planned for 1989 (possibly in North America; and a site in Eastern Europe) and 1990 (Barcelona). A periodic Newsletter keeps members abreast of each other's activities, relevant events, current developments, and the like.

This book is a selection of papers initially presented at the group's most recent meeting, the symposium on "Affordable Housing: from participation to self-help and shelter for the homeless", held September 16-20, 1987 at the University of Hamburg, Federal Republic of Germany, under the sponsorship of the Volkswagen Foundation. The preparations for this symposium took place on very short notice after a decision in August 1986 at the World Congress of Sociology in New Delhi to submit a proposal to the Volkswagen Foundation.

An Organization Committee consisting of Dan Ferrand Bechmann (France), Jane Darke (Britain), Jürgen Friedrichs (Federal Republic of Germany), and Jaspal S. Marwaha (India) wrote the proposal. Following its positive reception by the Volkswagen Foundation, Jürgen Friedrichs, who headed the committee, did an exemplary job in making the needed local arrangements in a very short time span and in securing publication of this volume soon thereafter. We hope that this timely dissemination of the papers that were presented, discussed and subsequently revised will enhance their usefulness as contributions to the ongoing discussions of ways in which decent housing can be provided so that it is within everyone's reach.

Elizabeth Huttman, Willem van Vliet--
January 1988

AFFORDABLE HOUSING AND HOMELESSNESS: A COMPARATIVE VIEW

Jürgen Friedrichs

The contributions in this book indicate a housing shortage and for some countries a dramatic increase in the number of homeless in advanced industrialized societies. Both problems, affordable housing and homelessness, are related. If a society cannot provide affordable housing, for instance by subsidizing rents, the number of homelessness will increase.

It is the market segment of lower-income households which has posed the problem of adequate provision in all capitalist societies. Over the last two decades, in most cities of these countries, it has been argued that a market equilibrium exists despite some deficits in the low-income segment of the housing markets and in some regions. Now we face, in this segment, a much larger deficit than initially assumed, furthermore, a growing number of homeless people. How can these changes be accounted for?

First of all, they are neither based on manipulations of statistics nor do they seem to be a temporary problem of the next five years. This is evident, if we link the problem of affordability to economic changes in advanced industrialized societies.

These societies transform from goods production to information processing and services. This process has been documented in detail for many countries, for instance the United States (e.g., Bluestone and Harrison, 1982; Stanback and Noyelle, 1982). Production and profit declines in those industries where the product cycle has reached its final stage, such as in shipbuilding, mining, steel production, and - if no process innovations have occurred - in textiles (see, Markusen, 1985). New jobs require either a high qualification or are restricted to lower service entry-level jobs. The decrease in the number of jobs in old industries has not been compensated by new jobs, and even if this were possible, the changes in the qualifications required ("mismatch") still lead to mass-unemployment and a rising number of households on public assistance (see, Kasarda and Friedrichs, 1985). Cities such as Liverpool, Lille, Duisburg, Barcelona, and Detroit may serve as examples for the resulting social problems.

The consequences for the homeless are vividly described in the contribution by Culhane and Fried. To cite one homeless, Manny, and his perception of the situation: "These things, when I began to smell myself, these things told me something about society. These things told me that society says ‘You are now unprotected. You are now no good to us‘".

The exact number of homeless in a country is difficult to estimate. The figuress supplied for France by Bechmann-Ferrand, and for the U.S. by Huttman, indicate the magnitude of

Affordable Housing and the Homeless

the problem and their alarming increase. The term "new" homelessness as used in West Germany to denote the situation - at least for West Germany - appropriately. In the early 1960s there was a large number of homeless as a result of the post-war housing shortage, their figure dropped considerably in the following decades, and rose again in the mid-1980s, this time due to economic problems.

Relating the problems of affordable housing and homelessness to structural economic changes, we may further assume that both problems will aggravate. The number of dwellings available for rent at affordable prices is continuously decreasing. First, the stock is reduced by demolishing old buildings and by modernization of buildings resulting in higher rents. Second, apartments are converted into condominiums, supporting the trend from rent toward ownership. This is documented in the contributions by Thorns and van Vliet--.

In addition, as the U.S. experience shows, hotels often used to house homeless are transformed into appartments, a process described by Huttman. Second, new construction is done in Europe on a very small scale if compared with construction figures in the 1960s and even the 1970s. New construction no longer compensates for the losses in the stock.

Thus, we may forecast a declining supply. On the demand side, there is little hope for an economic recovery in general, and hence an increase in renters able to pay their rent or an even higher rent. Taking West Germany as an example, the Research Institute of the Federal Agency of Labour has calculated that the unemployment rate will increase beyond the year 2000 if the economic growth rate remains below 2.5 percent, and the female participation rate does not increase. Over the last three years, the GNP in West Germany has grown by 2.0 percent (1985), 2.5 percent (1986), and 1.7 percent (1987). In the same period, the unemployment rate was around 9 percent, up to 9.9 in 1987 with a high variation among regions. In addition to these 2.5 million unemployed more two million persons were on public assistance (2,058,000 already in 1985).

Even in those large cities exhibiting economic growth and low unemployment rates such as Munich and Stuttgart in West Germany, London in the United Kingdom, Boston or New York in the United States, growth did not affect all social strata. The number of persons unemployed or on public assistance and the number of homeless did not decrease. Instead, we observe a growing social polarization (e.g., by income). As Murie and Forrest phrase it in their contribution: "Homelessness is one symptom of multi-dimensional exclusion from the social consumption norms of the majority". Processes of gentrification in inner-city neighborhoods are one of the spatial outcomes of these social changes (Berry, 1985; Smith and Williams, 1986).

There is little doubt that the problems of affordability and homelessness will continue to accompany the structural economic changes. As a further consequence, "affordable housing", supplied to a large extent in new housing estates is no longer affordable for many households living there.

Affordability of housing is--like poverty--a relative term, depending upon the level and quality of provision a country wants to supply and can supply. At present, the problem seems to be aggravated by the rising social disparities which were outlined above. It is poverty amongst the plenty. If such processes occur, the "relative deprivation", as conceived by Merton (1957), increases and will result in growing social antagonism.

Socialist Countries

Having discussed the problems of affordable housing in cities in capitalist countries, we may now turn to cities in socialist countries and ask how their local (or federal) administrations try to solve the problem. The contribution about Prague by Kerner gives some clues; to put them into a broader perspective, some data for other cities in Eastern Europe shall be added. (For a more detailed analysis, see Friedrichs, 1988.) The article by Kerner demonstrates the tremendous efforts made in Czechoslovakia, and in Prague in particular, housing is heavily subsidized, rents and repair costs are extremely low compared with prices in capitalist countries. However, neither Prague nor other major cities in socialist countries have managed to cope with the excess demand for housing.

In these countries, the basic problem is to provide housing for all social groups. The estimated housing shortage in capital cities as by 1979/1980 were (Friedrichs, 1988): Budapest: 96,000 dwellings, (stock: 726,691 dwellings), Moscow: 844,148 dwellings, (stock: 2,542,000 dwellings), Prague: 65,728 dwellings (stock: 448,034 dwellings), Warsaw: 80,658 dwellings (stock: 513,501 dwellings).

The considerable housing shortage, in turn, has led to several problems related to the question of affordable housing. First, to cope with the shortage, both in Budapest and Warsaw, communal dwellings are sold to households. Certainly, this is not socialist in a strict sense. The reasoning behind this strategy is twofold: to acquire funds for further communal construction and to benefit from private savings. One of the consequences is that housing is made accessible only to those with a high amount of savings, a further consequence is a reduction in state/communal control over the housing "market".

Second, in Budapest, Prague and Warsaw we find a trend to reduce communal housing construction in favor of cooperative housing. This may be interpreted - irrespective of the extent of this measure in each of these cities - as a trend towards withdrawal from state intervention into the housing market or housing supply.

Third, we can observe the advent of a crisis in affordability of housing. Some of the problems of large new housing estates, as described in the contribution of Friedrichs for West Germany, also refer to such new housing estates in socialist countries. Rents are extremely low, in contrast, prices for consumer goods are very high, but the costs for new construction and repair are increasing. Discussions with representatives from planning departments and universities in Budapest, Prague and Warsaw in two conferences on "Housing Problems in Socialist Countries" (Andrzejewski et al.; 1986, Borovicka and Kerner, 1986; Brenner et al., 1986) revealed that prefabricated elements and the concrete itself show dramatic symptoms of decay in both Western and Eastern European new housing estates. To cope with the rising costs for repair, tenants in Prague, for example, will have to pay a larger share of repair costs. In addition, it is planned to raise the rents.

Policies

The crisis of affordable housing and shelter for the homeless is a result of economic changes, therefore, it is impossible to solve these problems by urban planning by just providing homes or by transfer payments. This brings us to the question of policies to ameliorate these "new" social disparities.

The articles in this volume do refer to highly industrialized societies, which are as well rich societies. However, none of them has solved the problem of affordable housing. Excluding socialist countries, we may argue that all mechanisms of state or local intervention into a capitalist housing market have not achieved - or not secured - equal justice in housing provision for all social groups.

We are facing a situation of rich industrial societies not capable or not willing to supply a sufficient number of affordable dwellings for both the lowest income groups and the homeless. The policies described for Great Britain (Darke and Darke, Murie and Forrest), Australia and New Zealand (Thorns), and the United States (Huttman, van Vliet--) seem to have some elements in common: governments rely upon home-ownership to a growing extent and seem to have little propensity to subsidize social housing on the necessary larger scale.

A different position is proposed by Karyd. He argues that "dwellings are only to a very limited extent substitutes for each other". If this were a correct empirical proposition, we may conclude that only a broad range of dwellings offered would meet the more differentiated demand - which in turn is the result of greater differentiation of lifestyles in advanced societies. However, the situation is more complex: As noted above, we observe differentiation *and* in a larger segment of these societies and a growing social underclass (Wilson, 1985) at the same time. It is this underclass of low-income or transfer-payment depending households which are in need of affordable dwellings; for them substitution is more feasible.

A more provocative point is Karyd's assertion, that housing policies ignoring market laws - like Sweden - are using an "oystrich approach". His assumption, that subsidies to households will rise rent levels and have only a marginal effect on the quantity of housing supplied will be shared by many economists. This is one of the reasons why in West Germany a double subsidy-system was introduced after the Second World War: to subsidize households below a defined net household income and to subsidize the construction of dwellings in social housing projects, and to rent such dwellings by a local administration only to households below that income limit.

As the articles by Darke and Darke and by Thorns show, neither socialist nor conservative governments have succeeded in solving the housing problem, even the socialist governments in Australia have dismissed their initial policies in favor of a free-market, anti-Welfarist, policy. In more general terms: In most countries we can observe a trend toward less state intervention and from collective to individual provision. This holds true even for socialist countries, such as Czechoslovakia, Hungary, and Poland, albeit on a different level and magnitude.

With respect to policy conclusions the contributions in this volume offer mixed suggestions. Most authors agree that it is the responsibility of the government or the society at large to help the lower income groups. Many European countries had the tradition of governmental subsidies for rental dwellings, which were then managed or owned by non-profit housing organizations - sometimes owned by the local government.

An additional strategy may be self-help as suggested in the article by Turpijn. He reports that already half of the Dutch population are self- builders. To increase self-help, the major target group, low-income households, have to be stimulated by local authorities to build and to conform to building standards or regulations. To be effective, one of the main problems of self-help has to be solved by local governments: to define building standards meeting the essential requirements but as well compatible with the financial means and qualifications of the potential self-helpers.

A historic example of self-help strategies is supplied by Andernacht in his review of the Goldstein project from the 1920s. Initially aimed at supplying dwellings for low-income households, the project failed to pass legislation and was suspended. When it was finally realized it served more to supply labour and jobs then to result in a large number of homes, as the author concludes. Could this, nonetheless, be a useful strategy? Can it be transferred to our time and to other countries? These questions remain to be answered.

The final conclusion to be drawn from these trends is pessimistic. Housing departments or private investors cannot solve national economic problems. They can at best alleviate them. The problem of affordable housing thus remains a problem of economic growth of a society.

References

Andrzejewski, A., Dangschat, J. and Gorynski, J., 1986: Wohnungswirtschaft in Polen. *Archiv für Kommunalwissenschaften* 25, 219- 239.

Berry, B.J.L., 1985: Islands of Renewal in Seas of Decay. In: P. E. Peterson (ed.): *The New Urban Reality*. Washington, D.C.: The Brookings Institution.

Bluestone, B. and Harrison, B., 1985: *The Deindustrialization of America*. New York: Basic Books.

Borovicka, B. and Kerner, A., 1986: Wohnungspolitik in der CSSR und in Prag. *Archiv für Kommunalwissenschaften* 25, 240-251.

Brenner, J., Szücs, I. and Kiehl, K., 1986: Die gegenwärtige und zukünftige Wohnungsversorgung in Budapest. *Archiv für Kommunalwissenschaften* 25, 252-266.

Friedrichs, J., 1988: Large Cities in Eastern Europe. In: M. Dogan and J.D. Kasarda (eds.): *The Metropolis Era.* Vol. 1. Beverly Hills-London: Sage, pp..128-154.

Kasarda, J.D. and Friedrichs, J., 1985: Comparative Demographic- Employment Mismatches in U.S. and West German Cities. In: E.L. Simpson and I.D. Simpson (eds.): *Research in the Sociology of Work. Vol. 3: Unemployment.* Greenwich-London: JAI-Press.

Markusen, A.R., 1985: *Profit Cycle, Oligopoly, and Regional Development.* Cambridge, Mass.: MIT-Press.

Merton, R.K., 1957: *Social Theory and Social Structure.* Glencoe, Ill.: Free Press.

Smith, N. and Williams, P. (eds.), 1986: *Gentrification of the City.* Boston: Allen and Unwin.

Stanback, T.M., Jr. and Noyelle, T.J., 1982: *Cities in Transition.* Totowa, N.J.: Allanheld, Osmun.

Wilson, W.J., 1985: The Urban Underclass in Advanced Industrial Society. In: P.E. Peterson (ed.): *The New Urban Reality.* Washington, D.C.: The Brookings Institution.

PART ONE:
GENERAL ISSUES

GROWTH RESTRICTIONS AND AFFORDABLE HOUSING: DWELLINGS VERSUS PEOPLE

Willem van Vliet

Introduction

In the United States, differential patterns of investment and concomitant population shifts have contributed to various regional inequities. Some regions are characterized by disinvestment, unemployment and loss of population, whereas others benefit from new opportunities for economic expansion and experience rapid population increases (Bluestone and Harrison, 1982; Sawers and Tabb, 1984).

In these widely divergent regional contexts, communities have developed quite different, indeed often contrasting, responses to economic and demographic growth. On the one hand, there are communities in depressed areas that go out of their way to offer enticements for private enterprises considering potential business sites. Generous tax abatements and the gratis provision of infrastructure are among the incentives commonly offered (see, e.g., Feagin 1983, ch. 2). A literature that has developed in this connection contains political, demographic and theoretical analyses of the forces favoring growth (e.g., Humphrey and Krannich, 1980; Humphrey and Buttel, 1980; Logan, 1978; Lyon, Felice and Perryman, 1981; Molotch, 1976). The timeliness of the concern with growth is illustrated by a meeting of the U.S. real estate and development industries held this fall, where it was a central agenda topic (Lowenstein, 1987).

On the other hand, there are communities that attempt to restrict growth for fear of adverse effects on the quality of community life. There are concerns, for example, that uncontrolled growth may cause excessive demands upon the community's existing transportation system, medical services, and schools. Other problems may exist with respect to the natural environment, including negative impacts on recreational resources, air quality, and water supplies. In light of these potentially serious threats to the quality of community life, a number of communities have adopted growth management schemes. The stated purpose of these controls is typically to restrict new residential construction. Among the techniques employed in this connection with varying degrees of success are impact fees on new development, building codes, construction moratoria, zoning ordinances, and sub-division regulations (see, e.g. Burrows, 1978; Dowall, 1984; Scott, 1975). There is a growing body of research on the characteristics of people who favor growth controls versus those who oppose it and on the degree to which public officials represent the views of the population at large or those of special interest groups (e.g.,

Affordable Housing and the Homeless

Baldassare, 1981, 1982; Baldassare and Protash, 1982; Connerly, 1986; Gottdiener and Neiman, 1981; Neiman and Loveridge, 1981; Protash and Baldassare, 1983).

This paper is concerned with a central controversy surrounding the use of growth restrictions. It has been claimed that one of the results of these practices, whether unintended or not, is the exclusion of moderately priced housing (e.g., Frieden, 1982). The scarcity of land, the limited number of building permits issued, and so forth, are viewed as driving up the price of existing stock and newly constructed dwellings. The adoption of such growth limitation ordinances is seen as posing a threat to the provision of moderate-cost housing at a time when home ownership problems are already viewed by many to have reached crisis proportions (Schwartz, Hansen and Green, 1984; Lillydahl and Singell, 1986).

In a recent study, Miller (1986) compared house prices in Boulder, Colorado, (and those in several surrounding communities lacking such controls), before and after the introduction of a growth-control plan in 1977, with those reported by Schwartz, Hansen and Green (1981, 1984) in their comparison of Petaluma and Santa Rosa in California. On the basis of his research results, Miller challenged the conclusion that growth limitations necessarily eliminate low-price housing, suggesting that in the case of Boulder various policy and market factors mitigated the anticipated price increases. Boulder's experience should be of interest to communities elsewhere in the country which face similar circumstances and which might want to consider adapting elements of Boulder's approach to their particular situation. In this light, careful examination of the developments in Boulder is of broader significance.

Without disputing the ostensible validity of Miller's observations, this paper proposes a broader perspective on the issue. Specifically, it argues that it is inappropriate to focus exclusively on (part of) the supply-side of the housing market (i.e., the dwellings and then only the ones sold) and that it is necessary to consider also the demand side (i.e., the people). Additionally collected data on the Boulder population lead to conclusions clearly at variance with the more optimistic assessment arrived at by Miller.

The rest of this paper is structured as follows. First, the methods, findings and conclusions of Miller's study are summarized. Several main points are highlighted. Against this background, the approach based on dwellings is contrasted with a people-oriented approach and corroborative data are presented. The paper concludes with comments that emphasize caution in conclusions regarding effects of growth management and underlines the importance of integral consideration of supply *and* demand in policy-related housing research.

The Dwellings

The purpose of Miller's (1986: 319) study was "to contrast the effects on moderate-priced housing of a growth control ordinance in Petaluma, California, with the effects in Boulder,

Colorado, whose growth control ordinance was modeled after Petaluma's." To this end, Miller examined availability of moderate-priced units, changes in the characteristics of houses sold, and sale prices of new single family homes both before and after enactment of Boulder's growth limitation ordinance, principally re-analyzing data previously collected from the County Assessor's record of transactions.

Results of the comparison point up two chief observations. First, in Petaluma, Ca., the proportions of moderate-price new detached homes (sold at or below $25,000 in 1970 dollars) dropped from 87% in 1973, the year its growth limitation ordinance was enacted, to 15% in 1974 and 3% in 1976. In Santa Rosa, 16 miles north of Petaluma and without a growth limitation, the proportion of new detached dwellings fluctuated around 38% throughout that same period.

In contrast, Boulder was already a relatively expensive housing market even before growth controls were enacted. In the preceding years, the proportions of houses that were sold at moderate prices ranged from 29% (1974) to 34% (1976). In 1977, the onset of the growth limitations, that percentage dropped to 18%, declining further to 12% in 1981, before rising back to 26% in 1984 (Miller, 1986: 322).

Second, Miller explains the continued existence of a relatively high proportion of moderate-priced homes in Boulder (in comparison with Petaluma) by a significant shift to owner-occupied attached housing. Indeed, the number of attached homes as a proportion of all homes sold in Boulder jumped from 3% in 1976, to 9% in 1977, to 32% in 1978, to 49% in 1984 (p. 323). This shift resulted from four factors: (1) the conversion of about 1,000 apartment units into condominiums; (2) incentives in the growth limitation ordinance and Boulder Valley Comprehensive Plan to construct attached units in the center of town; (3) a 1973 ordinance requiring that 10% of all new units be affordable to people of modest means; and (4) the natural market for small attached units associated with universities (ibid.). Miller concludes that the above policy and market factors combined to mitigate the effects of the price increase of detached homes on the housing market overall and, in addition, that Boulder was able to avoid homogenizing consequences to community demography and economy as seen in Petaluma after the adoption of growth restrictions (p. 325).

As phrased, the first part of this conclusion is correct, and we do not wish to take issue with. However, it only partially covers what has, in fact, happened and several additional observations are in order to get a fuller picture of the developments that took place in Boulder.

To begin with, as Miller himself points out (p. 322) the maintenance of a (comparatively) sizeable proportion of housing in the low- to moderate-cost sector in Boulder has been due to very significant changes in characteristics of the housing stock. These changes included in particular the already noted increase in the number of attached homes and a precipitous decline of 22% in the square footage of homes sold (from 1,620 sq. feet in 1973 to 1,260 sq. feet in 1984; p. 325). Significantly, Miller writes that "while Boulder homebuyers paid less, they also received less" (p. 325).

Indeed, when one examines strictly comparable data only, Miller's (1986) findings on the effects on house prices of the growth limitations in Boulder appear to be completely in line with those obtained by Schwartz et al. (1986) for Petaluma. In 1976, the year before the growth ordinance was initiated, a new house in Boulder was only $15,000 more expensive (in 1984 dollars) than like houses in the rest of the county and 16% of all Boulder sales in 1976 were of new detached houses. By 1984, new single-family detached houses were almost $37,000 more expensive than in the rest of Boulder County, and they represented only 3% of the sold stock in the city (Miller 1986: 323).

Figure 1: Assessed Median House Values in Boulder, Census Tracts, 1970-1980

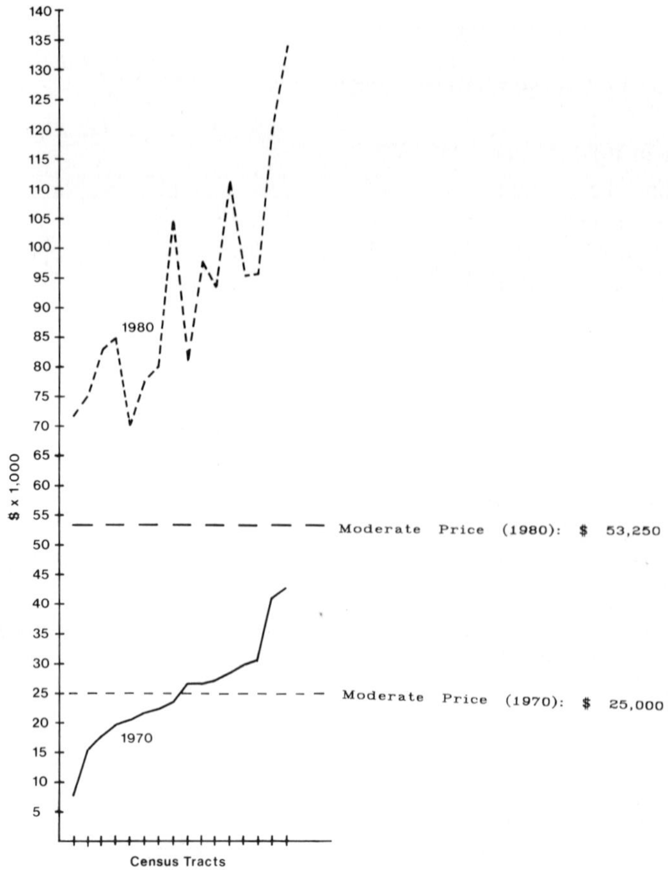

Source: U. S. Bureau of the Census, 1972: Table H-1, pp. H10-11; 1983: Table H-1, pp. 26-28.

To sum up, Miller's study leads to two conclusions. First, after a decline that coincided with the adoption of growth controls, the proportion of moderate-price housing in Boulder was maintained, thanks to various policy and market factors, at a clearly higher level than had been the case in Petaluma. Second, the maintenance of a low-cost housing stock could only occur because the stock underwent a metamorphosis, one which involved a very significant increase in the proportion of attached units and a steep decrease in the average square footage of houses sold.

A Broader View

The second of the above-mentioned conclusions is very important because it begins to give more meaning to the notion of moderate-price housing than a narrow focus on sale price alone. Indeed, labeling moderate-price housing so merely because of its price is misleading, as it says nothing about other important qualities of the house such as its size, type, structural condition and location vis-a-vis jobs, schools, shops, and the like.

It is also important to remember that Miller's analysis included only houses that had actually been sold. A fuller examination of the effects of growth limitations on housing should examine the entire housing market (i.e., owner-occupied and rental units) and not only part thereof (i.e., owner-occupied units that were sold). Such a broader analysis in the case of Boulder reveals several points (see Table 1). Among them, between 1970 and 1980:

1. The renter population *grew* by 19% from 39.7% to 47.2%, when the national figure *fell* by 8.2% to 30.7%.

2. The low-rent index declined by more than 22% to 12.4%.

3. The rental vacancy rate rose by 34%.

4. Median house values jumped up by almost 300% to $86,500 in 1980 (against a 1980 median value of $47,200 for the U.S. as a whole, representing a much lower gain: 178%).

5. Owner-occupied housing as a proportion of all housing units *de*creased by 7.8% when the national rate *in*creased by 2.4%.

6. The homeowner vacancy rate jumped by more than 400% (against 50% for the entire U.S.).

The preceding statistics appear to show that, in Boulder during the 1970's, escalating house values put ownership beyond the reach of a growing number of households, resulting, among other things, in higher vacancy rates. Concomitant to this trend has been an increase in renters who were faced with a declining number of low-rent units.

Table 1: Selected Housing Characteristics for Boulder and the U.S, 1970 and 1980

Housing Characteristics	1970	1980	1970-1980 % Change
Detached Houses (%)			
Boulder	54.3	45.3	-16.6
USA	66.2	66.2	- 6.1
Low-Rent Index (%)			
Boulder	15.9	12.4	-22.2
USA	39.8	37.0	7.0
Median House Value			
Boulder	$23,000	$86,500	+296.7
USA	$17,000	$47,200	+177.7
Owner-occupied Housing Units (%)			
Boulder	51.0	47.0	- 7.8
USA	2.9	64.4	+ 2.4
Renter Population (%)			
Boulder	39.7	47.2	+19.0
USA	33.4	30.7	- 8.2
Renter Vacancy Rate			
Boulder	3.5	4.7	+34.0
USA	6.6	7.1	+ 7.6
Homeowner Vacancy Rate			
Boulder	.7	3.6	+414.3
USA	1.2	1.8	+50.0

Source: Pay et al., 1985: 36, 38, 40, 47, 49, 50, 51.

Very clearly, the picture of moderater cost housing that now emerges is quite different from that found by Miller in his more restricted analysis of sold dwellings only. The salience of the shift in the proportion of moderate-price housing is perhaps most clearly illustrated in Figure 1. It shows that in 1970 in eight of the 16 census tracts on which data were available the median house value was below moderate cost ($25,000; the criterion used by Miller (1986: 322), while in 1980 none out of 19 census tracts fell in that category ($53,250 or less).

In view of the shift to attached housing, the decline in square footage, and the sharply increased cost of housing overall, one wonders how the growth restrictions affected people. Did incomes, in fact, increase in pace with housing costs or did cost-income ratios change? Do we find changes in population composition? It is to these questions that we turn next.

Table 2: Income Characteristics of the Boulder and U.S. Population, 1970 and 1980

Income Characteristics	1970	1980	1970-1980 % Change
Low-income Families			
Boulder	32.3%	34.9%	+ 8.1
USA	33.5	35.0	+ 4.5
Middle-income Families			
Boulder	43.0%	37.3%	-16.6
USA	43.1	40.5	- 6.1
High-income Families			
Boulder	24.7%	27.8	+21.0
USA	23.4	24.6	+ 4.9
Families Below Poverty Level			
Boulder	5.2%	6.9%	+32.7
USA	10.7	9.6	-10.3

Source: Pay et al., 1985: 23, 30-32.

The People

Let us first look at income. Table 2 shows a polarization trend, as the proportions of high- as well as low-income families increased, while that of middle-income families declined. These trends are in line with, but very much more pronounced, that those seen for the U.S.

as a whole during the 1970-1980 period. Moreover, while nationally the proportion of families below the poverty line dropped by more than 10%, in Boulder it rose by almost 33%. In and of themselves, these figures are relatively meaningless because they must be seen in relation to changes in housing cost.Information in this connection is found in Figures 2 and 3.

Figure 2: Ratios of Mean Family over Median Assessed House Values in Boulder, Census Tracts, 1970-1980

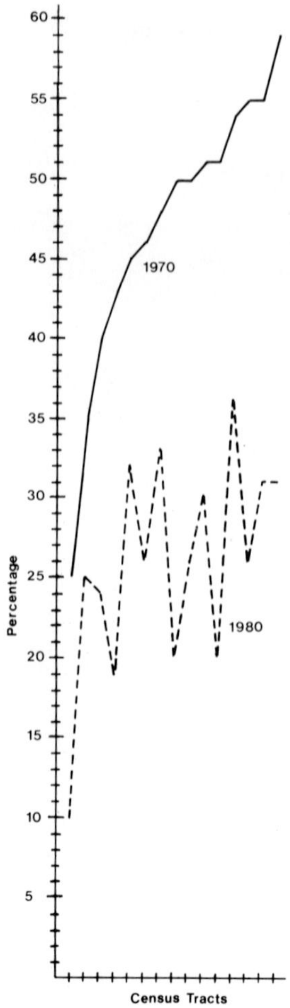

Source: U.S. Bureau of the Census, 1972: Table P-4, pp. P100-101; 1983: Table P-11, pp. P305-307.

Figure 2 shows the ratio of median family income over median assessed house value for Boulder census tracts in 1970 and 1980. During this ten-year period, this ratio declined very significantly without exception. This development provided existing owners with tremendous equity gains, but made home purchase greatly more costly for those wanting to trade up and much more so still for new and first-time buyers.

Figure 3: Median Rent as a Proportion of Median Family Income in Boulder, Census Tracts, 1970-1980

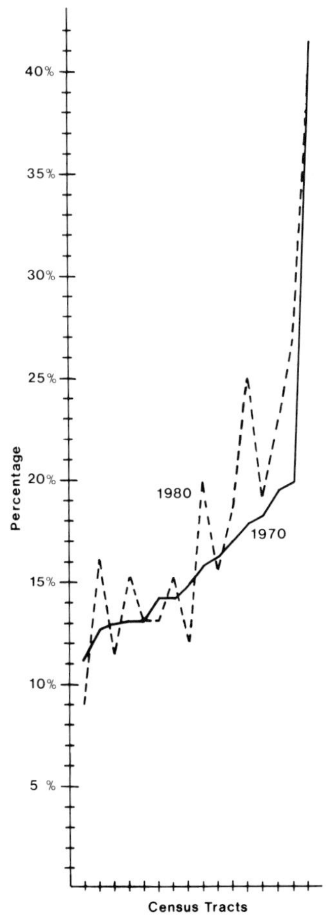

Source: Bureau of the Census, 1972: Table H-1, pp. H10-11; 1983: Table H-1, pp. H26-28.

Table 3: A Comparison of Selected Demographic Characteristics of the Boulder and U.S. Population, 1970 and 1980

Demographic Aspect	1970	1980	1970-1980 % Change
Family Households (%)			
Boulder	68.5	50.2	-26.8
USA	81.2	73.9	- 9.0
Population Under 5 (%)			
Boulder	7.5	3.9	-47.5
USA	8.4	7.2	-14.5
Population Between 5-18 (%)			
Boulder	24.2	13.4	-29.7
USA	25.8	20.9	-18.8
Single Parent Families (%)			
Boulder	10.3	24.2	+136.3
USA	12.3	19.5	+ 59.1
Married Persons (%)			
Boulder	55.5	38.1	-31.3
USA	68.8	61.7	-10.3
Ratio of Married to Unmarried Persons			
Boulder	1.04	.57	-45.2
USA	1.60	1.45	- 9.4
Divorced and Separated Persons (%)			
Boulder	4.5	9.9	+120.9
USA	5.9	9.3	+ 57.3
Total Number of Households			
Boulder			+ 21.8
USA			+ 24.6

Sources: Pay et al., 1985: 6, 7, 10, 12, 14, 15, 16, 18.

In a detailed study, the National Association of Home Builders (1981: 16) concluded that the artificial growth limitations imposed on. Boulder had accelerated house price increases to an extent that the majority of new and first-time buyers bought less expensive homes built in increasing numbers in surrounding towns. Similarly, Figure 3 shows how median rent in Boulder census tracts as a proportion of median family income rose steeply virtually without exception.

Furthermore, while median family income in Boulder increased by 100.7% between 1970 and 1980, this rise was less than for the U.S. in general (107.6%). More importantly, the gains in family income fell far short of the increase in housing costs. In fact, the house value to family income ratio rose by 84% from 1970 to 1980. In contrast, the income of unrelated individuals during the corresponding period rose by 243% and for them the house value to income ratio increased by only 1.1%.

Considering that between 1970 and 1980 the Boulder housing stock became less congent with family living (attached and much smaller units which had become also more expansive per square foot), one logically asks: did the Boulder population change, too?

The Boulder population did indeed change. Table 3 shows that family households decreased by 27% between 1970 and 1980 (U.S.A.: - 9%). The decline was most evident among families with children under five years (-48%). At the same time, the total number of households grew by 22%. Single-parent families and divorced or separated parents increased by, respectively, 136% and 121%, more than twice the national rate.

Only a more complete analysis than is possible here can clarify why fewer families stayed in or came to Boulder. However, it seems safe to conclude that a lack of affordable housing of the appropriate type and size ranks high among the reasons, notwithstanding Boulder's long-standing commitment to the provision of low-income housing. A 1985 survey of low-income households in Boulder (less than $15,000 per year) found that 27% mentioned affordable housing as a problem and 41% of those sampled complained about affordable rent (Kathlene, 1985b: 3).

Conclusion

The data presented in this paper indicate that following the enactment of growth restrictions in Boulder, the housing stock and the composition of the population have changed significantly. However, research on the effects of growth control on housing is fraught with many difficulties (Schwartz, Zorn, and Hansen, 1986). Obviously, there are other factors that should be considered as well. In the case of Boulder, the open space (Green Belt) program, the comprehensive plan, employment opportunities and a growing student population, no doubt, affected developments during the 1970's. The changes observed here are not exclusively attributable to growth controls.

The data presented in the preceeding discussions have several limitations. For example, it would be good to trace developments year-by-year, not constrained by the decennial interval of census data collection. It would also be good to compare the Boulder data not only with national figures, but with those for nearby communities as well (a task currently underway). Such a strategy would hold constant any effects that are specific to the region.

Of course, one would also want to know how many of the moderate-*price* houses sold were bought by moderate-*income* households, a question that requires information not available from accessible records. It would also be desirable to include a more encompassing analysis ramifications of growth control on the quality of public services and community infrastructure (cf. Huttman, 1979). A similarly broad approach is also argued in a pilot study by Anselin and Arias (1983) in which a multi-criteria framework is proposed as a decision support system for urban growth management.

Notwithstanding these and other limitations, the data that were presented suffice to make the argument that an examination of the implications of growth restrictions for housing must go beyond an analysis of the effects on the prices of houses sold. Also part of the housing market are the houses that are not sold (owner-occupied as well as rental) and the people living in and seeking these houses. The literature contains numerous examples of ill-fated housing polices, programs and projects that failed to recognize the needs of the very people they were intended to serve. In attempts to effectuate congruence between people and their housing environment, integral consideration of problems in the dynamics of supply *and* demand is essential (Studer and Van Vliet--, 1987).

References

Anselin, L. and Arias, E. G., 1983.: A Multi-Criteria Framework as a Decision Support System for Urban Growth Management Applications: Central City Redevelopment.. *European Journal of Operational Research* 13, 300-309.

Baldassare, M., 1981: *The Growth Dilemma: Residents' Views and Local Population Change in the United States.* Berkeley, CA: University of California Press.

----, 1982a: Predicting Local Concern about Growth: the Roots of Citizen Discontent.. *Journal of Urban Affairs* 4, 9-49.

---- **and Protash, W.**, 1982b: Growth Controls, Population Growth, and Community Satisfaction. *American Sociological Review* 47, 339-346.

Bluestone, B. and Harrison, B., 1982: *The Deindustrialization of America.* New York: Basic Books.

Burrows, L.B., 1978: *Growth Management: Issues, Techniques, and Policy Implications.* New Brunswick, NJ: Center for Urban Policy Research.

Connerly, C.E., 1986: Growth Management Concern. The Impact of its Definition on Support for Local Growth Controls. *Environment and Behavior* 18, 707-732.

Dowall, D.E., 1980: The Effects of Land Use and Environmental Regulations on Housing Cost. *Policy Studies* 8, 277-288.

Feagan, J.R., 1983: *The Urban Real Estate Game: Playing Monopoly with Real Money.* Englewood Cliffs, NJ: Prentice Hall.

Finkler, E., Toner, W. and Popper, F., 1976: *Urban Nongrowth: City Planning for People.* New York: Praeger.

Frieden, B., 1982: The Exclusionary Effect of Growth Controls. In: M.B. Johnson (ed.): *Resolving the Housing Crisis.* Cambridge, MA: Ballinger.

Gleeson, M.E., 1979: The Effects of an Urban Growth Management System on Land Values. *Land Economics* 55, 350-365.

Gottdiener, M. and Neiman, M., 1981: Characteristics of Support for Local Growth Control. *Urban Affairs Quarterly* 17, 55-73.

Humphrey, C. and R. Krannich, R., 1980: The Promotion of Growth in Small Urban Places and its Impact on Population Change, 1975-78. *Social Science Quarterly* 61, 581-594.

---- **and Buttel, F.** 1980: "The Sociology of the Growth/No Growth Debate. *Policy Studies Journal* 9, 336-345.

Huttman, E.D., 1979: Social Inequality and the "No Growth" Movement: a Further Barrier to Low Income Families' Entry into Desirable Residential Areas. In: A.J. Mayer and L. Gordon (eds.): *Urban Life and the Struggle to be Human*, pp. 191-197. Dubuque, IA: Kendall-Hunt.

Kamara, S.G. 1987: Effect of Local Variations in Public Service on Housing Production at the Fringe of a Growth-Controlled Multi-County Metropolitan Area. *Urban Studies* 24, 109-117.

Kathlene, L., 1985a: *Female Single Parents in Boulder County.* Boulder, CO: University of Colorado, Center for Public Policy Research.

----, 1985b: Low-income Households in Boulder County. Boulder, CO: University of Colorado, Center for Public Policy Research.

Lillydahl, J.H. and Singell, L.D., 1987: The Effects of Growth Management on the Housing Market: a Review of the Theoretical and Empirical Evidence. *Journal of Urban Affairs* 9, 63-77.

Logan, J., 1978: Growth, Politics and the Stratification of Places.. *American Journal of Sociology* 84, 404-416.

Lowenstein, R., 1987: When Developers Meet, Talk Turns to 'No-Growth' Trends. *The Wall Street Journal.* October 14, 1987, p. 35.

Lyon, L., Felice, L. and Perryman, M.R., 1981: Community Power and Population Increase: an Empirical Test of the Growth Machine Model. *American Journal of Sociology* 86, 1387-1400.

Miller, T. and Fitch, S., m.d.: *Impacts of the Danish Plan on Housing Prices in Boulder*. Boulder, CO: City Department of Human Resources/University of Colorado, Center for Public Policy Research.

Miller, T.I., 1986: Must Growth Restrictions Eliminate Moderate-Priced Housing? *Journal of the American Planning Association* 52, 319-325.

Molotch, H., 1976: The City as a Growth Machine: Toward a Political Economy of Place. American Journal of Sociology 82:309-32.

National Association of Home Builders, 1981: *The Danish Plan in Retrospect.* Washington, D.C.: NAHB, State, Local and Environmental Affairs Division.

Neiman, M. and Loveridge, R.D., 1981: Environmentalism and Local Growth Control: a Probe into the Class Bias Thesis. *Environment and Behavior* 13, 759-772.

Pay, W.S., Dane, S., Davis, J.N. and T. Miller, T., 1985: *The Handbook of Comparative Municipal Statistics.* Boulder: Division of Research and Evaluation, Dept. of Community Planning and Development.

Protash, W. and Baldassare, M., 1983: Growth Policies and Community Status: A Test and Modification of Logan's Theory. *Urban Affairs Quarterly* 18, 397-412.

Sawers, L. and Tabb, W.K., 1984: *Sunbelt/Snowbelt: Urban Development and Regional Restructuring.* New York: Oxford University Press.

Schwartz, S. I., 1984: The Effect of Growth Control on the Production of Moderate Priced Housing. *Land Economics* 60, 110-14.

----, **Zorn, P.M. and Hansen, D.E.**, 1986: Research Design Issues and Pitfalls in Growth Control Studies. *Land Economics* 62, 223-233.

Studer, R.G. and Van Vliet--, W., 1987: Sociophysical Congruence as Problem of Supply and Demand. *Architecture and Behavior* 3, 159-173.

Wolch, J.R. and Gabriel., S.A., 1981: Local Land Development Policies and Urban Housing Values. *Environment and Planning* 13, 1253-76.

WHO GETS HOUSED: THE CHANGING NATURE OF HOUSING AFFORDABILITY AND ACCESS IN ADVANCED CAPITALIST SOCIETIES

David C. Thorns

Housing Policy Context

Housing policy was a key ingredient of the post-war development of social-democratic style Labour administrations in a number of Western capitalist economies. These economies were shaped by the policies drawn from the economic theories of Keynes and as such emphasized an approach centered on the control of "demand" for commodities rather than upon the "supply" of money. The first two decades of the post 1945 period were generally ones of economic growth, interrupted by the short-term fluctuations associated with trade cycles. Over these years levels of inflation were modest, unemployment rates were low and economic growth was obtained. However, as the 1960s progressed the economies of western nations began to develop more acute problems. Inflation and unemployment became more pronounced leading to the growing realization that the capitalist state was moving into a new "crisis".

The crisis it was suggested resulted from the inability of the state to manage capital during a period when profitability was falling and restructuring was required to revitalize capitalist production and so increase the level of profits (Gamble 1979). State intervention into this process was re-fashioned during the 1960s with much rhetoric about the use of scientific and technological skills and improved economic management (Massey, 1984; Massey and Meegan, 1982). However, the limited ability of a particular nation state, during a general period of crisis within capitalist societies, to develop a viable strategy to reshape their economy increasingly became evident (Mandel, 1978).

The 1970s provided the decade in which the break with post war social democratic welfare state policy occurred. Nearly all western capitalist nations during this decade moved towards policies of fiscal austerity shifting attention from the "demand" side of the economic equation to the supply, especially of money.

The new emphasis on monetarism was accompanied by a revival of a new era of market individualism. The revival of economic well-being and consequently social progress was to be based on a new wave of entrepreneurial activity creating not a welfare culture but an entrepreneurial culture. This shift brought with it attacks upon the structure of the welfare state and an argument that this structure should be dismantled as it had

Affordable Housing and the Homeless

grown into a large and inefficient bureaucracy no longer able to deliver efficiently, health, housing, educational and social services to the population. This move was seen by many writers as one of "recommodification" (Forrest and Williams, 1980; Harloe, 1981), of "recapitalization" of capital (Miller, 1978). The more popularist presentation was of the "privatization" of services with the return to the individual of a greater capacity to choose the services or provisions required. The consequence of this has been growth in such areas as private medical insurance and in some western capitalist societies the expansion of owner-occupation.

One example of how these macro-changes have led to a re-direction of housing policy is the case of the United Kingdom. The policies followed by the Thatcher Government in the 1980s have led to the role of the State in housing being redefined. The state has become a residual provider only entering the housing arena when no other possibility existed with the normal expectations being that housing demand would be satisfied by the activities of the private market. Policy therefore has changed from one of support for public housing to one emphasizing the further expansion of home ownership, an attempt to revive the private rental sector and an attack on the level of existing public housing through vigorous sale policy (Murie and Forrest, in this volume). The shift in policy was based upon ideology as much as economics and cost cutting. This can be demonstrated by the increasing cost to the state of home ownership through the taxation system and through the policies adopted with respect to the homeless.

The taxation system provides assistance to owner-occupiers in the form of tax relief on mortgage interest payments, exemption from capital gains tax and inheritance tax, and discount on the sale of council houses. These varied forms of assistance collectively provide over 9 billion pounds annually (Darke and Drake, in this volume). The second area where the ideological thrust of the Conservative Government policy is clear is in the area of provisions for the homeless. In order to carry out these statutory obligations to house the homeless local authorities have increasingly had to spend large amounts of money on temporary accommodation in both hotels and bed and breakfast boarding houses. The costs of such provisions is now in many cases, especially in the London area, well in excess of the costs of providing a more permanent solution in the form of additional public housing stock. The permanent solution is, however, prevented by the Conservative Central Government's opposition to the expansion or maintenance of the public stock and its control over local authorities' capital expenditure (Murie and Forrest, in this volume).

The increased levels of home ownership that have resulted from the changes of the 1960s and 1970s has led to debate within the sociological literature regarding whether this movement from rental, both private and public, to home ownership has major social and political consequences. One position to emerge argues that housing changes lead to a restratification of the urban population around consumption sectors rather than production producing political changes in terms of voting behaviour, the formation of local social movements committed to the support of local property interests and a general resistance to change (Edel, 1982; Pratt, 1982; Saunders, 1979, 1984, 1986; Thorns, 1981).

The particularities of the British case need, however, to be seen in the light of comparative data. Not all western capitalist societies had this particular pattern of housing change, and it may well be that the tenure shift itself is not the most important consequence of the major structural changes that occurred during the 1960s and 1970s (Harloe and Paris, 1984; Kemeny, 1983, 1987). The shift to monetarist policies, the removal of housing's protected circuit of finance and the consequence of a much more mobile and global finance capital have all had impacts upon housing structure effecting the key aspects of housing policy, i.e., access, costs, construction and availability. In order to explore some of these impacts more closely it is necessary to examine some case study material. The next section of this paper will, therefore, focus upon Australian and New Zealand data.

Changing Housing Contexts: Australia and New Zealand

Australia

Owner-occupation for the whole of the post-war period has been the dominant form of tenure. However, it has increased over the period from 52% in 1947 to 69% by 1986 (see Watson, 1986, and Table 1). This broadening of the base of owner-occupation occurred during the 1950s and 1960s and was brought about through a combination of low rates of inflation of house and land prices, full employment, rising real wages and government policies designed to assist owner-occupiers. The mechanism of assistance chosen was through such devices as tax relief and incentive savings schemes and Commonwealth (i.e., Federal Government) State housing agreements which assisted in the provision of loans through building societies (Neutze, 1977).

The 1970s and 1980s, however, were in contrast to the 1950s and 1960s a period of rapid inflation in house and land prices with the result that considerable strain was placed upon the ability of households to gain access to housing, particularly in Sydney and to a lesser extent Melbourne (Burke et al., 1984; Kilmartin et al., 1985): During the 1970s, for example, the cost of an average (110 sq.m.) house in Sydney rose 238%, 220% in Melbourne and 141% in Adelaide. Within the total costs of house and land, the cost of land relative to the house changed markedly. For example, in Sydney in the 1950s land on average contributed to 14% of the total cost whereas in the 1980s this had risen to 50% (Daly and Paris, 1985). Over this period, the cost of houses and land, especially for those entering the market for the first time and not having the advantage of capital gains on their existing property, clearly escalated.

The impact of these changes upon the capacity of households to afford housing can be seen from the rising levels of deposit now required to purchase and in the increasing proportion of income that housing consumes (Burke et al. 1984, Australian Bureau of Statistics 1986). Research in the 1970s has shown evidence of a growing housing problem, more especially in Sydney and Melbourne, with the numbers of those living in caravans, boarding houses, emergency houses and homeless increasing (Daly and Paris, 1985; Fopp, 1986; Kilmartin et al., 1985; Paris and Stimson, 1986).

Table 1: Tenure Status of Occupied Private Dwellings/Households, Australia, 1911-1981

	1911		1947		1954	
	No.	%	No.	%	No.	%
Owner	402637	45.0	338025	44.7	1121814	47.9
Purchased by Instalments	39318	4.4	147677	7.9	353093	15.1
Owner/Purchaser undefined	na	na	na	na	na	na
Owner/Purchaser	441955	49.4	985702	52.6	14704907	62.9
Goverment Tenant	0	0.0	0	0.0	99376	4.2
Other Tenant	404371	45.2	812750	43.4	699854	29.9
Other Meth. of Occup.	48063	5.4	48867	2.6	56257	2.4
Not Stated	na	na	26304	1.4	13027	0.6
Total	894389	100.0	1873623	100.0	2343241	100.0

Table 1: Continued

	1966		1976		1981	
	No.	%	No.	%	No.	%
Owner	na	na	1306293	31.5	1548873	33.2
Purchased by Instalments	na	na	437770	34.7	1542282	33.0
Owner/Purchaser Undef.	na	na	17434	0.4	87110	1.9
Owner/Purchaser	2231913	70.8	2761497	66.7	3178265	68.1
Goverment Tenant	161722	5.1	204627	4.9	228938	4.9
Other Tenant	673357	21.4	839873	20.3	935543	20.3
Other Meth. of Occup.	59552	1.9	232477	5.6	190647	4.1
Not Stated	25382	0.8	102047	2.5	135516	2.9
Total	3151926	100.0	4140521	100.0	4668909	100.0

Source: Burke et al., 1984: 3

The collective impact of internal housing market changes and those of the external economic environment have created a housing situation in most of the Australian states in which waiting lists for public housing have grown, low vacancy rates exist in the private rental sector pushing up rental levels and high cost to income ratios from low and modest income earners are becoming common (Burke et al., 1984; Paris, 1984). The result is an increasingly differentiated housing market within which some substantial gains are sustained at the upper speculative end of the market, and money is available for loans but at a price many modest and low income earners cannot afford.

New Zealand

The tenure structure in New Zealand, like that of Australia, has been one dominated by owner-occupation rising from 55% in 1945 to 72% in 1986 (Thorns, 1983, and Figure 1). The 1950s and 1960s were decades of relatively stable prices, full employment and rising real incomes (Rosenberg 1986). The state provided considerable assistance to home owners through the operation of the State Advances Corporation which provided low interest loans to first home buyers purchasing a home. The loans were subject to income restrictions, thus ensuring they were available to households of low to modest income. The linkage of the loans to the purchase of a new house (until the late 1970s when the policy was changed) assisted in the growth of new housing subdivisions in the 1950s and 1960s and provided a ready market for the products of the larger group builders who became important suppliers of housing in the main urban centres, especially in New Zealand's largest city, Auckland.

Figure 1: Tenure, 1951-1986

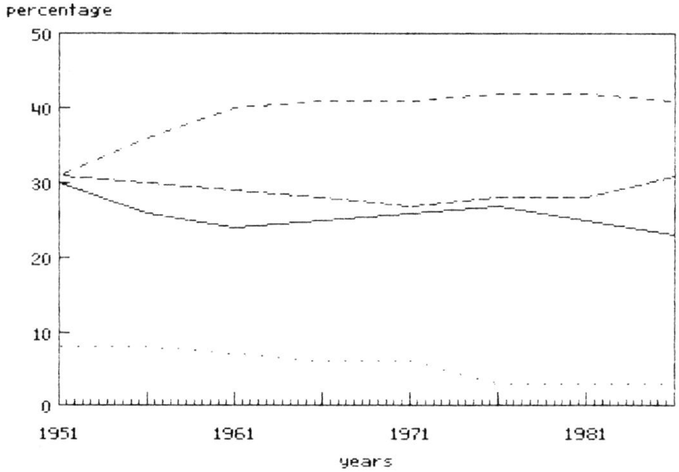

—— rent, ... rent free , - - - - mortgaged, ---------- freehold

The 1970s and 1980s, however, were in marked contrast, decades of high inflation, rising unemployment and falling real wages. These conditions have created a growing affordability problem especially for those attempting to enter the housing market for the first time. House and land prices have grown rapidly in a number of boom periods, from

1972-75, 1980-83 and 1984-85 (Figure 2). These booms are linked to construction cycles and also changes to monetary policy which encouraged the growth of credit in the early 1970s and the early 1980s (Thorns, 1986). The most recent boom, however, is different from the two earlier periods as it has resulted from a more radical restructuring of finance policies as part of a move towards a more general deregulation of the New Zealand economy after mid-1984 (Deane, 1985).

Figure 2: Graph of Percentage Increases per Year in House Prices, Weekly Wages and C.P.I.

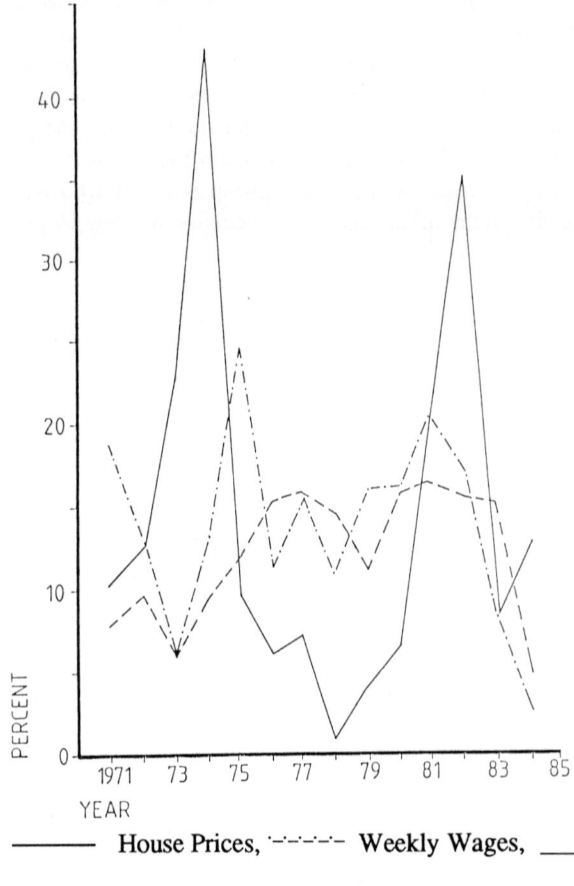

——— House Prices, -·-·-·- Weekly Wages, ______ C.P.I.

The changes to affordability of housing can be shown by examining the relationship of the average house and land price to the average weekly income. In 1974 it took 42% of the average weekly income to purchase an existing property and 49% to purchase a new property. By the mid 1980s this had changed to requiring 63% and 73% respectively

(National Housing Commission, 1986). Clearly such averages provide only a crude measure of change, nonetheless they indicate the direction of change and the erosion of many households' capacity to afford housing unless they have access either to capital or multiple incomes within the household.

Housing Policy Debate: The Retreat from Welfarism?

The growing problem of affordability of housing has now been demonstrated for Australia and New Zealand and growing housing pressures within the early and mid 1980s identified. In both countries the mid 1980s brought into office Labour Governments (1983 Australia, 1984 New Zealand) with housing as an area of priority in their election manifestos.

The Australian Labour Party's housing programme set out at the end of 1982, prior to the 1983 election campaign provided a traditional social democrat style solution to the perceived housing crisis within Australia. The policy aimed at increasing the supply of housing improving the planning and management of housing development and a firm commitment to public rental housing. The policy included specific commitments within this broad framework to increase the number of units built per year from 135,000 to 160,000 during the first three years of office of a Labour Government, to set up a Department of Housing and Urban and Regional Affairs and to expand public housing. Further the policy includes the rejection of the idea of deregulating the finance industry and so ending housing's protected position (Paris and Stimson, 1986).

The New Zealand Labour Party going into the 1984 election also campaigned with housing as a central area of concern. The housing policy that was advocated was based around increased assistance to home owners through the provision of "deposit gap" financial assistance to first home buyers. One scheme viewed as a possibility was the Australian Labour party's first home owner grant scheme. In addition the policy sought to encourage the construction of more housing with the restoration of the state within the public rental sector through an increased stock of public housing for rental and the reforms of landlord tenant relations to improve tenant security. Again an Australian model was chosen as a guide to reform. In this case the South Australian Tenancy reform legislation was chosen as a guide to developing New Zealand Law.

In office both the Australian and New Zealand Labour Governments have modified their housing policies from ones based upon equity and general Governmental assistance and involvement to policies which increasingly emphasize targeting of assistance to the "most needy" and the introduction of more "market" rents and interest rates for the users of public housing and mortgage loan assistance. Their moves have led to public housing occupying a much less prominent place within the respective Governments' housing policies. In the Australian case this has led to the abandonment of a commitment to double the size of the state rental sector and the adoption of a more general and non-specific commitment to increased funding. In New Zealand the Government initially stopped the sale of public housing, which had been strongly encouraged by the previous Government, and increased the rate of public house acquisitions. However, at the same time they have introduced a policy of adjustment to rents bringing them closer to the rates prevailing in the private market. The policy is designed in part to encourage the better-off tenants to vacate public housing and move into private home ownership. The adoption of this move to more modest rents provided a rent strike by state tenants in one area of Wellington in 1987.

The other major departure from their pre-election housing policies has been in the moves both Governments have made towards the deregulation of the financial sector and the resulting ending of a protected circuit for housing finance. This deregulation in both cases has made competition for money more intense driving up interest rates. Although it has not reduced the amount of funds available for housing within the economy it has increased substantially the cost of borrowing rather than decreased it as the advocates of deregulation forecasted. A consequence, therefore, of the deregulatory policies has been the necessity to produce new mechanisms to preserve access to housing for the low and modest income earning households who have been excluded from traditional financial arrangements by the increases in costs (Thorns, 1987).

The first question of interest is why did Labour administrations adopt macro-economic policies which were essentially anti-Welfarist? The answer here lies in the general trends of capitalist development as much as in the particularities of the two societies.

The end of the long boom of the 1950s and 1960s was a product of changes in the relative position of both countries with respect to their export commodities and world markets. The re-organization of Europe into the E.E.C. posed problems for the continuation of the export of primary products, important based for both societies. The 1970s recessions within the world economy further depressed raw material prices such as minerals which constituted another element of Australia's export income. Further the competition of cheaper products from especially South East Asia and Japan had important impacts upon domestic manufacturing with rationalizations and closures becoming a dominant feature of the 1970s and 1980s. The period, therefore, became one of extensive restructuring of both capital and State activity in an attempt to create conditions for continued economic growth (Martin, 1981; Rosenberg, 1986). Part of this process was to reduce the level of State expenditure on consumption and support for welfare provisions in order to re-direct subsidies and State assistance to the development of export industries. One victim of this change was the housing sector. Finance was removed from housing in part to finance other areas of Government expenditure. For example, in New Zealand the Government moved from subsidizing consumption in the form of welfare services to subsidizing production in the form of a "think big" energy related sector to develop among other things synthetic petrol and steel production (Pearce, 1987). The limited success of this strategy became clear by the middle of the 1980s when the level of unemployment was rising and the extent of control over the economy in New Zealand by the State was seen as the "most extensive of any western democratic nation" (Deane, 1985).

The new governments in the mid 1980s came to power at a time when market liberalism was re-emerging as a dominant economic theory. The experience of America and Britain notwithstanding, it was argued that the revitalization of the domestic economies of Australia and New Zealand required the re-emergence of entrepreneurial skills and these would only be facilitated through creating a climate of greater competition and new patterns of investment. The requirements for this were seen to be a less regulated and protected economy and society where risk-taking was encouraged. This produced the current paradox in which Labour administrations have become the champions of a free-market capitalism based upon a return to individualistic competition and action.

The shift with respect to housing policy in particular has been quite radical. In mid 1984 the New Zealand economy had been subjected to an extended freeze on wages, dividends, rents, prices interest rates and exchange rates. Further this freeze was imposed on an economy already subject to extensive import protection, export subsidies, compulsory ratio requirements for all financial institutions to invest in government stock, qualitative and quantitative credit guidelines and an array of other regulatory devices (Deane, 1985). The main elements of the new approach were the abandonment of wage and price controls, the abolition of interest rate and rent controls, a 20% devaluation followed by a floating exchange rate, the abolition of exchange controls over foreign currency transactions and a commitment to reducing the government deficit through a combination of cuts in Government spending, increases in charges for services and corporatization of Government departments. The Australian Government has also moved to de-regulate the finance industry removing the asset and interest rate controls that previously protected the housing sector.

The impacts of this welter of changes upon the housing sector have been extensive. They have pushed up interest rates, e.g. in Australia the deregulation of savings banks mortgages in April 1986 resulted in an immediate increase from a rate of 13.5% to one of 15.5%. In New Zealand the rate rose from 12% in July 1984 to 15% by December 1984. It has, however, continued to climb rather than to fall in the new more competitive environment with average first mortgage rates approaching 20% by March 1987 (Figure 3). Rent levels have also risen as has availability but at a much increased cost. In February 1987 the average weekly rental for a three-bedroomed house in Auckland was $235 which represented 67% of the average weekly wage (National Housing Commission, 1988). The increases in rents that have been charged for private rental accommodation have not led to an increase in the size of this sector as with the deregulation of the financial markets a higher rate of return became available in other sectors of the economy leading to a property and share boom during 1986 and into the first half of 1987. With the stock market crash of late 1987 money appears to be flowing into the banking system and again failing to stimulate the growth of accommodation. The removal of rent controls and financial deregulation therefore do not seem to have produced any direct benefits for the housing sector. Housing construction after an initial burst also does not seem to have been sustained by the new deregulated finance sector. For example, in New Zealand, housing permits grew through the latter part of 1984 and through 1985. However, towards the end of 1986 and into 1987 there has been a substantial fall in building activity especially outside of the Auckland area (Table 2).

Figure 3: Mortgage Interest Rates 1970-1987

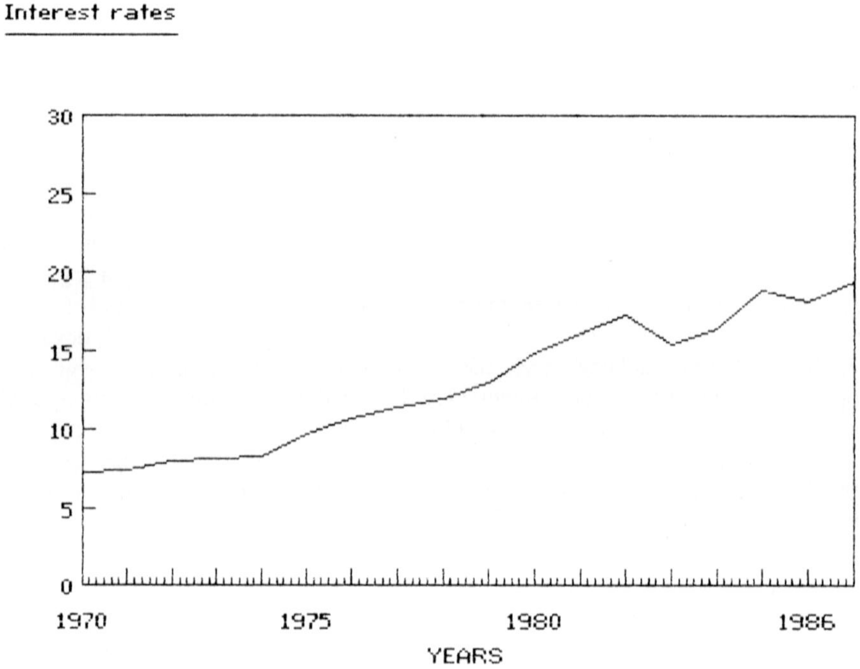

The Australian figures present a similar picture. The level of house building in 1982 was at a historically low point with 105,000 new units constructed which was the lowest since the 1950s. During the initial years of the Labour administration the numbers grew quite rapidly so that by the end of 1984 the annual rate had increased to 153,000. However, as the rising interest rate and prices of the mid 1980s caused growing affordability problems the rate of construction has declined. The final consequence of note is the extent to which the move towards market liberalism and a more deregulated economy has rapidly increased regional variations in house prices.

Absolute housing costs, for example, are highest in New South Wales, especially in Sydney (Henderson and Hough 1984), with the highest prices and rate of increase in values of land and houses and therefore the highest cost of home ownership. In 1983, the median house price in Sydney was $83,000, by 1985 this had risen to $91,000, this compares with $81,000 in 1985 for Melbourne. In New Zealand, the Auckland area stands out as the one with the highest prices and greatest housing pressures. In December 1986, for example, the average sale price of a house in Auckland at $153,653 was nearly twice the national average of $87,591. (Sydney Metropolitan area in 1986 contained 3,204,696 making it the largest urban centre in Australia. - Auckland Metropolitan area in 1986 contained 809,142 making it by far the largest urban centre in New Zealand. Wellington is next in size but has less than half the Auckland population.)

Table 2: Building Permits 1970-1987

Years	Houses	Flats	Total
1970	16990	6094	23084
1971	16230	7449	23679
1972	15577	8756	24333
1973	19916	12857	32773
1974	23582	16152	39734
1975	21436	11665	33101
1976	20932	11257	32189
1977	19160	10994	30154
1978	14358	6847	21205
1979	13669	5380	19049
1980	11687	3510	15197
1981	11108	3334	14442
1982	13996	5010	19006
1983	11854	4145	15999
1984	15488	4738	20226
1985	15664	6118	21782
1986	15907	7128	23035

Source: N.Z. Statistics Department

The Australian figures present a similar picture. The level of house building in 1982 was at a historically low point with 105,000 new units constructed which was the lowest since the 1950s. During the initial years of the Labour administration the numbers grew quite rapidly so that by the end of 1984 the annual rate had increased to 153,000. However, as the rising interest rate and prices of the mid 1980s caused growing affordability problems the rate of construction has declined. The final consequence of note is the extent to which the move towards market liberalism and a more deregulated economy has rapidly increased regional variations in house prices. Absolute housing costs, for example, are highest in New South Wales, especially in Sydney (Henderson and Hough, 1984), with the highest prices and rate of increase in values of land and houses and therefore the highest cost of home ownership. In 1983 the median house price in

Sydney was $83,000, by 1985 this had risen to $91,000, this compares with $81,000 in 1985 for Melbourne. In New Zealand, the Auckland area stands out as the one with the highest prices and greatest housing pressures. In December 1986, for example, the average sale price of a house in Auckland at $153,653 was nearly twice the national average of $87,591. (Sydney Metropolitan area in 1986 contained 3,204,696 making it the largest urban centre in Australia. - Auckland Metropolitan area in 1986 contained 809,142 making it by far the largest urban centre in New Zealand. Wellington is next in size but has less than half the Auckland population.)

Policy Initiatives

The high costs of housing access and the deterioration in affordability experienced in the 1980s have led to new policy initiatives in both countries based around new designs for mortgages. They do not, therefore, challenge the assumption that the continuance of owner-occupation is the most suitable form of housing tenure, they simply accept this as taken for granted and devote attention to trying to continue to facilitate it in the face of a deteriorating capacity of modest and low income earners to afford home ownership (Kemeny, 1983; Thorns, 1987).

oth the schemes devised have two main features. A cash grant to assist with the deposit for home purchase and a repayment plan which is designed around a constant real rate of interest and a fixed proportion of household income. In both cases the chosen levels have been a real interest rate of 3% and a repayment level of 25% of total household income. The nominal rate of interest in the scheme would be based on movements in the consumer price index and the capital sum outstanding would be adjusted by movements in the consumer price index over the previous twelve months. The repayments and the sum loaned are, therefore, indexed to inflation and so ensure a smoother repayments path and a more equitable return to the lender than a conventional mortgage.

The Australian scheme was launched in Victoria in 1984 with a pilot programme of 520 loans, subsequently in 1985 the state government changed all its housing loans to operate on this basis (Carter, 1986). Other state governments have also initiated schemes to try and reduce the costs of house purchase (see Bethune, 1986; Rose, 1986). In New Zealand the Government-controlled Housing Corporation has developed a scheme similar to the Victorian one and, since its inception in December 1985, 500 houses have been made available under its provisions. Evaluative data, available at present, suggests that these new schemes have assisted two groups of people, those with substantial deposits but with low income (e.g., those on benefits as a result of marriage splits, unemployment etc.) and modest income earners. The appeal of the scheme beyond these groups to middle and upper income earners is likely to be limited as they are unlikely to find it difficult to raise money from private sector financial institutions or be willing to forego the capital gains through sharing these with the lenders.

Future Directions

The restructuring process within most Western capitalist societies of the 1970s and 1980s brought in a new set of policies based around market monetarism and individual provision and away from the policies of collective provisions of welfare characteristics of the immediate post-war decades. Consequently, it is targeting rather than universalism, housing allowances and negative income tax rather than the building of state housing which become the dominant issues debated.

The failures during the 1950s and 1960s to promote continued economic growth are blamed on the inadequacies of state management and the growth of unwieldy bureaucracies. These in turn become cited as the cause of the fiscal and other crises of the 1970s and 1980s. Such critiques suffer from a limited analysis of the historical development of Western capitalist societies and a failure to carry out comparative analysis. Capitalist societies are characterized by sequential crises of varying severity and in this respect the 1970s and 1980s are yet one more such crisis (Mandel, 1983). However, each crisis comes with its own particular set of characteristics and its impact is not uniform across all societies.

The examination of the responses of two particular nation states to the prevailing economic conditions of the 1970s and 1980s has identified both common and unique features in their responses. They have both followed the path of economic liberalism, but at varying speeds. New Zealand has moved the most rapidly and extensively to deregulate and transform its economy through a restructuring of its finance system, corporatization of its public services and a progressive removal of support mechanisms to farmers and manufacturers, exposing both groups much more to the vagaries of international markets and flows of capital. The Australians while adopting a broadly monetarist strategy have been less wholesale in their adoption of such policies and have maintained a more corporatist style of economic management.

The consequences of these changes for housing provision have been similar and in both countries costs have risen and access to housing for low and modest income earners has got appreciably more difficult resulting in waiting lists for public housing growing, overcrowding increasing, pressure upon the cheaper end of the private rental market pushing up rents, and homelessness appearing.

The policy responses have been ones attempting to cheapen the costs of home ownership through new forms of mortgage arrangement rather than those which would confront the often outmoded building and subdivision practices, planning regulations, or attempt to tax or limit land speculation and the capital gains made through property sales. Further no real challenge has yet appeared to the continuation of home ownership as the main objective of public housing policy.

References

Australian Bureau of Statistics, 1986: *Household Expenditure Survey, Australia: Summary of Results. 1984.* ABS Cat No. 65300.

Bethune, G., 1986: *Lowering the Threshold: Recent Innovations in Housing Finance.* Paper presented at World Planning and Housing Congress. Adelaide.

Burke, T., Hancock, L. and Newton, R., 1984: *A Roof Over Their Heads.* Institute of Family Studies, Monograph No. 4.

Carter, R.A., 1986: *Innovations in Financial Mechanisms for Housing Markets.* Paper presented to World Planning and Housing Congress.

Daly, M. and Paris, C., 1985: *From the General to the Particular. Global Economic Re-structuring and the Local Housing Crisis in New South Wales.* Paper presented to a conference on Urban and Regional Impacts of the New International Division of Labour, Hong Kong.

Deane, R., 1985: *Financial Sector Reform: The Case of New Zealand.* Paper presented to a Conference on Financial Reform in the Pacific Basin Countries. San Francisco.

Edel, M., 1982: Home Ownership and Working Class Unity. *International Journal of Urban and Regional Research* 6, 205-222.

Fopp, R., 1986: *Youth Housing: Pre-requisites for Planning.* Paper presented to the World Planning and Housing Congress.

Forrest, R. and Williams, P., 1980: *The Commodification of Housing: Emerging Issues and Contradictions.* Centre for Urban and Regional Studies. University of Birmingham, WP.73.

Gamble, A., 1979: *Decline of Britain.* London.

Harloe, M., 1981: The Recommodification of Housing. In: M. Harloe, and E. Lebas. (eds.): *City Class and Capital.* London.

---- and Paris, C., 1984: The Decollectivization of Consumption. In: I. Szelenyi (ed.): *Cities in Recession.* Beverly Hills, 70-98.

Henderson, R. and Hough, D., 1984: Sydney's Poor Get Squeezed. *Australian Society,* 3, 6-8.

Kemeny, J., 1983: *The Great Australian Nightmare.* Melbourne.

---,- 1987: Toward a Theorised Housing Studies. A Counter Critique of the Provision Thesis. *Housing Studies* 2, 249-260.

Kilmartin, L., Thorns, D.C. and Burke, T., 1985: Social Theory and The Australian City. Sydney.

Martin, J., 1981: *State Papers.* Department of Sociology, Massey University. Palmerston North.

Massey, D., 1984: *Social Divisions of Labour.* London.

----, and Meegan, R., 1982: *The Anatomy of Job Loss.* .London.

Mandel, E., 1978: *The Second Slump.* London.

----, 1983: World Crisis and the Monetarist Answer. In: K. Jansen (ed.): *Monetarism, Economic Crisis and the 3rd World. London.*

Miller, S.M., 1978: The Recapitalization of Capitalism. *International Journal of Urban and Regional Research* 2, 202-212.

Murie, A. and Forrest, R., 1980: Wealth, Inheritance and Housing Policy. *Policy and Politics* 8, 1-19.

National Housing Commission, 1986: *Report for Year Ended 31st March..* Government Printer. Wellington.

----, 1988: *Five Yearly Report. 1983-1988.* Forthcoming. Government Printer. Wellington.

Neutze, M., 1977: *Urban Development in Australia.* Sydney.

Paris, C., 1984: *Affordable and Available Housing: The Role of the Private Rental Sector.* Australian Institute of Urban Studies. Canberra.

---- **and Stimson, R.**, 1986: *Housing Tenure, Costs and Policies in Australia.* Paper presented to World Planning and Housing Congress. Op. cit.

Pearce, G., 1987: *Where is New Zealand Going?* PhD. University of Canterbury.

Pratt, G., 1982: Class Analysis and Urban Domestic Property: a Critical Re-examination. *International Journal of Urban and Regional Research* 6, 481-502.

Rose, R.A., 1986: *Affordable Housing Finance..* Paper presented at the World Planning and Housing Congress, op. cit.

Rosenberg, W., 1986: *The Magic Square.* Monthly Review Society. Christchurch.

Saunders, P., 1979: Urban Politics. London.

----, 1984: Beyond Housing Classes. *International Journal of Urban and Regional Research* 8, 202-225.

----, 1986: Social Theory and the Urban Question. London.

Thorns, D.C., 1981: The Implications of Differential Rates of Capital Gains from Owner-occupation for the Formation and Development of Housing Classes. International *Journal of Urban and Regional Research* 5, 205-227.

----, 1983: Owner-occupation, The State and Class Relations in New Zealand. In: C. **Wilkes and I. Shirley** (eds.): *In the Public Interest.* Auckland.

----, 1986: New Zealand Housing Policy: Continuities and Changes. *Housing Studies* 1, 180-191.

----, 1987: New Solutions to Old Problems: Housing Affordability and Access within Australia and New Zealand. *Environment and Planning A,* forthcoming.

Watson, S., 1986: *Whose Great Australian Dream. Home Ownership and the Exclusion of Women.* Paper presented to World Planning and Housing Congress. Op. cit.

AFFORDABLE HOUSING: ROLES FOR THE STATE AND THE COMMUNITY

Jane Darke and Roy Darke

Introduction

At first sight affordability appears to be a useful objective with respect to housing, and one on which there would be substantial agreement: a dwelling should be affordable just as it should be structurally sound. Actually, the term conceals certain implications about the form of housing provision. An implication is that it is for the individual household to procure housing, according to its means, with the state intervening at the margins to render housing affordable. It recognises that poorer households in any society find it very difficult to afford adequate housing, but it still places responsibility for providing shelter with those households rather than the state which could provide "to each according to his needs". We suggest that the concept of affordability could be broadened to apply to expenditure by the state as well as by individuals, and that we need to examine what a state can afford to provide, or in some cases, whether a state can afford *not* to make certain provisions.

It might be thought that the idea of affordability has greater applicability in less developed countries. State provision in less developed countries, unlike the West, tends to be directed to the needs of middle income groups rather than the poorest, and often at lower paid government officials, where it is in the interests of the state as employer to have a contented workforce in good quality affordable housing. However, affordability applied to provision for the poorer sections has limited usefulness because these groups may literally be able to afford nothing, and obtain their shelter at present through occupying structures they find: ruins, concrete pipes etc. or through building makeshift shelters made of scrap materials. It is difficult to use affordability criteria as the basis for policy where the intention is to help households with very low and unpredictable incomes.

We return later to the idea of affordability but just note here that affordability is only one of several possible objectives of the state in intervening in the housing system.. The main part of this paper seeks to analyse different forms and degrees of state intervention. There is a tendency for state intervention to be seen as a single continuum, where a command economy would have a high score and a free market economy a low one. We wish to argue that state intervention has a number of different dimensions in relation to the changes in housing policy brought about in eight years of Conservative government in Britain.

Affordable Housing and the Homeless

Reasons for State Intervention in Housing

Before we look at various forms of state involvement, we should identify why, in principle, the state should have an interest in becoming involved at all in housing provision. There are various possible reasons.

Firstly, inadequate housing may be an actual or perceived threat to social order. It has been argued (Swenarton, 1981) that this was the main motivation behind the housing drive in Britain at the end of the First World War, with the threat of Bolshevism, as a potentially appealing option for the British working class, diffused by promises of excellent housing (in the event only partly delivered). More recently, inner city riots have often called forth increased investment in housing for the area concerned for the local authority, although it is also paradoxically the case that many neighbourhoods which have seen riots have also seen considerable housing investment *before* the disturbances (for example, neighbourhood offices and environmental improvements at Broadwater Farm, Tottenham, London; enveloping at Handsworth in Birmingham).

Secondly, there is a desire on the part of the state to produce a better quality population. In some cases, poor standard housing for the poor carried threats to the bourgeoisie: diseases resulting from poor sanitation that might then spread to all groups, or imperfectly inculcated sexual modesty due to overcrowding potentially leading to corruption of young men in other classes. Such risks in late 19th century Britain influenced the climate of opinion in favour of increased state intervention. There was also alarm at the poor physical health and condition of conscripts for military service. In analogous cases, employers have provided good quality housing in order to attract, retain and reproduce a high quality workforce (for example, Titus Salt who built Saltaire). In all these cases, apparently altruistic motives on the part of middle class legislators and opinion-formers may contain a strong admixture of self interest.

Thirdly, there is an idea linked with various forms of partnership between the state and households (individually or in small groups) to do with "housing as a verb" (Turner, 1972), namely, that the process of producing, acquiring or managing housing can empower the individual and engender new capacities and skills. This may be an important by-product of collective self-build projects in countries such as Nicaragua (Darke, 1987). Some such idea is a significant part of the newer housing objectives of the Thatcher government, including the breaking up of local authorities' large holdings of low cost rented housing. The first speech of the newly appointed Housing Minister, William Waldegrave, given at the Institute of Housing conference on 19th June 1987, promised to "wean people off the deadly drug of dependency" and to increase private sector involvement in public sector housing. .(Reported in the *Guardian,* June 20, 1987, p.3, and *Inside Housing,* June 26, 1987, p.3.).

Fourthly, the state may sometimes use housing production as a tool of macro-economic policy. In Britain this has more often taken the form of cutting production at times of economic difficulties, than being a positive element in employment planning. The "stop-go" policies of post- war governments have been one of the obstacles to developing an efficient construction industry. However, the policies on which the Labour party unsuccessfully fought the 1987 general election included a large increase in housing investment as a cost effective way of reducing unemployment. As an indication of the continued interest in the employment potential of housebuilding a national pressure group emerged in the mid 1980s under the campaigning slogan of "Homes and Jobs".

A final possible motive for state intervention, more characteristic of governments representing the interests of the working class or the economically weaker groups, is an objective to reduce inequalities in housing standards and to apply the resources of the state to collective benefit. The resources thus applied may include expertise in organisation, overheads such as research and development costs, interventions to achieve economies of scale and so on. In some instances, including Britain, there is a pooling of costs and cross subsidisation. Unlike owner occupiers, council tenants' costs are based on historic costs. Rent levels are pooled across all the properties in a particular authority's ownership and this pooling could be extended to a national sharing of costs. In countries where collective financing of housing and social equalisation through housing provisions are part of the state's objectives, housing intervention will probably be accompanied by extensive intervention in health care and education.

These five motives for state intervention can be summarised as: maintenance of social order, promotion of quality of the population, encouragement of self development, economic planning and collective equalisation. We return to them later.

Forms of State Intervention: Housing in Britain

We now turn to the various forms that state intervention may take. It has been suggested (Le Grand and Robinson, 1984) that state intervention in welfare goods is through *provision, subsidy or regulations*. These take place in the context of particular goals which relate to the five objectives described above. Obviously provision, subsidy and regulations are not *alternative* options: typically there is a mixture of all types of measure in government actions.

In discussing state intervention in housing in Britain, the situation is complicated by the existence of a local government system where the local authorities are responsible for housing provision in their own districts. In areas of greatest housing need, that is, the larger cities and in London (apart from the outer suburbs), most of these areas are controlled by the Labour party while since 1979 the national government has been Conservative: thus the two levels of government have been following different objectives, and each level carries different powers and obligations with respect to housing.

To expand on the question of housing goals, it has been suggested that, until the election of the Thatcher government in 1979, there was broad consensus on the need for state intervention to deliver welfare goods (Hall and Jaques, 1983). In the case of housing policy this is an oversimplification. Thatcherism *has* taken housing policy sharply into new directions but there were changes of emphasis before then.

To understand the goals of postwar governments we must look first at earlier phases of state housing. During the half century of state housing provision before the Second World War, the Conservative party never fully accepted that either state provision or a system of subsidies would be a permanent part of housing supply. In this sense Thatcher's housing policy *is* an extension of Conservative "victorian values". State intervention was seen as occasionally necessary to meet an exceptional situation: the high cost of removal and replacement of insanitary housing, the shortage of homes after World War One, the continuing high level of building costs, the threat to public health and social order posed by slums and overcrowding. The assumption was that the market could and would be the normal channel of provision for most households, including the working class. This provision was expected to take the form of private housing for rent rather than owner occupation.

Labour, by contrast, envisaged the provision of good quality housing by local authorities as a normal component of housing supply, potentially catering for most working class households. The housing policies of the first Labour government, a short lived minority administration in 1924, were based on this objective. In the Labour administration of 1945-51, this was extended to encompass households of all social classes (Merrett, 979). In this their housing policies paralleled their education and health care policies. It was thought potentially beneficial for professionals such as doctors and teachers to live among the communities they served. We see high levels of provision, subsidy and regulation from this government: controls over the building industry and building materials supply to ensure that these met social needs (although stopping well short of nationalisation of the industry), high space standards for new housing, a powerful system of town planning and so on. There was however a certain vagueness with respect to goal setting in terms of output targets (Merrett, 1979). This was exploited by the Conservative party during the 1951 election campaign in their promise to build 300 000 homes a year, and this was a significant factor in their victory.

The goal was still to achieve high housing output, but the emphasis gradually shifted to owner occupation as the mainstream housing provision, to which it was assumed all families aspired, with council housing as a second-best tenure for sections of the working class. Output of council housing halved between 1953 and 1959, while private sector output rose steadily until the 1960s. When Labour finally returned to power in 1964, it accepted this shift of ideology, as seen from the following statement of their objectives:

> "once the country has overcome its huge social problem of slumdom and obsolescence, and met the needs of the great cities for more houses let at moderate rents, the programme of subsidisied council housing should decrease. The expansion of the public programme now proposed is to meet exceptional needs...The expansion of building for owner occupation on the other hand is normal; it reflects a long term social advance" (Ministry of Housing and Local Government, 1964).

These broad assumptions continued under the Conservative government of the early 1970s and the Labour government of 1974-1979, although there were considerable fluctuations in output and subsidy levels. Thus, only between 1951 and 1979 was there some degree of consensus on national housing objectives.

British Housing Policy since 1979

The steady postwar improvement in housing conditions for the mass of the population was checked by the policies introduced in 1979. The goals of the Thatcher government have been to *reduce* the size of the state sector, expand home ownership and latterly to *revive* the private rented sector. The aim is to encourage and reward enterprise, and it is believed that dependence on a local authority landlord is peculiarly destructive of such enterprise. State investment has been cut, and for the first time since the war there has been a *decrease* in the numbers and the quality of the local authority stock. Numbers are shown in Figure 1, and the increasingly poor quality is evident from statistics on disrepair in successive House Condition surveys (Department of the Environment, 1973, 1978, 1982) and from a major "Inquiry into the Condition of the Local Authority Housing Stock" undertaken by the Department of the Environment in 1985, showing that 3.8 million of the 4.6 million council houses in England needed renovation and repair at an average cost of almost £5 000 each: a total bill of some £19 000 million at 1985 prices (Association of Metropolitan Authorities, 1984; Department of the Environment, 1985).:). In other words, the scale of *provision* is being reduced. The level of investment which the government permits local authorities to make has been reduced by 75% since 1978/79, although spending has been slightly greater than 25% of the 1978/79 level due to the forced sale of council houses and local authority land.

As well as reductions in stock through sales at a discount to tenants there are now to be opportunities for council tenants to vote for their existing home to be transferred from local authority ownership to a housing trust. he terms of the transfer, and what happens to the outstanding debt, have not been made clear. There are also pressures on local authorities to enter into various partnership arrangements with the private sector in order to increase housing provision, in particular through renovation and sometimes resale of run-down estates.

Home ownership has been supposedly made easier for people at the margins by a variety of initiatives, in addition to the right to buy their home (Whitehead, 1986). he aggregate effect of these measures has been slight compared to over a million dwellings sold under the Right to Buy legislation in Britain up to the end of 1987, representing one in six of council dwellings.

Figure 1: Post War Trends in Housing in Britain

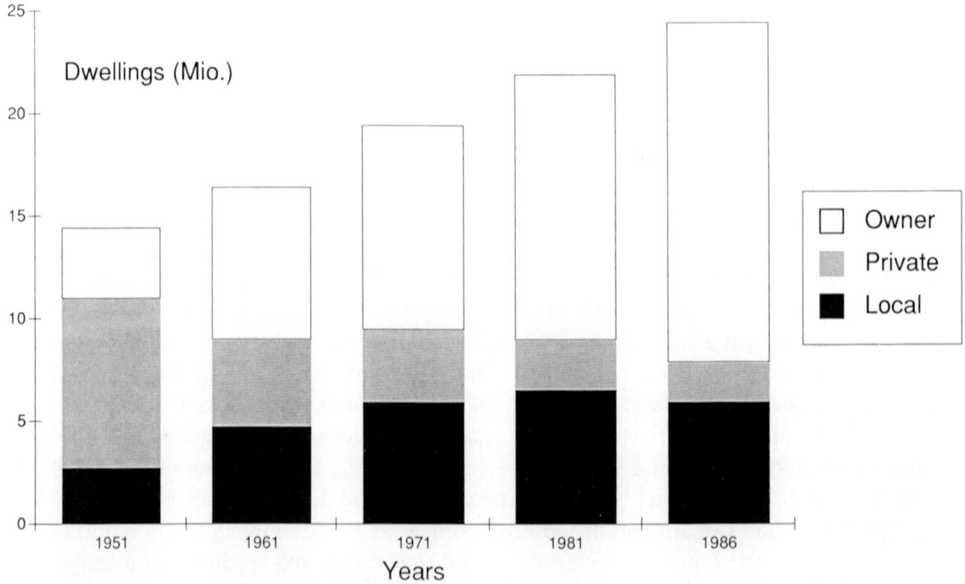

Source: Social Trends, No.17, 1987.

Initially the goal of privatising the public sector was obscured by an apparent objective to cut public expenditure. In adopting the LeGrand and Robinson framework, the category of subsidies must be expanded to include *capital* investment controlled by government, as well as current subsidies, although investment will appear under "provision". In the early years of the Thatcher government, with Michael Heseltine as Secretary of State for the Environment, the cuts in housing expenditure resulted in steep reductions in current subsidies to local authorities. Tenants faced large rent increases to compensate for this: between 1980 and 1982 rents rose by 75% while the retail price index rose by only 23%. Housing expenditure was cut very much more severely than other areas of welfare spending such as health and education. There were also severe reductions in *capital* expenditure which meant a drastic cut in housebuilding as we have already seen, and insufficient money to spend on repairs, maintenance and remedial work.

Yet it has become apparent in subsequent years that the housing goals of Thatcherism consist in an *ideological* attack on the public sector, rather than an objective of saving money. This is seen in various ways.

Table 1: Housing Statistics, Britain: Selected Comparisons.

	1978 or 1978/79	1980 or 1980/81	1985 or 1985/86	1987 or 1987/88
A.	114 000	94 000	33 000	12 700*
B.	£4 849m	£3 097m	£1 672m	£1 225m
C.	£1 258m	£1 393m	£ 457m	na
D.	£#2 100m	£2 720m	£4 750m	-
E.	£12 023	£17 533	£23 742	£27 444**
F.	£5.20	£7.71	£15.59	-
G.	53 000	63 000	93 000	53 450*
H.	100	134.1	189.6	200.4

* Figures for first six months; ** Figure for 1986.

A. Public Sector Housebuilding: Completions (England).
B. Housing Investment Programme Allocations (England), 1986/87 prices.
C. Exchequer Subsidy to Local Authorities (England).
D. Tax Relief on Mortgage Interest (Great Britain), 1985/86 prices.
E. Average House Price for First Time Buyers (UK).
F. Average Weekly Local Authority Rent (England and Wales).
G. Homeless Households accepted by Local Authorities (England).
H. Retail Price Index (Great Britain).

Sources: Dept. of the Environment., various dates, *Housing and Construction Statistics*; DOE., various dates, *Local Housing Statistics;* Association of Metropolitan Authorities; Parliamentary Written Answers, various dates; Public Expenditure White Papers; *Accountancy,* June 1987.

Firstly, the accounting conventions used in public expenditure do not include the cost of tax foregone through support to owner occupation, but in fact this represents a loss to the public purse far greater than the savings in housing subsidies. In the five years from 1980/81 to 1985/86, tax relief on mortgage interest increased from £ 720 million to £4 750 million: its abolition would have meant a 13.4% increase in revenue from income tax and surtax. Over the same period, Exchequer housing subsidies to local authorities decreased from £1 393 million to £457 million. Thus the increased subsidies to home owners were more than double the reduction in subsidies to council tenants with, of course, richer owners getting the greatest support.

Subsidies to housing costs of individual householders through housing benefit (including rate rebates) reach about 3.6 million householders each in the public and private sectors and cost about £2 300 million in each sector, so this does not increase the imbalance. However, support for owner occupation does not end with mortgage tax relief: if we add exemption from Capital Gains tax, Inheritance tax and discount on the sales of council housing, the total cost to public funds exceeds £9 000 million and even this leaves out supplementary benefit payments of mortgage interest, development grants and relief from Value Added tax.

Secondly, public expenditure is taken to include both *capital* expenditure by local authorities, where there is a real asset as a result of the expenditure, *and* current subsidies on costs. Capital expenditure is financed by borrowing through the money market, and we have the illogical position where such expenditure through an individual loan is seen as useful expenditure to be encouraged through tax incentives, but a similar house built by a local authority with a similar loan is seen as an intolerable drain on public resources.

A further instance where the anti-public sector project triumphs over saving in public expenditure is in provision for the homeless. This is an issue which Forrest and Murie address in their chapter. Suffice it to say here that there are some 100 000 households annually accepted as homeless and in priority need, a figure which has doubled since 1978, and a proportionof these will spend several months in temporary accomodation in bed and breakfast hotels at a cost of some £11 000 a year per household in hotel bills, where the actual costs of providing permanent rehousing would be half of this. (Figures given in the House of Commons in January 1987 by John Patten, then Minister of Housing.)

Another instance of state intervention over subsidies has been promised by the recently re-elected government which again affects the Treasury's costs adversely and will increase costs to some council tenants. There is to be a ban on transfers from local authorities' General Rate Fund (that is, their general income from property tax) to the Housing Revenue Account. Local authorities will not be allowed to subsidise their tenants, and in some areas (mainly London boroughs) this will mean doubling of rents. Where this impacts on the Treasury is that about two thirds of these tenants will be having some or all their rent paid by the Department of Health and Social Security as Housing Benefit. (Transfers in the other direction will not be banned, so the situation will continue where some ratepayers in rural areas are being subsidised by rents of council tenants which more than cover the outgoings from the Housing Revenue Account.)

In summary, the goal of reducing provision has taken precedence over that of reducing expenditure: provision *will* be cut even if this means *higher* costs, to say nothing of the social costs.

The Government's alterations in *regulations* significantly affected housing activity have shown greater consistency. Early in their term they abandoned regulations on minimum space standards to which local authorities had to adhere. The other main area where regulations have been relaxed is in rent controls and security of tenure in the private rented sector. There has already been a partial abandonment of fair rents, and fixed term "shorthold" letting is now permitted instead of the greater security previously enjoyed. It has been announced that this relaxation of controls will go further; that landlords should be allowed to make "a reasonable rate of return" and that they will not be subjected to a process of approval.. "Assured tenancies" introduced on a limited scale will be extended more widely.

One area of regulation introduced by the last Labour government may well be relaxed, although this prediction is the authors' supposition rather than any "promise" or advance warning by the government.. The Housing (Homeless Persons) Act of 1977 placed on local authorities a duty to rehouse homeless families, provided they had dependent children, or were vulnerable (includiing being pregnant, elderly or ill), *and* had a "local connection", *and* had not brought about their homelessness intentionally.

These conditions are fairly restrictive and exclude most homeless households, but for many authorities, particularly in London, the incidence of homelessness is greater than the incidence of available vacancies, given other obligations such as transferring tenants subject to violence or harassment. Unless the flow of homeless households can be reduced, the government will not be able to achieve its aim of reducing the size of the council stock in these areas. We would therefore expect an enforced change in the regulations on who qualifies for rehousing by the local authority when homeless, to make them even more restrictive.

The aggregate effect of all these changes, some merely outline proposals, is virtually impossible to calculate. Expenditure on housing takes many forms and there is little sensible correspondence between those having an impact on the national economy, those regarded as public expenditure, and those which the government seeks to control. However, if the cost of all forms of support for owner occupation is taken into account, the total cost of the government's housing policy has certainly increased massively, despite the continued emphasis on pressing the nation to live within its means. Government assistance has been heavily redistributed from poor to rich. The aim is not to render housing affordable but to de-collectivise housing provision.

Summary

To summarise the case of Britain under the Conservatives, the evidence shows that state intervention cannot be seen as a single dimension. The ousing objectives of previous governments were, first to meet the overall *shortage* of housing then to tackle *unfit* housing. The Thatcher government has aimed firstly to reduce public expenditure, then reduce individual households' dependence on a local authority. We have seen that public sector newbuild has been severely cut, and that together with disposal of existing public sector stock this has resulted in a shrinking public sector, for the first time this century. Regulations have been relaxed to supposedly provide the conditions where private landlords can meet the needs that local authorities are prevented from meeting. Taking all forms of expenditure on housing, these have massively increased, mainly in order to achieve the objective of extending owner occupation. Yet there has been *no* action with respect to the main problem facing prospective housebuyers in the prosperous South East, that of rapidly inflating house prices.

Affordability is not a useful concept for understanding the objectives of the Thatcher government. The word may be used by government ministers as in the promise of "affordable rents": a piece of Orwellian 'newspeak' referring to rent levels very much higher than present fair rents or council rents; that is, *unaffordable* rents.

In terms of the original five objectives for state housing policy, the maintenance of social order has been achieved by increasing police powers and more sophisticated weaponry rather than by housing provision. Quality of population is scarcely an issue when those in steady jobs are increasingly in owner occupation: the state shows little interest in maintaining health, morale or dignity in a population without an economic role, and dependent on state benefits.

The social costs and damage to quality of life arising from occupation of an area where not only are *you* poor and trying to cope with the associated problems, but this is also true of all your neighbours, have not been recognised by the government, still less addressed. The government has deliberately rejected the idea of planning to reduce unemployment, believing that market forces will in time bring this about provided that workers do not price themselves out of the market through excessive wage demands. The encouragement of self sufficiency, in a highly individualised form, is clearly paramount. any merits in a collective approach, from support for research through overall direction of resources to meet the particular targets, to allowing individuals' housing costs to be based on historic costs, have effectively been ignored.

State Intervention in Housing Policy: The Developing World

Turning to Third World countries, the pattern of state intervention is very different. Concern with the objective of maintaining social order is often significant for governments in the developing world although social unrest is rarely precipitated by poor housing conditions alone. The fight for survival against the tyranny of hunger and poverty is so dominant in the life of many families in the less developed countries (LDCs) that political organisation and collective mobilisation is less widespread than might be expected. Where poverty is widespread and social change relatively slow, expectations of improvement may be limited. On the other hand the state in the developing world is also much more likely to exert coercion and direct force in quelling unrest. Open use of power may be used on a scale and in a manner that would not be considered legitimate in the West. Indeed, state power has frequently been used in LDCs to *reduce* housing provision directly, for example, by the bulldozing of barrios and squatter settlements built without state approval.

The second principal objective for the state is a concern to improve the health and physical well-being of the population. However, in the LDCs the burgeoning population with large numbers of young people capable of carrying out unskilled tasks means that labour supply outstrips demand. Many workers or prospective workers turn to the service sector in order to earn some money. The conventional wisdom about strategies for development in LDCs stresses the need for investment in human capital but priority normally goes to educating professional and highly skilled workers leaving the majority without adequate education and training. In the advanced nations a similar position may be emerging with mechanisation in production and advanced communications in other sectors resulting in smaller workforces for similar levels of wealth creation. A consequence is that governments show less interest than before in sustaining social and welfare programmes for all.

Enhancing self sufficiency and creating opportunities for development of skills as a third aim of government with respect to housing policy has come to prominence over the past decade. Self build housing programmes as a principal policy in the poorer nations has been given prominence by the World Bank's emphasis on "sites and services" schemes (Williams, 1984; World Bank, 1972, 1975). How far governments go in terms of treating self build as a means to develop the abilities and skills of the population depends on the circumstances within particular nations.

The goal of employment planning takes on a different form in the less developed countries. In most such countries there is plentiful cheap labour, although technical, organisational and building craft skills may be scarce. Economic planning related to housebuilding may centre on other objectives such as reducing dependence on expensive imported materials and construction plant.

The final objective of reducing inequalities and achieving redistribution through some form of pooled costs or central sharing of resources is on the agenda for many governments in the developing world. Progress towards this aim is limited given the relatively low levels of GNP, high levels of international debt and small size of the surplus in most LDCs. The experience of housing programmes has often shown that beneficiaries are from the middle economic strata rather than those households in greatest need (Dwyer, 1975; Harms, 1972). An explicit commitment to equalisation of housing conditions has been associated with socialist and collectivist governments.

Conclusions

Many people have seen the self actualising potential of participation in decision-making from Plato to Habermas whilst it is also said that the broader the participation the more democratic the process becomes (Pateman, 1970). When the organisation of housing provision is undertaken at the broader level, cross subsidisation and redistribution can be more easily effected. We believe this ability to pool resources in order to achieve equalisation was a principal benefit from state intervention in the housing system in the UK during the mid 20th century and that this remains a principal justification for maintaining a major governmental presence in the housing systems of the developed world today. Whilst not wishing to underplay the problems that have beset programmes of state housing in Britain particularly since 1956 when the subsidy system was altered to encourage the building of high rise housing, the record is not all bad. Against the catalogue of unpopular high flats, technical mistakes, bad construction, "sink" estates, poor repairs services and indifferent management, there are recent efforts to improve that reputation.

Principal among these are decentralisation of housing management in order to provide a more accesible and approachable service. Often decentralisation has been accompanied by some degree of greater tenant consultation and participation in the decision-making process. rogress is slow and some of the changes appear limited but they are pointing in the right direction in order to overcome the unpopularity of past management practices. Compared with other agents of housing provision (housing associations and private landlords), local authorities can be more effective and more responsive to tenant demands. In the realm of housing management, modernisation of dwellings and newbuild, the more adventurous efforts to obtain tenant participation in decision-making have been in the public sector. On the other hand those households on the margins of owner occcupation who have sought to buy their homes when on low incomes are faced with escalating difficulties of debt, as the scale of disrepair for which they have responsibility increases and the lack of experience to tackle these problems threaten to overwhelm them (Karn, Kemeny and Williams, 1986).

The rising scale of disrepair and lack of maintenance shows the limits to a vision of a property owning democracy in Britain. This growing problem will only be resolved by some form of collective state-led intervention such as direct provision and management (for example, enveloping) or subsidy (for example, grant aid). With a widening disparity in the developed nations between the well- and poorly-housed the case for greater equalisation of housing conditions and collectivisation of housing policy grows more pressing. Affordability as a concept might be turned on its head from its conceptual basis in the notion of individual responsiblity to offer a revised definition which indicates that the developing and developed worlds cannot neglect housing distress or decline in the quality of the housing stock. The corollary is that nations cannot afford *not* to develop collective programmes for improvement of housing conditions. Affordability would then become a matter of national accounting which presents housing costs as an input to national well-being and not a drain on resources.

Thus we do not decry the present British government's aim of promoting participation and reducing passive dependence on a local authority, but feel that this can be achieved through increased tenant participation in decisions about their housing. Where we disagree with the present government's approach is that these measures are not offered within a broader context of collective improvement or equalisation of housing conditions nor within a framework which offers wider democratic opportunities. Local authorities, being elected bodies, are accountable to local people; as stated above, the system of financing state housing through local authorities has many advantages and despite their failings, local authorities have a much better record of involving their clients than other agencies providing housing.

References

Association of Metropolitan Authorities, 1984: *Submission to the Inquiry into British Housing*. London: The Association.

Darke, R., 19xx: Housing in Nicaragua. International Journal of Urban and Regional *Research* 11, 100-114.

Department of the Environment, 1973: House Condition Survey 1971: England and Wales London: Her Majesty's Stationery Office.

----, 1978: *English House Condition Survey 1976*. London: Her Majesty's Stationery Office.

----, 1982: *English House Condition Survey 1981*. London: Her Majesty's Stationery Office.

----, 1985: *Inquiry into the Condition of the Local Authority Housing Stock*. London: The Department.

Dwyer, D., 1975: *People and Housing in Third World Cities*. London: Longman.

Hall, S. and Jaques, M., eds., 1983: *The Politics of Thatcherism*. London: Lawrence & Wishart.

Harms, H., 1972: The Housing Problem for Low Income People. In: J.F.C. Turner and R. Fichter (eds.): *Freedom to Build: Dweller Control of the Housing Process*. London: Collier-Macmillan, pp. 73-94.

Karn, V., Kemeny, J. and Williams, P., 1986: Low Cost Home Ownership in the Inner City. In: P.A. Booth and A.D.H. Crook (eds.): *Low Cost Home Ownership: An Evaluation* of *Housing Policy under the Conservatives*. London: Gower, pp. 149-169.

Le Grand, J. and Robinson, R., 1984: *Privatisation and the Welfare State*. London: Allen and Unwin.

Merrett, S., 1979: *State Housing in Britain Londo*n. Routledge and Kegan Paul.

Ministry of Housing and Local Government, 1964: *The Housing Programme 1965 to 1970*. Cmnd. 2838. London: Her Majesty's Stationery Office.

Pateman, C., 1970: *Participation and Democratic Theory*. Cambridge: Cambridge University Press.

Swenarton, M., 1981: *Homes Fit for Heroes: The Politics and Architecture of Early State Housing in Britain.* London: Heinemann Educational.

Turner, J.F.C., 1972: Housing as a Verb. In: J.F.C. Turner and R. Fichter (eds.): *Freedom To Build: Dweller Control of the Housing Process.* London: Collier-Macmillan, pp. 148-175.

Whitehead, C.M.E., 1986: Low Cost Home Ownership in the Context of Current Government Policy. In: P.A. Booth and A.H.D. Crook (eds.): *Low Cost Home Ownership: An Evaluation of Housing Policy under the Conservatives.* London: Gower, pp. 59-79.

World Bank, 1972: *Urbanisation: Sector Policy Paper*. New York: World Bank.

----, 1975: *Housing: Sector Policy Paper.* New York: World Bank.

Williams, D.G., 1984: The Role of International Agencies: The World Bank. In: G.K. Kayne (ed.): *Low Income Housing in the Developing World.* Chichester: Wiley, pp. 173C. Exchequer Subsidy to Local Authorities (England).

PART TWO:
THE PROBLEM OF AFFORDABLE HOUSING

AFFORDABLE HOUSING AND THE MARKET

Arne Karyd

Introduction

In his lifetime, a physician will probably perform many deep sighs over what he perceives as mere supersticion and misconceptions among the people surrounding him. Staying outside in chilly weather without proper clothing neither makes you catch a cold nor brings pneumonia around; it just lowers your resistance against contageon. Probably the same kind of problems face most professionals whatever the art of their profession. The situation for the economist revealing his occupation at the cocktail party is most accurately described as the dealing with myths, some of which displaying extreme survival capability.[1] For example, it is commonly believed that the optimal state of any activity is maximum, sufficient or at least profit. Any deficit-producing activity should preferably be abandonned. Among all myths of economics, this is probably the worst and its origin is often to be found in completely erroneous parallells between the economy of the nation and the economy of the household. The economy of the nation cannot be derived or described as a mere sum of every household. The assumed eternal life of the nation is but one crucial difference.

A closely situated illustration is the traffic policy of Western Europe and the Federal Republic of Germany (FRG). In the FRG, the state railways - impressivly effective to a foreign utilizer - display an annual deficit of some four billion DM. Many people are alarmed by this fact and advocate the reallocation of traffic from railways to roads. However, if the financial result of the roads was measured in the same way as the result of the railways, the deficit would render most business accountants unconscious. Consider for instance the annual interest and depletion on the capital invested in the 9000 km FRG highway net.[2]

1. It should be kept in mind that economists deal with questions of economy facing a nation, region, branch, socio-economic layer, group of people etc, normally disregarding organizational boundaries. The science dealing with economy within an organizational framework, e.g. costs and revenues of a business firm, is labeled business administration..

2. Note, that although - contrary to a widespread misconception - German highway construction began as early as 1913 less than one third of the present net was completed by the end of World War II. Hence even the nominal cost of production is immense.

Affordable Housing and the Homeless

In addition, it can be shown that there is an optimal price level for railway transport as well as any other service or merchandise. To the economist, "optimal" means optimal to the society rather than to the railway administration. It can also be shown that in the railway case this price level is very low and will bring about a substantial deficit. The conclusion is that railways should be run with a certain deficit. If a profit is displayed, this normally indicates too high a price level, insufficient volume of production or both. This conclusion is probably backed up by the relatives of some 10,000 men, women and displayed, this normally indicates too high a price level, insufficient volume of production or both. This conclusion is probably backed up by the relatives of some 10,000 men, women and children annually killed by road traffic in the FRG. To them, to the transportation economist and to those distressed by dying woods, the railway deficit removed from its economic context means less than nothing.

Now the connection between this line of reasoning and affordable housing may seem more than obscure. My point is the following: If basic economics is disregarded, the effects on society might be more profound and widespread than most policymaker realize.

Although there may be no lives to be saved by altered housing olicy, vast sums now spent in vain may be saved and used better. The aim of this paper is to discuss o the nature of the "market" in the housing framework o some frequently disregarded market-related facts of economics within the housing policy sector o some effects of this neglect.

Swedish Housing Conditions

Housing policy and housing conditions in Sweden differ significantly from those of continental Europe. 178 years of peace, rapid urbanization, a high rate of economic growth, powerful unions and a powerful construction industry, a high level of ambition in social policy etc. all put their marks on development. It is also obvious that housing policy makers in a country slightly larger than the FRG, Austria, Switzerland and the Benelux together inhabited by a population comparable to that of greater Paris (8,4 million) face different problems than those facing their continental colleagues. However, these differences apply to the size of the problems rather than to their kind. In other words, probably all questions troubling Occident housing policy makers can be found in Sweden but their extent and severity are less pronounced. A possible exception is the problem of homelessness. Facing winter, social authorities in Gothenburg, our second largest city, scanned the city for outdoor sleepers. Their total findings were one man sleeping in his car as a victim of a raging wife rather than housing policy (Göteborgs-Posten, Nov 22, 1987). In Stockholm, comparable to Hamburg in size, conditions are somewhat harsher and in a recent TV-programme social authorities estimated the number of outdoor lodgers to less than 100.

The Present Swedish Housing Situation

In order to save paper space for discussion rather than description, the present situation and its background will be summarized into a few points. Details are found in the Benton and Karyd (1986) paper.

- As far back as in 1970, Sweden probably outstripped most if not all comparable countries in housing standard measured as the number of occupied dwellings per 1.000 inhabitants (Luijanen, 1981). The same conclusion is valid for the average size of *completed* dwellings by that time but not for the average size in the existing stock.

- Basic housing objectives (discussed at length in e.g., Lundquist, 1981; Malmsten, 1969) were fulfilled in the mid-1970s, at least on the macro level (see Jussil, 1981).

- By this time, construction activity dropped to one third of its 1970 peak level which was some 110.000 completed dwellings. Simultaneously, construction price index *increased* its rate of growth (Wickman, 1987) and housing subsidy volume started skyrocketing.

- Construction of new dwellings has from time to time turned into "houseomania". From 1949 to the present day, some 2.6 million dwellings have been completed. The whole population could be very well housed without utilizing any part of the housing heritage from centuries past. The ratio of post-war dwellings to all dwellings is roughly the same as in the FRG, a country which - to put it mildly - had a slightly different starting point (see the contribution by Friedrichs).

- Direct governmental financial support - housing allowances, interest allowances and miscellaneous supports - amount to some SEK 20 billion at present. In comparison, the defence budget is some 25% larger.

- The financial burden of interest allowances to already existing dwellings will continue to grow for about 18 years at the present inflation level (Wickman, 1987).

- Strong evidence suggest that income distributive effects of housing subsidies conflict with fundamental housing policy objectives in Sweden as well as in the other Nordic countries (Åhren, 1986, and to some extent also Turner, 1986).

- In spite of alleged severe conditions on urban housing markets, hardly any attempts have been made to use the second hand market for housing policy purposes although this sector comprises vast policy opportunities (Brzesky, 1986).

Affordable Housing Policy

Most developed countries recognize the responsibility of government to provide housing to its citizens. How, and to which extent, government should intervene in the housing sector is an issue of considerable debate. The disagreement is extremely profound when the attitude of government towards "housing markets" is under debate. In order to provide a point of departure for the subsequent discussion, I will characterize two different types of opinion in this field and trace their economic implications.

Market believers: "Almost every kind of services and goods are available on a market which means that there are sellers as well as buyers. There are markets for single-dwelling houses, condominiums and multi-dwelling houses. Although illegal in Sweden, there is also a market for rent agreements in the big cities. The need for housing will be satisfied by the forces of the market - demand and supply. Compared to these real forces, the power of government is small. Because of its limited power and because the market is the best way to distribute housing, the role of government should be confined to lubricate and facilitate activities on the markets. If extremely high rents or sales profits are observed, this is not an indication of unsufficient government control but a sign of improper market function. The reasons are often to be found in vainful attempts from the government to offset the market, e.g. by constraints on construction and supply".

Market opposers: "Adequate housing is a basic human right, not a merchandise. The influence of markets over such an essential sector of human life should be removed or at least rendered harmless. Government should excise control over physical planning, construction of new housing, rent levels and price levels. Although private-owned single- and multi-family dwellings may be tolerated, realized capital gains occuring at sale should be heavily taxed. For multi-family dwellings, prospective buyers should be subject to approval by the local tenant organization. The forming of condominiums should not be encouraged. In general, housing should be subsidized to prevent people from choosing inferior housing conditions in order to use the money for other kinds of consumption".

For reasons of discussion, the opinions characterized above are somewhat exaggerated. Although there may be straightforward advocates of each version, most opinions encountered in every-day life are compromises between the two. This should be kept in mind but has no impact on the following discussion.

The Nature of the Market

Part of this antagonism is explained by the fact that "market" is a word with very different meaning to different groups. To the believer, it is a nice sunny place where neatly behaving sellers and buyers agree upon fair deals to the benefit of all and the omnipotent, wellinformed consumer is free to choose. To the opposer, it is a ghastly location where top-hat- dressed, tax-evading sharks already well off make incredible profits by exploiting basic needs and ignorance among powerless people.

No more than anyone else could the economist supply a description of the market that both parties would agree upon. Another approach is to find the necessary conditions for the existence of a market. In other words, which factors must be present before we can say that the situation is best described as a "market"? Economics shows that only three factors are necessary:

- There must be buyers, i.e. someone willing to increase his possession of the merchandise and pay a price for it;
- There must be sellers, i.e. someone in possession of the merchandise but willing to dispose of it at a price;
- Finally there must be some way for sellers and buyers to find each other: A market place, advertisements, brokers etc.

In particular, it should be noted that the approval of government or of society in general are not necessary conditions. This is proven by the perpetual existence of semi-legal and illegal markets like those for prostitution, narcotics, and even housing (see the contribution by Kerner). If the market offers profits high enough, it will resist almost any kind of extermination attempts.

From this scenario it should be clear that the market exists whether you like it or not. Housing policy can make it shrink or expand and improve or obstruct its activities but housing policy can never make the market disappear. Facing this harsh reality, the best way to act for the housing policy maker is to travesty the proverb If you can't beat them - join them and say: I can't beat the market, so I will accept its existence and use it for my housing policy purposes. Unfortunately this confession is slightly too much for many a housing politician. The result is an at least in Sweden frequent attitude, namely the ostrich approach to housing policy. This is characterized by the denieing, neglecting or disregarding of the market in the futile hope that if you pretend it is not there, it will cause you no harm. 1) I will provide some examples in section 4.

Market-Believer Policy Implications

Even the most superficial glance at 20th-century housing history clearly reveals the inability of a market left to its own to provide adequate housing for the poor. Market believers are seldom crude enogh to deny this conclusion. More often, the market believer escapes this lacking feature of the market: If the poor are poor, then general social policy and general subsidies like allowances, not housing subsidies, should relieve the poor from their poverty and make them fit for fight in the market. In the market, existing whether we like it or not, income redistribution by means of subsidizing specific goods like housing causes price- and behaviour adjustments and in the end, the redistributional effect may be offset or inverted. In short, poverty should be fought by social policy, not housing policy, and the latter is fairly useless even as a tool in social policy. A possible exception is the housing voucher system used in the U.S. contribution to This is not a general subsidy - it is directed towards housing - but its use can be confined to those who really need it.

Normally the inability to combine housing policy tools with such a restriction is put forward as a major disadvantage by the market believer. This line of reasoning is quite powerful and necessitates a brief discussion of the housing policy advocated by the market believer. For goods and services in general, the quantity can be sufficiently described by using units as number, weight, volume or number of man-hours. Measuring the volume of housing is immensely more complicated. Popular units as sq.m. or number of dwellings do not incorporate the quality and equipment standard of housing. Consequently these measurements provide only a very rough estimate of housing volume.[1]

For the discussion we will disregard this complication and assume that square meters, is an adequate measurement of housing volume. Then the main argument of market believers can be sketced as follows.

Figure 1: Market Believer Housing Market

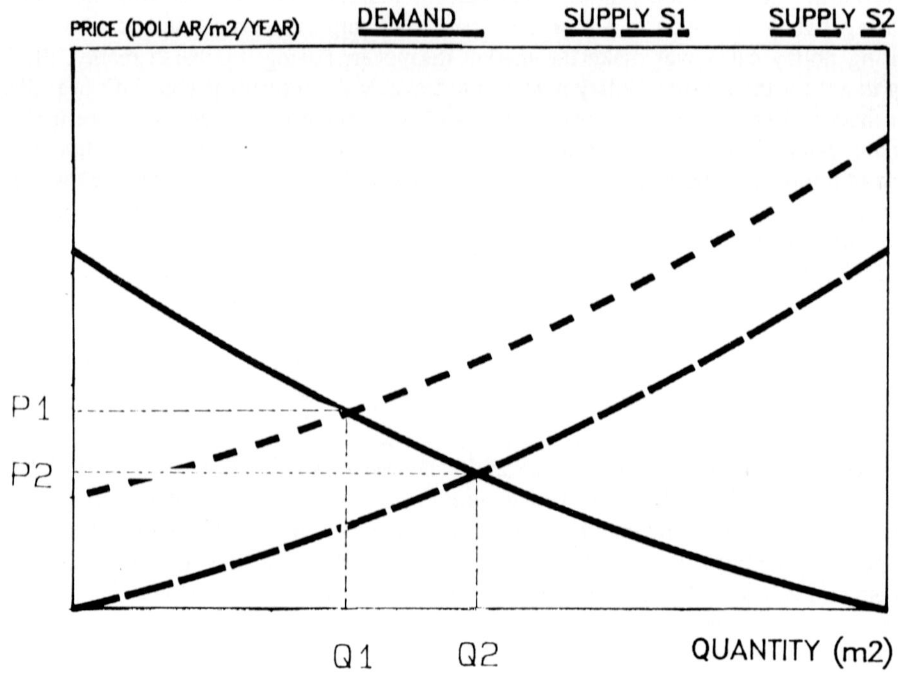

1. See Eriksson (1981) for a discussion of the relation between "useful floorspace" and "floorspace for housing purposes". Comparing 1970 and 1978, Eriksson concluded that in spite of a 50% drop in the number of dwellings annually produced, the produced useful floorspace.

In Figure 1, the vertical axis measures the price of housing in SEK per square meter and year. (The precise nature of this price - rent, costs for a condominium or cost for a single-family dwelling - has no bearing on the discussion.) The "quantity of housing" is measured along the horizontal axis in square meter. The demand for housing is downward sloping, i.e. the lower the cost for housing, the higher the quantity of housing demanded. The supply for housing is upward-sloping, i.e. the higher the price for housing, the higher the volume of housing offered on the market.

While the *exact* properties of the demand and supply curves are very hard to establish, there is no doubt whatsoever regarding the general relationships between price and volume. The market, if left to its own, will find a point of equilibrium at the quantity q_1 and the price level p_1. (It can be shown that some combinations of slopes will make the price and quantity fluctuate around the equilibrium point rather than reaching it. This possibility is disregarded in the following.)

The prevailing price level p_1 may be unattainable to large groups of citizens. According to the market believer, the first commandment is that this situation never should be attacked by interfering with the market. Instead, general subsidies to the low income earners should make them able to face the price level p_1. Hence no "housing policy" is necessary. If, however, a housing policy really must be implemented it should be directed towards the supply of housing.

The demand curve is a reflection of consumer preferences and these should not be tampered with. Instead, action should be taken in order to shift the supply curve to the right. Possible steps are the introduction of construction-encouraging policy instrument such as (more) favourable tax rules for the owners of multi- family dwellings, conversion of abandoned industrial sites into housing sites, changers in the building code, etc. (The existence of a building code - a book of technical construction requirements - is justified inter alia by the fact that the lifespan of a building normally exceeds the lifespan of its constructor. Hence society, as heir to the building, has the right to impose rules otherwise neglected by the constructor. This point is normally accepted also by market believers.) The supply of housing will increase to the S' curve and the market will reach a new equilibrium at the lower price level p_2 and the higher volume level q_2. Everyone but landlords are better off than before.

This sketchy example is of course a very rough description of the market believer line of reasoning. Nevertheless it serves fairly well as a basic tool for evaluating a market-centered policy. The rough sketch also contains the main objection to this kind of policy.

Macro- and micromarkets

The Swedish word for real estate, "fastighet", has the same inherent meaning as the German "Immobilien" and the French "immeubles", i.e. the basic property of sites and buildings of not being movable. This means that "housing" at the macro level discussed above is a fairly useless concept. Dwellings are only to a very limited extent substitutes for each other. Normally the housing consumer is faced with a micro housing market within reasonable range from his work..

Most people, especially in the lower income groups, cannot choose their housing first and their work later. Their choice of housing must be confined to available opportunities within a few hundred square kilometers. In addition, this limited market can be further divided into markets for tenancy agreements (where the price is the rent), condominiums and single-family dwellings. In the latter cases, the "price" is the paid or lost rent for the necessary capital plus, in the condominium case, the yearly fee.

In urban areas, all these markets are characterized by next to vertical supply curves, i.e. the quantity of housing offered at the market will remain practically constant regardless of the housing price level. The offered quantity is not totally insensitive to the price level because very high price levels would make the conversion of present non-housing premises into dwellings profitable and even tempt some owners of single-family dwellings to offer a room or two for rent. In general, though, the supply of housing is quite stiff because there are very few sites suitable for housing construction and very few dwellings not already occupied. Under these circumstances it is impossible to implement a housing policy aiming at increased supply and furthermore, the real cost of housing (the cost expressed in e.g constant 1987 dollars) may rise all by itself. According to a disputed but interesting theory of economist Södersten (1976), three factors contribute to a long-run upward push of market-determined housing costs: The growth of cities, making remote areas less and less remote; inflation, raising the general price level more than the costs of owning multi-family dwellings; and finally the fact that productivity (production per unit of input, e.g. man-hours) tends to grow slower in the construction industry than in general, thus raising the cost of new construction and pushing the price of existing buildings upward.

The Vicious Circle

However, even if the market works like the ideal case depicted in figure 1, the general subsidies preferred by market believers will affect the market. If the subsidy works as intended, it will rise the income level of the recipients. Consequently, their demand for all goods and services *including housing* will rise. The demand curve in Figure 2 is shifted to the right.

As a result, the price level will rise to p_2 and the quantity of housing to q_2. Landlords and property owners will also receive part of the subsidy, materialized in a higher price level. The rising price level will create a need for additional subsidies which in turn will rise the price level still further and so on. This vicious circle will not continue for ever but the final subsidy level might be much higher than originally calculated.

Applied to the small urban markets discussed above, the conclusion will will be that the subsidy will have but marginal effects on the quantity of housing offered to the market. Instead, the housing price level will rise and the bulk of the subsidy will be received by landlords. Summing up, a policy tool such as general household subsidies requires more than the existence of a market in order to work as intended by market believers. It requires a market with a *price-sensitive supply* of housing. This complication is frequently overlooked by market believers.

Figure 2: Subsidy Effect in the Market

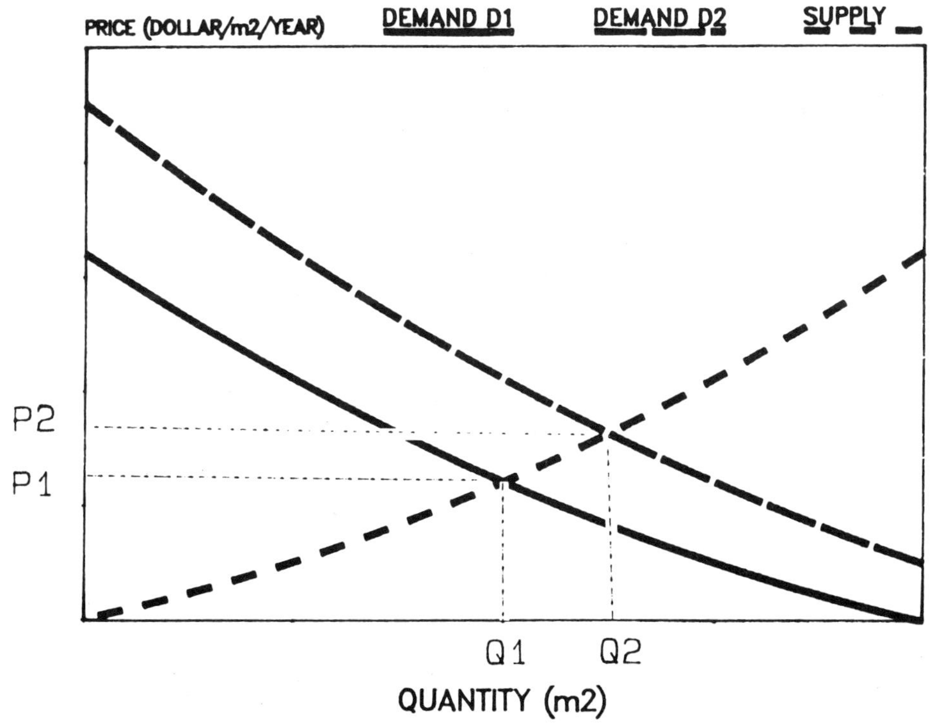

Market-Opposer Policy Implications

For the market opposer, the correct ways to act differ somewhat between the different kind of dwellings. For reasons of space I will confine the discussion to one specific issue. The example concerns rent levels for rented dwellings. If market rents are too high, the market opposer will advocate the replacement of market rents by some other standard, e.g. dictated or negotiated rents. To the lawyer and the policy-maker contaminated by the ostrich approach, this is done by adding an additional paragraph to the law. The economist would say that the task is slightly more complicated.

Negotiated Rent Levels

In Sweden, rent levels are set in negotiations between the tenant organizations and their landlord counterpart. Semi-public bodies are assumed to be rent leaders. (A detailed discussion of negotiated rents versus market rents is found in Nyman and Torne, 1985). Differences in location have a profound effect on the demand but are only to a minor extent reflected in the negotiated rent levels. Compared to the rent levels emerging in a free market, the central city rents will be lower and the remote suburban rents higher. This means empty dwellings in the suburbs and excess demand in the center (Figure 3).

To the economist, as separated from the business administrator, both empty suburban dewellings and excess demand in the center indicates ineffectiver housing policy. In the first case, we could all agree upon the fact that if the house already exists, it will normally stand there for fifty or a hundred years and in fact it will deteriorate more rapidly if it is not occupied. Nothing is to gain by keeping the rent level so high that none finds it worthwhile to live in the house. Instead, the rent level should be lowered, the house filled with tenants and we will all benefit from the fact that still another part of our common capital is utilized. (Provided, of course, that the deterrent factor really is the rent level. As indicated in the contribution by Friedrichs in this book, also the physical and social environment and the constructive quality of the house may serve as intimidating factors. These factors may be too powerful to be offset by rent decreases and in that case demolition or drastic reconstruction may be the only remedies.)

Under negotiated rents, the counterpart of empty suburban dwellings is normally excess demand in the central parts of the city. "Excess demand" means that at the prevailing rent level, there will be a queue of prospective tenants for each available dwelling because the benefits associated with these dwellings are perceived as having a value greater than the rent.

. Suppose a centrally located, attractive dwelling has a negotiated rent of x dollars per month. If the rent was determined at a free market instead, it would be x plus an additional z dollars, i.e. someone is willing to pay not only x but x+z dollars for the benefit of occupying this dwelling. Anyone moving into the dwelling would, though, only have to pay x dollars monthly because this is the negotiated rent. Realizing that if I could get hold of the dwelling and will have to pay only x dollars per month, I may conclude that it would be profitable to offer the present inhabitant a sum of money for the lease contract. In fact, it would be profitable to offer a sum up to the present value of the z dollars per month I would be willing to pay but do not have to pay if I get hold of the dwelling. Further realizing that if I pay this sum of money the money is not lost but constitutes an investment, the value of which I will be able to recover if I sell the lease contract, my willingness to pay the present inhabitant for his contract increases additionally.

Figure 3: Negotiated and Market Rents

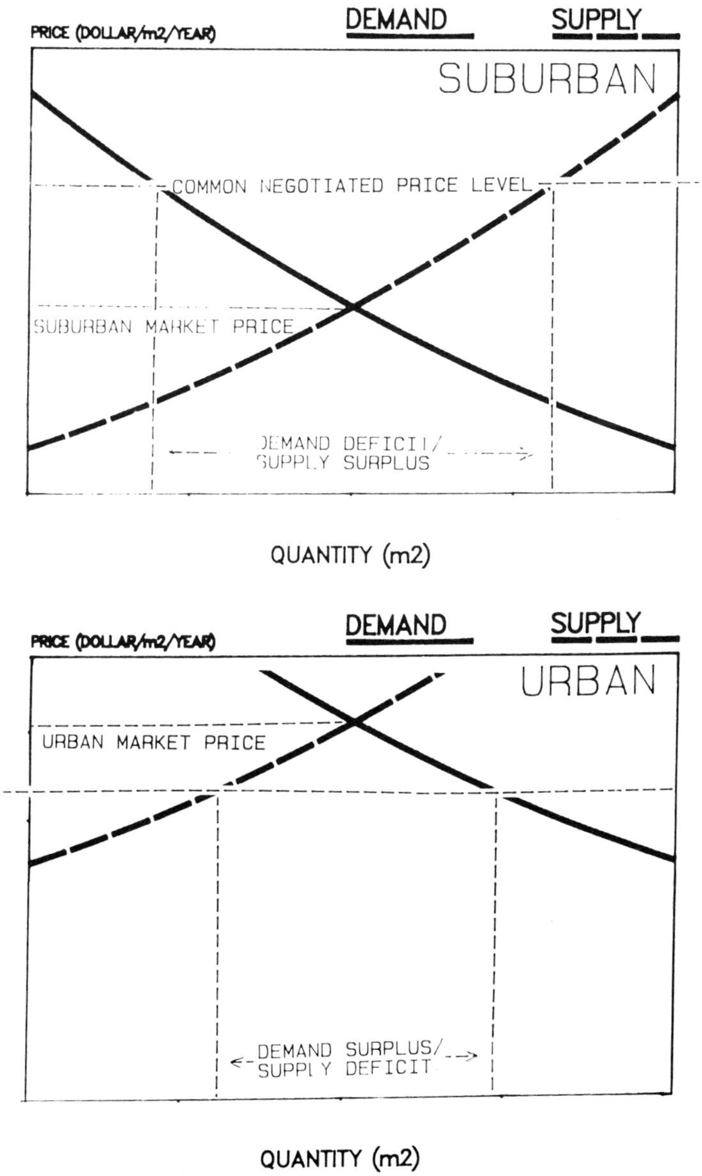

The prospect that a small group of happy central dwellers should be able to make vast profits just because they happen to inhabit an attractive dwelling is unacceptable not only to the market opposer. Consequently this kind of business arrangement is prohibited in Sweden. Unfortunately - as we have already seen - the approval of government is not a necessary condition for the existence of a market. In other words, the market cannot be banned away.

For the present Swedish government, active regional policy is hardly a hallmark and the urbanization pressure is back to its 1960s level. This means increased demand for centrally located dwellings and a rising difference between negotiated and market rents. As mentioned above, one is not allowed to sell ones tenancy agreement but to switch it for another or hand it over to the seller of a single-family dwelling one is buying. These possibilities set the stage for profitable circumvening. If someone switches his tenure against another of less market value, he can always capitalize the difference in market value by simultaneously selling some furniture or your 1972 Volkswagen wreck for 10,000 dollars. This may be illegal but no one can do anything about it because the car price is never made public. Accompanying rising demand, these transactions are performed less and less tacitly and at present may find notes in the most popular areas offering thousands of dollars to anyone who will hand over a lease contract. While the offer is not illegal, accepting it is doubtlessly illegal.

In the case where a tenant moves to a single-family dwelling and the former owner will take over the tenancy agreement, the situation is even more advantageous. The seller will pay the tenant the whole market value of his tenure by simply reducing the price of the single-family dwelling. For reasonable proportions between selling price and tenure value, this transaction is invisible, unattackable and probably not even illegal.

Capitalizing market value by circumvening the law is a phenomenon rapidly aggravating the problem of implementing a rent level policy. Law enforcement when the criminal action is totally confined to two *consenting* parties is next to impossible. Even the market opposer must give the market believer some credit for the statement that government power is small compared to the real forces of demand and supply.

To this problem no easy remedies are visible. My impression is that negotiated rents perform their redistributional task reasonably well as long as the difference between negotiated and market rent is not too big. When this difference reaches a certain magnitude though, negotiated rents have to take at least part of the market pressure into consideration. This will give rise to new problems, for instance rapid increases in the price of centrally located buildings, but the alternative is inevitably black- market adjustments described above. These adjustment can be assumed to be even less desirable than increased rents and property values from a social point of view.

The Problem of Subsidized Single-Family Dwellings

Practically all single-family dwellings constructed in later years are financed by means of heavily subsidized government loans. One salient problem with such an arrangement is how to confine the subsidy to those who really need it. Until mid-1986, the construction of a government-financed house was surrounded by tight regulations on maximum floorspace and equipment standards. For instance, a sauna occasionally disqualified the house for government loans. The same effect was brought about if the maximum permissable floorspace was exceeded. Such regulations are sitting ducks for the ingenuity of the construction industry: Attics with no staircase (to be delivered later) and the windows hidden behind the wooden panel, spaces remarkably similar to saunas but labeled closet, supply room or something else. In 1986, these rules and the production cost control, equally circumvenable, were simply lifted. This was the right thing to do because these restrictions did not work. However, one could raise the question whether the social profile of the housing policy still remains when a castle-building millionaire receives a heavy subsidy for the first 5-6 rooms.

While the subsidizing of single-family houses regardless of size and standard in itself is enough to cause hesitation, the trouble really starts when the house is being sold at the second-hand market. Real estate broker advertisements clearly reveal an evident feature of a subsidized loan connected to the house and not to the inhabitant: The loan has a market value corresponding to the size of its remaining subsidy content. The second-hand buyer will buy not only the house but also the subsidized loan at its present value. Consequently the subsidy, intended to last for some 15-20 years, may be cashed at present value by the first owner if the market is functioning reasonably well. This is probably the most obvious and most omitted property of a subsidized loan. A detailed example is given by Benton and Karyd (1986: 311); a remedy - attaching the loan to persons instead of houses - is also suggested. If at all recognized, the problem has been attacked only by vague and easily circumvenable means like transfer price control.

Conclusions

In a research report as well as in a discussion paper the author should be granted the right to use the last lines at his own discretion, e.g. to present the deductions he wants to present regardless of the degree of background support in the preceding text. Straining this freedom to the limit, I would suggest that the "Swedish model" housing policy is mainly influenced by the ostrich approach to housing markets. It is tacitly assumed that if you refuse to see or discuss the market, it will cease to exist. Unfortunately, the market does not require the approval of anyone to be fully operational and it will tend to offset the most ambitious policy programs insofar as these programs are designed without due consideration to basic laws of the market. Housing policy could make use of the market (see, Brzeski, 1986) but this possibility is rarely utilized. Out of the immense volume of housing subsidies, the bulk will serve to boost the housing standard of people who do not really need it. Only to a marginal extent will the provision of affordable housing to those who cannot afford it be promoted by this system.

Furthermore there does not seem to be much hope of rapid recovery from the ostrich syndrom. On the contrary, even recent actions reveal ignorance of basic market laws. According to the municipalities of Gothenburg, the best way to stop black market transactions with tenancy contracts would be to force the landlord to sign an affidavit that no money was involved when a tenancy agreement was taken over. Sancta simplicitas would be the comment from the market believer and also from those who do not believe in but understand the market (Göteborgs-Posten, Sept. 22, 1987: 7).

Another policy instrument recently introduced confirms the prevailing ostrich approach. In order to enable low income earners with children to buy used single-family dwellings, acquisition loans were introduced during 1987. Someone having at least two children and a low household income is entitled to a very favorable loan. This fact is of course known to the seller. Hence the price will be pushed upward and this effect cannot be offset by transfer price control for reasons stated above. Furthermore, the fact that one may be entitled to a vast subsidy if his household income is low enough makes income tax evasion even more profitable than before. Note that the income requirement is assesed for one year only while the subsidized loan will yield revenue for many years (Göteborgs-Posten, Sept. 9, 1987: 4, "Sydost" enclosure). Finally, this kind of arrangement divides the buyers on the market into one non-subsidized and one extremely subsidized group on the very dubious basis of taxable income. The members of the latter group will be much more competible in the housing market than even high-income earners of the former group. It is a riddle how the housing policy can go on and on creating such profound cleavages.

References

Åhren, P, 1986.: *Housing Subsidies in the Nordic Countries*. Discussion paper to the 1986 International Research Conference on Housing Policy at the National Institute for Building Research

Benton, L. and Karyd, A., 1986: *How to Spend Billions. Waste Aspects of the Swedish Housing Loans System*. Discussion paper to the 1986 International Research Conference on Housing Policy at the National Institute for Building Research.

Brzeski, W.J., 1986: *Resale Home Finance and Market Reallocation of Households - a Viable Option for Swedish Housing Policy Research*? Discussion paper to the 1986

International Research Conference on Housing Policy at the National Institute for Building Research.

Eriksson, J., 1981: Har vi byggt bort trångboddheten? Contribution to the anthology *Bostadsfrågan inför 80-talet*. Stockholm.

Jussil, S., 1981: Kredit- och skattepolitikens samband med bostadspolitiken. Contribution to the anthology *Bostadsfrågan inför 80-talet*. Stockholm.

Luijanen, M., 1981: Svensk bostadspolitik vid internationell jmfrelse. Contribution to the anthology *Bostadsfrågan inför 80-talet*. Stockholm.

Lundqvist, L.J., 1981: Bostadskostnaderna. Statens Institut för Byggnadsforskning t:19.

Malmsten, B.: Bostadsbyggandet i plan och verklighet. *Byggforskningsrådet* R69:84

Nyman, B. and Tornée, P., 1985: *Marknadsmässiga hyror för en rättvisare bostadsmarknad.* Discussion paper to the 1985 housing seminar at the National Institute for Building Research.

Södersten, B., 1976: Bostadsförsörjning och bostadspolitik under efterkrigstiden. In: B. Södersten (ed.): *Svensk Ekonomi*. Stockholm.

Turner, B., 1986: *Housing Finance in the Nordic Countries*. Discussion paper to the 1986 International Research Conference on Housing Policy at the National Institute for Building Research.

AFFORDABLE HOUSING IN A SOCIALIST COUNTRY THE CASE OF PRAGUE

Antonín Kerner

This chapter focusses on experiences in a socialist country, the CSSR, and in particular its capital, Prague, with no housing "market" but a housing policy with a strong impact on social interventions. The non-existence of a housing market, however, does not imply that there are no economic problems with regard to housing policy and other services connected with dwellings.

The Socialist Economy

The Czechoslovak national economy is being developed on the basis of social ownership of the means of production. It is the state-owned socialist enterprises together with co-operative enterprises that play a decisive role, even though there is a relatively wide range of various organizational forms differing in their ways of management and financing, in the scope of economic activity etc. Private ownership of small-scale producers in agriculture or in services (craftsmen) is of little importance.

The practice of building up socialism in Czechoslovakia is based on Marx's thesis that it is not the realization of private ownership of the means of production but only human labor that can be the source of individual income.

The socialist economy is a planned economy. The system of overall economic balance-accounting is a precondition for economic growth and balance. The system of balance-accounting of income, investments, manpower and external economic relations is a prerequisite for future-related decision-making. The quality of balance-accounting also influences the quality of decision-making processes which are outlined in the general scheme in the objectives of the plan. Further working out of the balance-accounting method and all other information systems makes possible approaching the drafting of middle-term and long-term structure plans. Middle-term plans (for five years) can perform their target and programme function. The five-year plan integrates main targets such as the number of flats, subsidies, capital investment in the form of technical and social infrastructure.

First of all the planning scheme programme is orientated towards locating capital investments and the labor force as the main conditions for economic equilibrium. The real economic growth rate and the proportion of all kinds of goods and services depend on many other circumstances. The responsibility of enterprises to fulfill the main targets laid

Affordable Housing and the Homeless

down in the state plan on the one hand and to introduce marketing on the other hand are the important points of today's socialist economy. The decentralization of decision-making processes is very important for the material and moral initiative.

The system of economic planning is a very important background for the social policy. Economic and social policy are very closely integrated. Positive results in economy policy influence social policy.

Social policy safeguards important social rights and certainties for all people. Czechoslovakia is a country with full employment, a country in which everyone can work corresponding to his education, training and abilities. In Czechoslovakia today social security covers the entire working population - mothers, children, old and sick people.

Young families with children receive help, free education and free health care is provided for the whole population. The socialist state is also increasingly caring for retired people (men over the age of sixty and women aged between 53 and 57 depending on their number of children).

Housing Policy

The housing problem seen as an imbalance between the number, size, and location of flats on the one hand and the real demand for them on the other hand was the historical problem. Socio-economic and technological progress which is the basis for the development of productive forces has led man to engage in constant improvements in his way of living and has improved his real possibilities to satisfy his demand for housing. However, in the past the use of these possibilities depended not only on the socio-economic level of society as a whole but mainly on the status of a given social stratum or group in the process of the production and distribution of the national product.

The basic housing paradox of the past was the massive deterioration of the housing conditions of the industrial proletariat and the impoverished lower middle classes, despite the general economic growth which could easily have fully satisfied the housing requirements of those days.

Industrialization also spurred great social changes, in particular a rapid growth of cities which became industrial and economic centres. City populations continued to grow much faster than national populations - a fact attributed to the influx of people from rural areas.

The developing industries drew new blood not only from the villages, but their labor force was also reinforced by smallholders and minor craftsmen pouring in from smaller towns.

This process inevitably led to the worsening of their housing situation compared with their earlier smallholder existence as craftsmen or farmers. The transition to hired labor meant the separation of work and home - earlier a harmonic unity. No sooner had a smallholder been denied the possibility to use his own means of production and forced to seek employment in the city than he lost the benefit of keeping his own house or apartment. His options narrowed to renting a flat either from his employer or a landlord.

Many things have changed after the Second World War in the period of the construction of the socialist system. Radical changes that occurred in this period led to a broad democratization and to the humanization of housing with standards rapidly improving. The main objective was to satisfy the housing needs of workers, providing each and every family with their own flat. A new housing policy was formulated as part of the social policy characterized by a strong government influence.

Housing policy can be defined as an inventory of means and methods applied by any society to achieve certain goals in the sphere of housing. These goals differ depending on which class rules society or, better still, whose interests are pursued by those who formulate and implement such a policy. The socialist housing policy strives to eliminate the housing shortages which in the past affected most strongly the low-income, poorly qualified and socially underprivileged classes.

The socialist society with its political and management bodies provides all citizens equal access to housing. In this process it gives priority to the improvement of the conditions under which those on a lower social level must live. To ensure that housing needs are met is primarily the job of social institutions. These include first of all the national committees, i.e. local bodies of state power and administration, social organizations and co-operatives.

An inevitable part of housing policy is the consistent satisfaction of housing requirements in harmony with the requirements of production and society, and with the social needs of the different groups of the population. Czechoslovakia's socialist housing policy emphasizes a comprehensive approach to housing, comprising both housing construction and the provision of all basic amenities for residents. Its goal is to create a hygienic and first-rate housing environment consistent in all aspects with the modern demands of housing culture.

The architectural solution and physical planning of housing complexes stem from the tenet that newly built and existing housing projects must ensure equal access to the basic components of social consumption of finance from public funds, such as education, health care and culture.

In the post-war years Czechoslovakia experienced positive demographic trends resulting in an upswing in new families and new households. This, conversely, dramatically increased the demand for housing, especially in newly industrialized regions. The new organization of the national economy naturally changed the national demographic pattern. The housing problem became a hot issue, largely because of the ever fuller satisfaction of the other vital needs of the population. Thus, housing emerged as a crucial condition for keeping the rapidly growing living standards in good proportions. With regard to the number of finished flats per 1,000 inhabitants, Czechoslovakia in the mid-seventies ranked among the leading European countries.

The following Table 1 shows the gross total of housing construction in ten-year periods since the end of the Second World War (all types of dwellings):

Table 1: Housing Construction in Czechoslovakia, 1946-1985

Period	Number of finished homes
1946-1955	307,000
1956-1965	722,000
1966-1975	1,055,000
1976-1985	1,133,000

Current estimates stand at 336 housing units per 1,000 inhabitants on a national scale. More than two-thirds of all Czechoslovak citizens live in houses and flats built after the year 1945. The rapid growth of houses during the sixties and seventies brought with it the need to use pre-fabricated elements and to apply industrial elements in constructing new districts. Concerning quantity this was a big advantage. On the other hand there are many problems with technical and architectural standards, with maintenance, and with regard to social aspects.

It goes without saying that the satisfaction of housing needs, just like other spheres of consumption, is limited in socialist societies by the means and resources accrued. Thus, economic progress and consequently even housing construction are determined by the level of social production reached so far. They do not depend exclusively on individual wishes or the co-operativeness of state organs, but also on the objective availability of resources that can be realized for housing projects in the spheres of financial investment, material or capacity. Demands are rising as far as the quality of housing and related services is concerned. The situation is better in villages and small towns; demand is higher in cities, especially in Prague, the capital city.

Forms of Housing

The following forms of housing construction co-exist in Czechoslovakia: state (communal), based on state ownership, co-operative based on the principle of group socialist ownership and construction of family houses which are the personal property of citizens. It is possible for private citizens to buy state-owned apartments.

Housing policy as part of social policy is not only realized through state-owned housing. This form dominates in big cities but not in the country as a whole. The majority of all houses are in personal property (family houses). Czechoslovak Constitution Law distinguishes between private property (means of production) and personal property (means of consumption, originating in labor income). It is also possible to buy apartments from state ownership in personal property (newly built or older ones). This is not common, however, mainly because of the price compared with the low rents in state housing.

The forms of housing in Czechoslovakia in 1986 were: state ownership: 24%, co-operative based: 16%, and personal ownership: 60%. In total, there are 5.4 million flats of all forms of ownership in Czechoslovakia. Their average age was 35.6 years in total Czechoslovakia, 39.4 years in the Czech Republik, and 26.1 years in the Slovak Republic.

Determining the proportion of each form of housing construction and to make decisions regarding overall scope, location and standard are component parts of the housing policy of the central government (technical standard, financing) and also of local governments (location, distribution etc.). The influencing and limiting factors include in the first place the building, material and financial considerations but also the need to save and protect such priceless resources as farm land, water and other components of the living environment. Another important factor influencing decisions about the location and form of construction in different parts of the country is the actual state of development and the distribution of the labor force.

Social subsidies concern all forms of housing construction and are granted predominantly from state funds. The investment process of housing and related construction starts with physical planning in regions and districts. The national committees decide about the use and functions of different areas and allocations for housing, economic and other public ventures. Among other things they mark off areas designed for housing projects, zones of rest and recreation, protected areas, reserves etc.

The national committees are also responsible for the protection of farm land and therefore offer non-farm land for housing construction without any fee or with a very small fee for family houses (permanent personal land use). In fact the cost of land for housing construction has no important role. Some administrative rules are more complicated.

The national committees therefore function as direct sponsors of housing and related projects. This arrangement is called "communal housing construction" and also includes, apart from state-financed housing construction, the construction of technical amenities of housing estates - roads, parking lots, parks and public green, playgrounds, water supply, sewerage networks, gas, electricity and heat distribution etc. Moreover, communal housing projects also include the social infrastructure, i.e. creches, kindergartens, basic schools, health care centers, communal services, retail networks, restaurants, cultural centers, sports centers. All these projects are financed by the state irrespective of whether they serve the occupants of state-owned, co-operative or private houses.

The national committees and their organs do not have to fulfill all functions prescribed by the law. They are free to appoint special agencies to work in their stead in certain areas, e.g. building project investments. Completed projects are handed over to organizations which manage them. Housing complexes pass over to the so-called housing economy enterprises (non-profit organizations) which also report to the national committees. Their task is to provide services relating to the use of flats. They oversee the maintenance and servicing of flats and keep in touch with their occupants.

The national committees also function as construction authorities issuing building permits for all projects, be they executed by socialist organizations or private builders. The construction authority also checks building projects for their societal aspects, such as safety, aesthetic value, environmental considerations etc. In the final stage it decides whether the project meets all functional requirements and authorizes its use. The construction authority also sees to it that buildings are properly maintained.

Social housing (communal dwellings) are financed completely from the budget of national committees (in fact there are subsidies from the state budget according to the number of flats, because local revenues are insufficient). The subsidies also include the technical and social infrastructure. Furthermore, the state bears the bigger part of the maintenance costs. Rents per sq.m. have been constant for a long period, at present since 1964. They equal about 8% of the household income.

The legal regulations for the distribution of housing proceed from the following main principles:

- Homes managed by the national committees are primarily for bigger families with lower incomes.
- The distribution of homes is subject to public control.
- State control and supervision prevents speculation and ensures proper use of flats.
- The right of tenancy can be suspended only in cases specified by the law.
- Nobody may be evicted from his home without being assigned an alternative apartment or another form of accommodation.

Homes rented from the state are distributed by the local national committees. This distribution is a direct instrument of the state housing policy. Applicants are put on the housing list. Here, the national committee will give priority to applicants without a home of their own in the constituency, married couples living in separate households and persons who have flats of their own in other communities than their place of work. Priority is further given to applicants whose flats are considered in unsanitary condition or unsuitable in any other way, and to applicants who have been ordered to move out through a decision of a court or a national committee.

The "unsanitary" status applies to premises marked by the health officer or the construction authority as unsuited for habitation because of technical flaws adversely affecting human health. The Czechoslovak legal system thus defines circumstances under which applicants are put on the housing list so that all legitimate reasons for citizens to apply for a new flat are covered.

Homes are distributed to applicants who are on the waiting list. One criterium is that priority should be given to applicants in urgent need of housing, who should be assigned flats before others on the grounds of their housing situation and other circumstances (e.g., the social importance of their work). Thus waiting lists are drawn up following guidelines similar to those binding for housing lists, i.e. the applicant's housing situation in his community, the sanitary condition of his flat, his state of health etc. The more points an applicant has accrued the sooner he qualifies for a new flat. The importance of the applicant's work is classified according to the significance of his profession and his professional results.

Rents in state-owned homes are dependent on the respective housing quality. According to their amenities flats are divided into four categories that determine their rents:

I. Category - Flats with central heating and complete facilities
II. Category - Flats without central heating with other facilities
III. Category - Without central heating with some facilities
IV. Category - Without any facilities

The basic rents are determined according to floorspace. If a dweller undertakes private efforts to modernize his flat this does not change the category of the flat and thus the rent. Of course the other communal services are paid for individually depending on the amount consumed (e.g., water, gas, electricity, etc.). The rent (excluding services) is then modified by different social considerations. It is reduced progressively for families with children: one child: 5%, two children: 15%, three children: 30%, four children: 50%, etc. Rents are determined according to fixed legal regulations and do not rise with the tenant's income. Rents for communal flats have not been raised since 1964.

Once a flat is assigned by the national committee nobody (except in cases specified by the law) has the right to prevent the user from moving in. The right of tenancy can be voided either by the user (through death or other circumstances, e.g., renunciation of his right of tenancy, moving to another flat etc.) or by court order or the national committee.

In no case of suspension of user right for whatever reason must the user be left without shelter. In most cases he has the right to be assigned an adequate substitute home or accommodation. The substitute flat must be either of the same quality (not in unsanitary condition, unsuitable or inadequate) or at least adequate to the user's requirements.

Housing Construction Co-operatives

Czechoslovakia has gradually evolved several types of people's co-operatives differing in their economic orientation. In the first place there are agricultural co-operatives engaging in livestock and vegetable production on co-operative farmland which is still the property of its original, now associated smallholders. Then there are producer co-operatives in which former smallholders are associated and consumer co-operatives engaged in trading. Finally, there are the housing construction co-operatives.

Their role is to satisfy the housing requirements of their members and to provide economic, social and cultural services of vital importance in the sphere of housing. They build and secure construction of co-operative flats for their members as well as of non-residential structures (studios, garages etc.). In addition, the housing construction co-operatives

- assign co-operative flats and non-residential facilities to members;
- secure users' unobstructed exercise of rights ensuing from the use of these flats etc. by conducting proper and timely maintenance and servicing of co-operative property;
- ensure the proper provision of services related to the use of flats and organize additional projects and works connected with the building of co-operative flats.

A housing construction co-operative is set up by a founding meeting of members which admits founder-members, approves the statutes of the co-operative and elects co-operative bodies. Membership is open to all citizens who do not join co-operatives for speculative reasons and who, by fulfilling their financial duties (deposition of an acceptance fee and the basic membership deposit) demonstrate their preparedness and ability to meet their obligations towards the co-operative.

Membership rights include the personal use of the flat, the right to participate in all co-operative activities, to enjoy all advantages ensuing from membership, to use the flat for the accommodation of relatives and other persons with whom the user intends to live in one household, the right to have the flat at one's disposal and to decide about the transfer of membership after one's death.

The supreme body of the co-operative is the general meeting which decides on all crucial affairs, endorses the housing statutes, outlines the main directions of the co-operative's work and its activities. It decides over the lists of applicants and the waiting lists that are binding for the distribution of flats. The executive organ of the co-operative is its presiding committee which steers co-operative work and decides on all matters unrelegated by the statutes to other organs. The smallest organizational and economic units of the co-operative are the self-management committees of groups of resident and non-resident members. They operate only in larger co-operatives and their purpose is to active and coordinate the direct participation of members in their co-operative's activities.

The Czechoslovak housing co-operative movement acts on the assumption that *one* flat satisfies the personal requirements of an individual. Therefore, a citizen can be a member of only one housing construction co-operative - except under precisely defined circumstances. This, however, does not prevent a member of a housing construction co-operative from simultaneously being a member in another type of co-operative, e.g., one dealing with the construction of family houses, the building and administration of garages etc. Apart from admission as a member, a citizen can also acquire membership of a housing construction co-operative through the transfer of membership rights from another member under an agreement whereby he replaces the former member, or by inheritance.

Co-operative housing construction enjoys full government support through either direct assistance of state organs and subordinated organizations in the preparation and execution of co-operative housing projects or financial aid. Direct assistance implies primarily free-of-charge allotments of construction sites for co-operative housing schemes. If a co-operative develops a housing estate the local national committee, by means of its investment engineering organization, helps safeguard predesign stage blueprints and handles, on behalf of the co-operative, all matters involving qualified personnel for investment-type projects.

The financing of co-operative housing projects is based on two sources: First, state subsidies, consisting of a fixed sum per flat and of a sum per sq.m. of the actual usable floorspace. Apart from this basic contribution the state also provides special payments to compensate for higher costs which may arise, e.g. due to the size of the building. These subsidies amount to about 30% of total costs. Second, the co-operative itself. Funds needed are drawn from membership shares and special investment credits granted by the Czechoslovak State Bank.

Organizations committed to stabilizing their labor force can grant special aid to co-operatives. This type of housing construction is widely used by virtually all Czechoslovak organizations whose employees are entitled compensation of the full amount of their co-operative membership shares. This compensation presents a kind of loan written off after the employee has worked for the enterprise for a given period.

This sponsored or "stabilization" housing construction is very popular in Czechoslovakia and has by now largely replaced earlier forms of enterprise-sponsored state housing schemes. All other costs such as for maintenance are financed with the co-operative's own funds. Therefore, "rents" are approximately three times higher than in state-owned flats.

The co-operative housing system is an example of participation, of a self-help system in housing policy. It has many favorable consequences for the economic and moral initiatives of citizens. The interest of citizens in the maintenance of buildings and in saving money for running costs etc. is enhanced. On the other hand there is the competition with state-owned flats, which are sometimes of the same quality level but with cheaper and fixed rents.

The Family Houses

The Czechoslovak socialist legal system guarantees the protection of personal property. This concerns property acquired by virtue of work for the benefit of society and which serves the personal needs of the citizen and his family. The remaining amount of certain means of production still owned by individuals, such as a certain small acreage of farmland or a negligible proportion of the housing stock, is not considered personal property but private property which does not fall under the above-mentioned legal protection. A small house in personal ownership enjoys protection just like all other personal property.

To avoid conflicts over the question which houses can serve for renting and which are explicitly designed to suit the needs of their owners and their families, the Czechoslovak Civil Code sets a certain objective limit for houses considered as personal property. Such buildings are called family houses.

First of all, such houses must be designed for non-seasonal residents. Since many village buildings serve both housing purposes and farm production, even a part of a farming estate can be considered a family house. Size is further criterium. A family house must not have more than five habitable rooms, excluding kitchen, bathroom, entrance hall, basement, attic etc. If there are more than five habitable rooms, then the total floorspace must not exceed 120 square meters.

The Czechoslovak housing policy strives for every citizen to build a house of his own, to be able to acquire a plot of land of basically the same quality and size to suit the needs of housing in personal property. However, densely populated Czechoslovakia cannot afford to waste farm land. Therefore the Czechoslovak legal system prescribes certain limitations to ensure that these building sites are adequate to the builder's needs and also to the capacities of our society concerning the distribution of such priceless natural resources as land. The right of personal use is a new type of civic liberty designed to enable citizens to use sites in socialist ownership for their private benefit.

Society even supports individual housing projects with its resources. It mainly helps the individual to acquire the building site for his family house. Apart from the low charges for the right of personal use of the site, the state may under certain conditions grant this right free of charge. In order to minimize the loss of farmland the state gives particular support to the "group building" of family houses which, by its nature, requires less space. In this case the user rights are free.

Family housing construction is an efficient tool for the economic use of labor and a major factor for stabilizing the workforce where it is needed most badly. Employees of socialist organizations can claim family housing construction loans from their employers. Such loans are granted under agreements between the employee and his organization provided that he has worked in the enterprise for a specified period of time. If an employee meets his obligations the organization will refrain from claiming the sum back.

A similar type of loan is granted to citizens who do not fulfill the conditions of this "stabilization" agreement with socialist organizations. These are granted non-returnable loans by national committees. Apart from non-returnable loans, individual builders may also be granted loans returnable in not less than thirty years from the banking system. The interest rate is fixed at 2.7%, in the case of group building at only 2%.

Newly built family houses are exempted from housing taxes for a period of fifteen years. On average, family houses are financed as follows: 25% by social resources, 25% by loans from savings banks, the rest by the builders private financial resources. The family houses project is more popular in the countryside than in cities where total costs are higher. In the cities there are many problems with the land, with the technical infrastructure, with the cost of transporting materials etc.

The previous facts have demonstrated the ways and means used by the Czechoslovak state to regulate new housing construction projects and what is possible in affordable housing. But it should be stressed that in the past emphasis was placed less on a maximum increase in the number of homes than on the replacement of inadequate housing.

Between 1961 and 1970 for example some 455,000 homes in Czechoslovakia were phased out from permanent use, and this number went up to 534,000 in the period 1970-1980. Thus, not less than 47.8% of all newly built homes were used to replace outdated housing. Over the past forty years housing has been subject to major modernization programmes as shown by the steep increase of the share of flats built after 1945 whose quality is incomparably higher than that of the majority of older flats. In 1980, 65.1% of all Czechoslovak citizens (CSR: 57.8%, SSR: up to 80.2%) lived in houses and flats not older than 35 years.

Over the same period the number of occupants per housing unit declined. Thus, in 1961 there were 278 housing units per 1000 inhabitants on a national scale (296 in the Czech Lands and 236 in Slovakia). In 1970, that number increased to 296 (CSR: 315, SSR: 253), and according to the 1980 census, the national figure was 321 (CSR: 340, SSR: 283). Thus the number of occupants per housing unit has dropped since 1961 by about 15.4% (CSR: 14.9, SSR: 19.7). Current national estimates are 336 housing units per 1,000 inhabitants.

Together with the increase in floorspace and the number of homes there were improvements in basic equipment and amenities. The percentage of homes with bathrooms or shower facilities increased from 24.8% in 1961 to 79.7% in 1980 and is now estimated at 85%. Heating arrangements also changed. The percentage of centrally heated flats increased over the same period from 8.6% to 56.8% and is now believed to be in the neighborhood of 65%. Coal-heated flats have all but disappeared from the cities, and where central heating is not available, coal stoves have been replaced by electricity or gas. The percentage of households connected to natural or city gas supply networks rose from 19.7% in 1961 to 40.4% in 1980. At present, about 45% of all flats and the majority of city households use this amenity.

Apart from its quantitative aspects the housing problem also has a qualitative aspect indicated by shortcomings with regard to the size and standard of flats. The general rise of living standards leads to increased demands on housing standards and thus a new housing problem.

Man's needs (at least from a subjective point of view) continue to grow much faster than the possibilities to satisfy them. This concerns not only the quality of flats and other housing amenities but also their quantity. Not even the extensive housing construction drive that has been going on in Czechoslovakia has until now succeeded in satisfying all applicants. One reason is the growing concentration of people in big cities due to the increasing number of urban housing projects. Hence the relative shortage of housing in some big cities despite the fact that the number of buildings completed actually exceeded the quotas previously planned by more than three times. On the other hand housing is more than abundant in other places. This does not mean that some families are left without shelter. We have in fact no homeless people. Rather, some young families simply cannot break free as soon as they would like and have to continue, at least temporarily, living with their parents. Also, divorced younger couples face problems finding new suitable flats within a short period of time.

In evaluating housing quality not only the size and equipment of a flat are taken into account, but also its location within the house, housing complex, architectural unit and neighborhood, e.g. relating to the living environment and lifestyle of a given group of residents, its distance from places of work, shopping amenities, transport routes, sports and recreational facilities.

Solving the housing problem in Czechoslovakia, i.e. the creation of housing whose availability, size, quality and location correspond to existing structures and the needs of both entire households and individuals, is obviously a continuing process which is unlikely to end at a certain future date. For both the individual and group concepts of housing are subject to constant change and development.

Prague

All the above information on housing policy is valid for the capital of Prague, too, although some of the problems are multiplied by the population density. Prague is not a giant city, but with its 1,2 million inhabitants and its size of 498 sq.km it shares many of the problems of big cities everywhere in the world.

The first problem lies in the historical character of the city. Prague has many monuments from medieval times, from the 14th century but also from earlier and later periods. All styles of architecture and various building systems can be found. It is our duty to save historical monuments not only for our generation but also for future ones. This maintenance creates many problems, not only financially, but also materially and technically. The old town square and the King's way (finished in 1987) are good examples.

But the city's history is not based exclusively on public monuments. There are also simple flats (the majority being inhabited by older people) with a generally very low standard. Some of them, dating back to the last century when they were built in suburbs during the industrialization boom, will be demolished and replaced by new houses (for example Prague 3 - Zizkov). Some that were built at the beginning of this century are in relatively good condition but need modernization.

In Prague, like in other cities, we started after World War II with new districts which were built in the new areas using pre-fabricated elements. Of course many people were drawn from the inner city to these districts. The inner city now has less residential dwellings and a large share of older people. Modernization in Prague started ten years ago and we now have the first experiences. The project will continue with the modernization of whole blocks of units and single houses. The necessary funds will come from the city budget, and the majority of flats will remain state property. We also support all initiative steps of individuals intending to modernize their flats (fixed rents).

The types of housing in Prague differ somewhat from the rest of Czechoslovakia. While in Czechoslovakia as a whole more than 70% of all flats are in individual houses (personal property and co-operatives) and the remaining 30% are state flats, the situation in Prague is different (see Table 2). The average size of a flat is 20 sq.m., whreas the average in newly constructed flöats is 48 sq.m.

Table 2: Flats in Prague, by Proprietor (a) and by Category (b), 1986
a) Proprietor

Proprietor	abs.	%
State	296,474	63%
Co-operative	100,030	21%
Personal	65,315	14%
Other	10,000	2%

b) Categories (State and Co-operative Property)

I.: 224,590; II.: 108,889; III.: 27,582; IV.: 49,000

The majority of the flats are in communal ownership, and therefore there is strong pressure from applicants who need a flat. Two groups stand out in this respect: young and divorced couples (with or without children). Very often these applicants need small flats, whereas the majority of new communal flats has three or more rooms.

On the other hand the big share of communal houses is based on the great responsibility for the maintenance of buildings. The Civil Code strictly regulates the duties of house owners, and people are well aware of their rights and strongly criticize any shortcomings regarding maintenance, cleaning etc.

True, it is sometimes impossible to fulfill all these needs. Therefore we also find self-help, do-it-yourself etc. Tenants can receive materials and tools to paint corridors, windows, doors etc., and also for maintaining lawns, parks etc. Such activities take place on a voluntary basis without remuneration. The problem is sometimes to organize such self-help activities on a larger scale. People are more initiative when the maintenance of their flats is concerned than that of whole buildings.

The tendency in city-funded flat modernization is first of all to improve the flats of categories III and IV. A pressing need is to improve some older districts constructed with prefabricated elements. Architectural design, roofs, walls, green spaces etc. have to be improved. Other special problems are presented by important communal services closely connected with housing policy (water supply, sewage systems, gas, electricity, cleaning, urban transport, central heating).

In Czechoslovakia, the prices of major communal services are subsidized and will remain so in the future. The problem is only that the subsidies are higher every year because the technical infrastructure is getting ever more complicated (underground, water supply, sewage systems etc.). Since it also depends on the population density, we do not intend to stimulate the further growth of Prague's population.

Outlook

In 1986 the master plan for the growth of the capital Prague until the year 2000 was completed. It lists the main goals in all aspects of urban development including housing. It is estimated that the population will grow very slowly from 1,192,000 in 1985 to 1,228,000 by the year 2000. The number of households will rise only slightly: from 551,000 in 1985 to 567,000 by the year 2000. The project of housing policy is to increase the number of flats from 487,000 in 1985 to 567,000 by the year 2000. The goal is to have one dwelling for each household. During the period 1986-2000 it is estimated that 110,000 new flats will be constructed in newly developed areas and 7,000 flats in modernization areas. During this period it is planned to modernize 28,000 flats in the city and historical areas.

Czechoslovakia's experiences during the last 40 years clearly demonstrate the necessity of social efforts in housing policy. In the period ahead popular participation in solving housing-related problems will increase. We will support all forms of co-operative and family housing through state subsidies. We wish to continue providing communal housing but not to increase its share of total construction efforts. The construction of new buildings will continue in the large estates located at the periphery but also in the inner city.

The present and future problem is to modernize the existing housing stock with private financing for the smaller units and state financing for the larger ones. Among the more recent elements of the housing policy are a decentralization of the administration especially in the communal dwellings and the promotion of self-help in small-scale maintenance.

LARGE NEW HOUSING ESTATES: THE CRISIS OF AFFORDABLE HOUSING

Jürgen Friedrichs

The Problem

After the Second World War, in the territorry of West Germany 2,1 million dwellings were destroyed (18% of the pre-war stock), in addition, it is estimated that two to three million dwellings were damaged. In many cities the figures were even higher, such as in Hamburg, where out of 560,00 dwelling more than 270,000 (54%) were destroyed and further 60,000 damaged (Kinder and Pause, 1964). As a consequence, a large percent age of the population lived in poor housing conditions, often barracks at the periphery of the city. The enormous housing shortage was aggravated by the influx of more than eight million refugees, residents of the eastern parts of the former Reich.

Hence, West Germany (as well as East Germany) was confronted with a tremendous housing shortage and new construction became one of the major tasks of the country. The main instrument to cope with this shortage was a program of social housing which started in the late 1940s.

Since during the war period rehabilitation and repair of residential buildings was neglected, and the housing shortage was to be alleviated soon, the construction of new housing estates was given absolute priority over rehabilitation of older residential buildings in inner-city residential areas. Furthermore, a rent control did not allow a sufficient amount of private investment in multi-story residential buildings.

The new housing estates were predominantly built on large sites at the periphery, but inside the central city, where larger lots of vacant or agricultural land was available at low prices. This post-war policy of solving housing problems can be found in most cities in Western and Eastern Europe.

In Table 1, data on the housing production in West Germany are presented. They indicate the high percentage of social housing compared to other forms of construction (cooperative, private). The figures indicate as well the decline of social housing in the late 1970s, mainly due to high construction costs. As the construction became more and more industrialized, the new housing estates became larger, often scheduled for more than 40,000 inhabitants. By 1985, there were more than 233 new housing estates, of 52% are large housing estates (LHEs), defined as estates with more than 1,000 dwelling units. The are distributed over 100 cities of the F.R.G., comprising a total of 500,000-600,000 dwelling units (Schmidt-Bartel and Meuter, 1986: 15).

Affordable Housing and the Homeless

Table 1: Dwelling Units Completed, F.R.G., 1949-1980

		Social Housing	
Year	Total	abs.	%
1949	221,960	153,340	69.1
1950	371,924	254,990	68.1
1955	568,403	288,988	50.8
1960	574,402	263,205	45.8
1965	591,916	228,606	38.6
1970	478,050	137,095	28.7
1975	436,829	126,660	29.0
1980	388,904	103,700	26.7
1984	387,607	77,808	20.1

Sources: Statistisches Jahrbuch für die Bundesrepublik Deutschland, 1986: 219, 223; Ziercke, 1982: 96.

By 1980, more than 16,5 new dwellings had been completed since 1949, the average rate per 1,000 residents was 8,8 new dwellings. A considerable amount of these dwellings were owned by the non-profit housing organizations, as the data in Table 1 show. In the LHEs, they often own and manage more than 70 percent of all dwellings. From the total stock of 26,8 million dwellings in 1984, the non-profit organizations held 12.9%.

The basic aim of these LHEs was to make housing affordable for families with lower incomes (below a defined limit) and to those living in bad housing conditions, either due to the war or due to substandard dwellings in inner-city neighborhoods. Note, that the programs of modernization for inner city areas came much later (in the mid-1970s) than new construction. This priority for new construction over modernization of the existing stock can be observed in many cities in Western and Eastern Europe (Friedrichs, 1985, 1988).

Despite the impressive amount of new construction especially social housing in the LHEs experienced several problems since the early 1980s (e.g. BfLR, 1987; Herlyn, 1986; Köhler, 1981; SAGA, 1980; Schmidt-Bartel and Meuter, 1986; SRL, 1986; Strubelt and Kauwetter, 1982). The major problems these estates exhibited were:

- A growing non-occupancy rate (defined as a dwelling unit continuously not occupied for three month, later revised as empty for six month). For 1984 the rate for the entire stock of social housing is estimated to be one percent (Thoss, 1986: 2), but up to 3.2 percent in new estates (Schmidt-Bartel and Meuter, 1986: 25). Mainly apartments of 70-80 sq. m. are vacant (Schmidt-Bartel and Meuter, 1986: 26; Pohl, 1986: 34).

Table 2: Demolition, Fluctuation, and Non-Occupancy, Selected Cities
a) Demolition

	Construction Period	Dwellings	Demolition
St. Louis (USA), Pruitt-Igoe	1950-54	2780	1972/76
Newcastle (UK), Noble Street Flats	1956-58	434	1975
Leeuwarden (NL), Linneasstraat	1947-55	414	1977

b) Non-Occupancy

City, LHE	Rate	Year	Dwelling Units
Kiel (D), Mettenhof	11	1984/85	7300
Bremen (D), Osterholz-Tenever	15	1985	2600
Malmö (S), Rosengaard	17/9	1977/85	7000
Lyon (F), Les Minguettes	16	1980	9200
Briey-la-Foret (F), Unit	59/100	1983/85	339
Amsterdam (NL), Bijlmermeer	25	1982	12500
St. Louis (USA), Pruitt-Igoe	66	1969	2780
Boston (USA), Columbia Point	75	1984	na
Boston (USA), Mission Main	60	1984	na

c) Fluctuation

City, LHE	Rate	Year
Hamburg (FRG), Kirchdorf-Süd	16	1985
Bremen (FRG), Osterholz-Tenever	21	1985
Essen (FRG), Hörsterfeld	25	1984
Leeds (UK), Hunslet Grange	40	1976+
Amsterdam (NL), Bijlmermeer	30	1984

Source: Autzen and Becker, 1985: 138.

The major problems these estates exhibit are:

- an increasing fluctuation of renters, resulting in high costs for renovation of the apartment and administrative costs;

- a negative image of the LHEs, in particular, the negative evaluation of the low accessibility and insufficient infrastructure (shops, crafts, cultural facilities, jobs);

- a negative evaluation of the dominant (especially concentrated) high-rise apartment buildings, hence, perceived high density;

- increasing incidences of crime and vandalism;

- a growing concentration of "problem families", such as families living on transfer payments (public assistance, unemployment aid), foreign-born;

- a growing number of households in delay with their rent payments;

- increasing deterioration of the buildings, especially defects in the pre-fabricated concrete segments, resulting in high costs of repair not calculated in the rent, for instance of DM 500 million for the 95,000 dwelling units by the nonprofit organization SAGA in Hamburg.

The crisis of the affordability of affordable housing was indicated and officially recognized be a program "The Amelioration of Large New Housing Estates from the 1960s and 1970s", launched by the Federal Department of Housing in 1982.

Most of these problems are not specific to LHEs in West Germany, but can be found in many other countries. In Table 2, some data pertinent to these almost intricable and universal problems of LHEs are presented. The main reasons for this crisis of LHEs were: an overall equilibrium in the housing market (yet deficits in the submarket of low-cost housing), the financing system of social housing resulting in a higher increase in rents in social housing than in private, construction costs and rents rising faster than incomes (see Table 3), a growing tendency to rent social housing apartments to "problem families", a declining population but increasing number of households, amongst them many young unmarried seeking inner-city locations.

Table 3: Construction Costs for Residential Buildings With Three or More Dwelling Units, F.R.G., 1970, 1975, and 1980

Indicator	1970	1975	1980
Construction costs			
(DM per square meter)	914	1,523	2,227
Index	100	166	244
Net income (DM/month)*	1256	2200	2993
Index	100	175	238
Index Living costs	100	134	162
Expenditures for rent (DM/month)	168	280	401

* Four person blue collar household, medium income

Source: Ziercke, 1982: 123, 1258.

To analyze the problems of LHEs greater detail, in the following section one of the largest new housing estates in Hamburg will serve as an example. In the final section, the findings will be discussed in the context of LHEs in general.

Figure 1: Mümmelmannsberg and its Neigborhoods

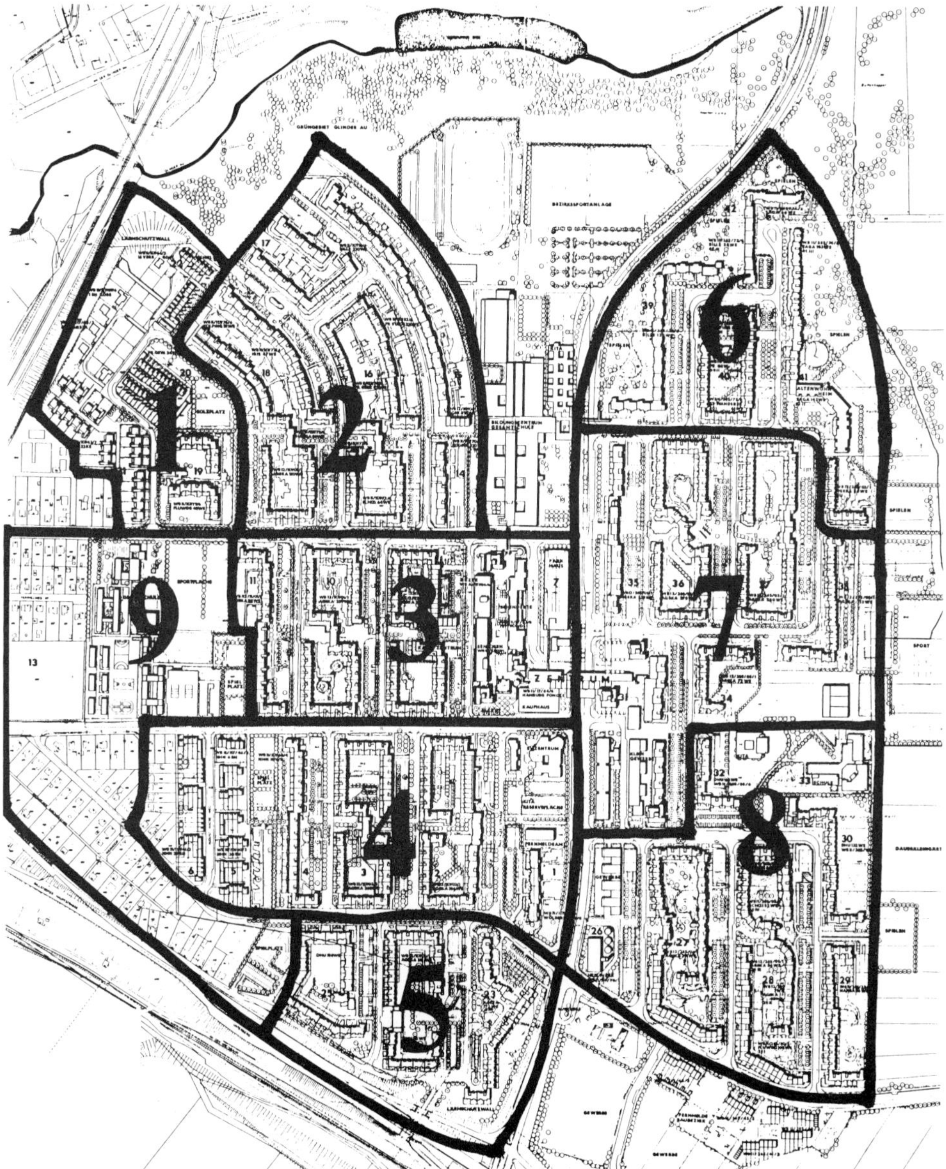

The Example: The New Housing Estate "Mümmelmannsberg"

The estate of Mümmelmannsberg (in the following abbreviated as "MMB") is located at the eastern fringe of Hamburg; the layout of the residential area and its component nine neighborhoods are shown in Figure 1. MBB was built between 1972 and 1984 and has 7,200 dwelling units. In 1985, it had 18,228 inhabitants with a percentage of foreign-born of 19.1 (Hamburg: 9.7%) and with 29% of all households living on public assistance.

To analyze the existing problems and to implement an amelioration program a study was conducted in 1986; field research was done in September/October, and the report was completed in December of 1986 (Friedrichs and Dangschat, 1986). A random sample of residents, drawn from the Central Directory of Residents, were interviewed either by telephone or - if the household had no telephone - face-to-face. From a total of 1,217 addresses 727 interviews were completed, 82% by telephone. The non-response rate of 40% was mainly accounted for by incorrect addresses, households that had moved and - to a smaller extent - refusals to be interviewed. Due to the fact that the 1981 census had been postponed in West Germany, there are very few data on the population structure; judged by these, the sample is not biased; however, the percentage of foreign-born is only 11.5% compared with 17.5% according to official statistics.

Some important characteristics of the population composition and housing conditions are shown in Table 4. Compared with Hamburg, the residents of MMB are younger, households are larger, and figures for income (as far as data are available) and years of schooling are lower. Net monthly household incomes are considerably lower in social housing apartments than in cooperative or private apartments; a similar difference can be found for years of schooling. Many households pay relatively high rents per square meter.

Population Change. The population in MMB changed considerably between 1980 and 1985. The total number of residents dropped by 11%, in the section constructed first (neighborhoods 1-5, 9) even by 17.6%, and in neighborhood 2 by almost one-third (886 residents). Since more German than foreign-born residents moved out, the latter percentage rose, increasing by 80% between 1980 and 1985. A particular increase was shown by the number of foreign-born residents from non-European Community countries such as Polish citizens or Asians seeking political asylum - their figure tripled. By 1985, they accounted for half of the foreign-born population. The highest concentration of foreign-born residents with 55% was in block 222 in neighborhood 1, followed by two blocks with over 27% in neighborhood 4.

Fluctuation and Non-Occupancy. As indicated by the data on population change, the fluctuation rate rose in MMB. Data were available only for the dwellings owned by two non-profit organizations, Neue Heimat and SAGA. The fluctuation rate for the apartments of the former was 20% in 1985 (Handwerkskammer, 1986: 20), for the latter, the state-owned SAGA, fluctuation rose from 6.7% 1981 to 9.9% in 1985.

The non-occupancy rate in non-profit social housing was 14% for the Neue Heimat apartments in July 1986, but 30% for one particular block in neighborhood 2 (Ziercke,

1986: 5). The highest rates were in neighborhoods 2, 3, 4 and 7. In summer 1986, the total number of vacant apartments was 581.

Table 4: Socio-Demographic Composition of Mümmelmannsberg Residents, in Percent

Age		**Household Size**	
14-18 years	9.4	1 person	7.7
19-34 years	29.8	2 persons	27.5
35-59 years	52.2	3 persons	23.1
60+ years	8.7	4 persons	23.1
		5+ persons	11.6
Years of Schooling		**Household Net Income**	
9 years	61.8	DM -1499	14.0
10 years	24.9	DM 1500-2999	22.4
13 years	13.2	DM 3000-3999	22.4
		DM 4000+	8.0
Owner of Dwelling		**Size of Dwelling in sq.m.**	
Non-Profit	57.9	-69	25.8
Cooperative	32.0	70-79	32.0
Respondent	10.1	80-99	35.4
		100+	6.9
Monthly Rent (incl. Heating)		**Monthly Rent per sq.m.**	
DM -699	33.6	DM -7.99	6.0
DM 700-799	32.4	DM 8.00-9.99	59.4
DM 800+	34.0	DM10.00-10.99	23.5
		DM 11.00+	9.5

Source: Friedrichs and Dangschat, 1986

Problems Perceived by Residents. The residents were asked (in open-ended questions) to state their content and discontent with the estate. The responses given revealed a broad range of problems - the number of responses to the question what was disliked was 20 percent higher than to the question what was liked. Responses to both questions can be grouped in three major areas: the dwelling, the environment (area around the dwelling), and the estate. In Table 5 the distribution of responses for both questions is given.

The responses exhibit a plausible pattern: People moved into the area for low-cost housing in a green environment, hence we find more positive responses for both the dwelling and the environment, and "the green" is the most often cited reason in the category "estate".

In contrast, dislike concentrates on features of the estate in general. The four most often mentioned topics were: "high-rises, architecture, concrete" (20.0%), "vandalism, crime, antisocial people, unsafe" (12.4%), "dirt" (11.6%), and "social environment" (11.3%). Respondents living in cooperative or private houses showed less criticism of the dwelling but more of the environment and the estate.

Table 5: Major Areas of Content and Discontent with Mümmelmannsberg, Multiple Responses

Resposes Pertaining to	Content	Discontent
Dwelling	15.6	8.6
Dwelling Environment	16.3	6.2
Estate	58.9	84.5
"Nothing"	8.3	0.1
Other	0.8	0.6
Total %	100.0	100.0
Total Responses	1397	1847
Total Respondents	678	696

Source: Friedrichs and Dangschat, 1986: 69, 71.

Analyses of responses by socio-demographic characteristics revealed some surprising results. Among respondents critical of the architecture ("high-rises", "concrete") a higher percentage had a higher education (more than 13 years of schooling) and income. However, respondents criticizing dirt, crime and vandalism were overproportionately those with a low education and a low income. In seeking to explain this finding, we assumed a social segregation correlated with unpleasant living conditions in the neighborhood. Indices of segregation (Duncan's IS) resulted in low values for both education and income (9.8 resp. 23.9).

Segregation alone cannot explain the attitudes met. Hence, to account for the higher rate of low-status residents complaining about "crime" and "dirt" we may refer to social norms: Persons with low status are oriented toward middle-class values and react more strongly when the respective norms are violated. Furthermore, we may assume that for the majority of this group moving into the new estate represented a social achievement which they do not want to be spoiled by a negative image resulting from crime. In this context, two further findings are important.

1. As noted above, many negative responses pertained to the "social environment". To explore this dimension the respondents were asked a) whether they agreed or disagreed with the statements "Some people say there are too many antisocial people in MMB" and "Some people say there are too many foreign-born people in MMB". Two-thirds of the respondents agreed with both statements; for the second statement there was *no* statistically significant difference between German and foreign-born residents. Clearly, the residents perceive the social problems of the estate and the unfavourable social mix as detrimental to their conceptions of a good neighborhood and the image of the estate.

This conclusion is supported by two additional findings: When asked for their opinion about MMB today compared with the time when they moved in, 41% did not state any change, 13% said it had changed to the better, and 46% responded that MMB had changed to the worse, predominantly due to changes in its resident structure. The second finding refers to the image of the estate. Respondents had to rate it on a six-point scale ("1" being the best grade), for themselves, the presumed note friends and relatives would give the estate and the presumed note Hamburg residents would give. The average notes given were 3.5 for respondents, 3.9 for friends, and 4.5 for Hamburg residents indicating the negative image MMB residents think the estate has in Hamburg.

How to Improve Living Conditions in MMB. Besides exploring the deficits of the estate as perceived by its residents the major aim of the study was to explore the type and feasibility of measures to improve living conditions. This was done in two ways: by asking the respondents what sort of improvements they thought of or wished, and by presenting a catalogue of possible improvements, asking respondents to grade each of these improvement by importance. The main suggestions emerging from both types of questions were: 1. improvement of infrastructure, e.g. shopping facilities, improvement of shopping center, give tenants individual gardens, more small craftmen's businesses; 2. demolition of high-rise buildings, in particular of one block in neighborhood 2; 3. other building-related changes, e.g., "more color", "painting of facades", "more green"; 4. to improve the social structure; 5. to lower rents.

The results of the study summarized here require several interlocking measures of amelioration quickly to be implemented; many of them will cause enormous costs if conditions are to be stopped from further deteriorating.

Conclusions

Initially, the LHEs supplied favorable housing for low-income families. When first surveyed, most residents were satisfied with their new apartments and - contrary to preconceptions of many social scientist and architects - with their environment and the estate as well. This is well documented in the numerous studies published in the early 1970s (e.g., Dittrich, 1973, 1974; Dorsch, 1972; Heil, 1971; Kob et al., 1972; Lüdtke, 1973; Sample, 1974; Weeber, 1971; Zapf, Heil and Rudolph, 1969). At that time, the housing shortage resulted in positive responses which can be explained by the transfer of positive judgements on dwellings to the estate in general. However, by this time many deficits had already become apparent, such as the lack of infrastructure and job facilities and the poor accessibility.

Rents at this period were low and took only a relatively small percentage of the disposable household net income (see Table 3). Over the last five years this major advantage - to have a well-equipped apartment at a low rent - has changed dramatically. The major reason that accounts for this change lies in the German system of financing social housing.

Capital subsidies (repayable mortgage loans) are granted for the construction of social housing, implying rent limits to secure rent ceilings. Apartments can be rented legally only to families with lower incomes; the present limit, e.g. for a family with two children, is an average gross monthly income of DM 4,417.

These subsidies were granted for a period of 20 years. As instalments are repaid and interest rates rise, rents rise automatically as well. As a result of this financing system the rents rise higher in older LHEs whereas the more recently constructed LHEs have low rents. For example, a dwelling in one of the first blocks constructed in 1973 had a monthly rent of DM 6.76 per sq.m. In 1985, the subsidized cost rent was DM 14.03, of which the tenants had to pay DM 11.14 and the owner, a non-profit housing organization, DM 2.89 (Ziercke, 1986a: 72). In contrast, in more recently constructed LHEs, which are smaller and better designed, the rent will be DM 7.30. Social housing thus competes with social housing.

The system of degressive loans was based upon the premise of rising incomes, so that income and rent increases would ideally be in equilibrium. This has apparently not been the case, in contrast, since 1982 households in the lower income brackets either had no net gain or even lower net incomes. In addition, the rising number of persons unemployed or on public assistance has aggravated the problem of renting older social housing apartments.

Furthermore, the financing system became a burden for the budget of the city, the city-state of Hamburg in this case. The Hamburg Senate had to raise the initial rent (not including heating) from DM 3.47 in 1970 to DM 7.80 since 1984 (Plesner, 1986: 64). As more and more social housing apartments exceed this limit the city has to finance the difference between DM 7.80 and the actual rent by a "post-subsidy". The dramatic increase in the number of dwellings above this limit is documented by the amount of money spent by the Hamburg Senate for this post-subsidy: it went up from DM 2 million in 1986 to DM 40 million in 1985 (Plessner, 1986: 65). Finally, subsidies became higher due to rising construction cost; at present the cost per square meter (without heating) is DM 19-22, the maximum rent in new social housing is DM 7.80 - the difference has to be subsidized.

The second major reason for the problems faced by LHEs is the change in their social structure. Social housing apartments, constituting the majority of the entire dwelling stock in LHEs, are let by governmental agencies - as outlined above - to persons or households under specific conditions. This already limits the social range of households living in these apartments, and due to their large share - as compared with dwellings owned by cooperatives or privately - also determines the overall mix in LHEs.

Over the last five years more vacant apartments were let to "problem families" (low income, homeless, single-parent) and to households from inner-city modernization areas. Furthermore, to supply housing for foreign-born residents, their households were often directed toward LHEs, in recent years especially foreigners seeking political asylum in West Germany. As the findings of our study of MMB indicate, residents do not approve of the present social composition.

Judged by the sparse empirical evidence available, the imbalanced social composition of the LHEs has led to a selective outmigration of households with a (meanwhile) higher social status (Kob et al., 1972; Wiemann, 1978; cf. Herlyn, 1986: 46). A recent survey of 194 new estates showed that these changes take place particularly in LHEs with more than 5,000 dwelling units (Schmidt-Bartel and Meuter, 1986: 30). This tendency was also apparent in the study on MMB: Two-thirds of the residents interviewed intended to move out of the estate, 22 percent of all respondents had already actively searched for a new apartment, of these the majority had above-average social status judged by income and education.

The combination of the three factors: increasing rents, an imbalanced social structure and the perception of competing new and better social housing has led to a *spiral of decline* and impaired the market position of the apartments within LHEs.

As a consequence, urban governments are faced with an almost paradoxical situation: Either they regard social housing as a means of social policy and hence rent apartments in LHEs mainly to low-income German or foreign-born households, thus facing a continuation of the spiral of decline (higher fluctuation and non-occupancy rates causing financial losses), or leave the apartments to the market, diminish losses and eventually break the spiral, but at the price of being blamed for an "unsocial" housing policy.

Hamburg's Social Democrat government has taken the latter position. In March 1987, they decided to abolish the income limit for social apartments in MBB, to reduce the rents by DM 0.50 per sq.m./month, and to let non-profit housing organizations rent their apartments themselves - instead of a governmental agency. This market-oriented decision has drastically reduced the number of non-occupied dwellings from 581 in 1985 to 80 by July 1987, and to almost zero by early 1988.

Additional measures have been implemented to ameliorate the living conditions in MMB and other LHEs in Hamburg. Residents were asked to participate actively in improving the environment ("parliament of tenants"), and some of the above-mentioned deficits perceived by residents may be reduced. *The long-run results and the improvement of market chances are to be awaited.* For instance, the question of whether to demolish part of the high-rise buildings in LHEs has created a considerable controversy in West Germany (e.g., Feldhusen, 1986; SRL, 1986). (Note, that 66% of the respondents in MMB voted for the demolition of one block.) Planning authorities and non-profit organizations have in general reacted negatively to such suggestions, for reasons of costs and the loss of apartments, but also, presumably, for fear such acts would visibly acknowledge prior errors of architects and planners.

A further problem needs attention. The correct decision to break the spiral of decline by attracting middle-income families to LHEs does not resolve the question of where to locate families with an even lower income or living by transfer payments. The price for ameliorating the conditions in one LHE seems to be to shuffle the latter groups to another LHE - thus posing the question of affordable housing even more dramatically.

References

Autzen, R. and Becker, H., 1985: Moderne Zeiten: Aufwertung, Rückbau oder was sonst? *Stadtbauwelt* 86, 134-142.

Dittrich, G., 1973: *Neue Siedlungen und alte Viertel.* Stuttgart: Deutsche Verlags-Anstalt.

----, 1974: *Menschen in neuen Siedlungen.* Stuttgart: Deutsche Verlags-Anstalt.

Dorsch, P., 1972: *Eine neue Heimat in Perlach. München: Piper*

Feldhusen, G., 1986: Rückbau oder Gnadentod? Das komplexe Problem der Großsiedlungen in der BRD. *Bausubstanz*, 3/86, 6-13.

Friedrichs, J. (ed.): *Stadtentwicklungen in West- und Osteuropa.* Berlin-New York: de Gruyter.

-----, 1988: Large Cities in Eastern Europe, In: M. Dogan and J.D. Kasarda (eds.). *The Metropolis Era. Vol.* 1. Berverly Hills-London: Sage (in print).

----- **and Dangschat, J.**, 1986: *Gutachten zur Nachbesserung des Stadtteils Mümmelmannsberg.* Hamburg (Unpublished research report).

Handwerkskammer Hamburg, (ed.), 1986: *Zukunftswerkstatt - Entwicklungschancen* des *Stadtteils Mümmelmannsberg.* Werkstattbericht No. 2. Hamburg: Handelskammer.

Heil, K., 1987: *Kommunikation und Entfremdung.* Stuttgart: Krämer.

Herlyn, U., 1986: Lebensbedingungen und Lebenschancen in den Großsiedlungen der 60er Jahre. In: R. Guldager (ed.): *Wohnquartier im Wandel - in Braunschweig und anderenorts.* Braunschweig: Seminar für Planungswesen (Veröffentlichungen Heft 25).

Kinder, H. and Pause, G., 1949: Soziographische Untersuchungen im Raum Hamburg. In: *Schriften zum Bau-, Wohnungs- und Siedlungswesen,* Ausg. 2. Hamburg: Hammonia.

Kob, J., Kurth, M., Voss, R. and Schulte-Altedorneburg, M., 1972: *Städtebauliche Konzeption in der Bewährung:* Neue Vahr. Bremen-Göttingen: Vandenhoek und Ruprecht.

Köhler, H.-J., 1981: *Neuere Wohngebiete - Wohnlager der 80er Jahre?* Denkschrift der SAGA. Hamburg: SAGA.

Lüdtke, H., 1973: *Bauform und Wohnverhalten.* Hamburg:: Hammonia (Gewos-Schriftenreihe, Neue Folge 8).

Plessner, R, K., 1986: Lösungsansätze aus der Sicht der Mieten- und Belegungspolitik. In: SRL 1986.

Pöhl, H., 1986: Wohnungsleerstände in Westfalen-Lippe - Marketing auch in der Gemeinnützigen Wohnungswirtschaft gefragt. In: R. Thoss et al. (eds.): *Wohnungsleerstände - Was tun?* Münster: Institut für Wohnungs- und Siedlungswesen.

SAGA (Gemeinnützige Siedlungs-Aktiengesellschaft Hamburg) (ed.), 1980: *Neuere Wohnungsgebiete - Wohnlagen der 80er Jahre?* Hamburg: SAGA (Unpublished paper).

Schmidt-Bartel, J. and Meuter, H., 1986: *Der Wohnungsbestand in Großsiedlungen in der Bundesrepublik Deutschland.* Bonn-Bad Godesberg: Schriftenreihe des BMBau.

SRL (Vereinigung der Stadt-, Regional- und Landesplaner e.V.) (ed.), 1986: Nachbesserung von Großsiedlungen der 60er und 70er Jahre. In: *SRL-Information* 20. Bochum: SRL.

Strubelt, W. and Kauwetter, K., 1982: *Soziale Probleme in ausgewählten Neubaugebieten ausgewählter Städte der Bundesrepublik Deutschland.* Bonn-Bad Godesberg: Schriftenreihe des BMBau.

Thoss, R., 1986: Wohnungsleerstände als volkswirtschaftliches Problem. In: R. Thoss et al. (eds.): *Wohnungsleerstände - Was tun?* Münster: Institut für Wohnungs- und Siedlungswesen.

Weeber, R., 1971: *Eine neue Wohnumwelt.* Stuttgart-Bern: Krämer.

Wiemann, U., 1979: *Wohnungswechsel bei Bewohnern von Neubausiedlungen.* Hamburg: Universität Hamburg (Unpublished Diploma thesis).

Zapf, K., Heil, K. and Rudolph, J., 1969: *Stadt am Stadtrand.* Frankfurt/M.: Europäische Verlagsanstalt.

Ziercke, M., 1982: *Entwicklungen auf den Wohnungsmärkten der Bundesrepublik Deutschland.* Hamburg: Verlag Weltarchiv.

----, 1986: *Vorschläge für ein umfassendes Handlungskonzept zur Verbesserung der wirtschaftlichen, sozialen und technischen Situation in Hamburg-Mümmelmannsberg.* Hamburg (Unpublished research report).

SHADOW-HOUSING
SELF-HELP OF DWELLERS IN THE NETHERLANDS

Wouter Turpijn

All that is of interest occurs
in the shadow, decidedly. One
knows nothing of the true
history of man.
Céline, 1952

Introduction

The central questions posed in this chapter are the following: What is the present relationship in the Netherlands between the self-help of dwellers and the care of the authorities and other professional institutions for housing; which historical developments have led to this relationship, and what perspective does the subject offer for the future?

Self-help by dwellers is defined hereby as all activities concerning the realization and maintenance of the built environment, carried out by the dwellers themselves for the benefit of their own housing, with a minimum of interference from authorities and other professional institutions.

It will be clear that this chapter is mainly concerned with the situation in the Netherlands. At certain points, however, in particular in section two, general comparisons are made with the situation in other countries. Moreover, the ideas and theoretical concepts of writers such as Illich (1971, 1972, 1981), Gorz (1980) and Turner (1976) form an important basis for the analysis of the current phenomenon of self-help of dwellers in the Netherlands.

Historical Developments in the Netherlands and Other Countries

As in many other countries the care for housing in the Netherlands has become increasingly subjected to the rule of government and other professional institutions since about the middle of the nineteenth century. While in times long past the building and maintenance of houses and housing areas were largely a matter for the dwellers

Affordable Housing and the Homeless

themselves, nowadays in the Netherlands we are confronted with a government policy that emphasizes the role of professional institutions in building and maintenance. In other words, the Netherlands has not only become a welfare state regarding social security and medical, educational and social-cultural services, but also regarding the field of housing.

In this development the activity of the Dutch government has always been concentrated on the financing and subsidizing of the construction of rented dwellings which are managed by housing associations or local authorities. This is an important point of departure in the Housing Act of 1901, for instance. The consequence in the present situation is that of the more than 5 million dwellings in the Netherlands about 45% are let by (semi-governmental) housing associations or local authorities and 15% by private enterprises or individuals, 40% are owned by dwellers. Many dwellings of the latter two categories are also subsidized by the government.

Emphasis on the building of rented dwellings has meant that until now the Dutch government, formally speaking, has hardly made any allowance for the self-help of dwellers. For rented dwellings are not the property of the dwellers. When moving out tenants are obliged to leave the dwelling "in the original condition" as it was when they moved in. If they have permission from the owner/landlord to rebuild the dwelling, the owner is in principle not obliged to give any remuneration. Financially, therefore, it is hardly worthwhile for tenants to go beyond painting and decorating the interior. In practice, however, do-it-yourself tenants do much more, with or without the owner's permission, and regardless of the financial consequences upon discovery or when they move house.

Apart from the emphasis in governmental policy on the building of rented dwellings, and its effects on the self-help of dwellers, the Dutch government has never generally stimulated the self-help of dwellers as defined in my introduction. Although the government and other professionals have allowed for dwellers' participation in the building and management of dwellings since the 1960s (involvement in discussion and decision-making), we are in fact dealing here with a controlled organ of governmental policy. In this respect, dwellers' participation procedures are dominated by the negative aspects of inflexibility and technocracy. The government and other professional institutions continue to pull the strings while the influence of dwellers is usually limited. The activities of squatters and the squatters movement are sometimes even considered as a reaction to the "participation ideology" (Nelissen, 1980; Van der Loo, Snel and Van Steenbergen, 1984). In this context the fact that many do-it-yourself dwellers build without governmental subsidy and/or building permit (Turpijn, 1987) is also worth mentioning. To me these seem to be clear examples of a development from dwellers' participation to self-help of dwellers.

In the 1970s and 1980s in addition, local authorities, especially in Rotterdam, embarked on several projects in which dwellings were actually built for a large part by dwellers themselves. But in this case too strict governmental regulations were of decisive influence, while the Rotterdam projects were not followed up due to strong protest and political lobbying on the part of employers and employees in the building trade who perceived their position as threatened.

It is remarkable that in spite of the current austerity policy in the Netherlands the authorities and other professional institutions in the field of housing still do not show much intereste in the self-help of dwellers. This situation is quite different from the situation in other already mentioned fields of the Dutch welfare state. In the fields of medical services, services for the elderly etc., the government nowadays pleads for a "caring society" with extensive self-help and less services paid for by the state and provided professionally.

The situation in the Dutch field of housing is also quite opposite to the assumption of Harms (1982) that in times of crisis governments like to stimulate the self-help of people. Even in the 1930s the Dutch government did not stimulate the self-help of dwellers. To my knowledge Dutch governmental policy concerning the self-help of dwellers differs considerably from that in other welfare states. In Sweden, Danmark, the United Kingdom, West Germany and Belgium the historical development has certainly been towards increased care of government and other professionals for housing. In comparison with the Netherlands, however, the governmental policy of these countries has been more strongly geared towards encouragement of home-ownership. The owner-status implies that the legal possibilities for self-help of dwellers are considerably greater than those of tenants.

Generally speaking, indeed, self-help housing is more strongly propagated by the governments of these countries than in the Netherlands. In the United Kingdom the government and the national Housing Corporation stimulate self-help housing in several ways (e.g., tax and mortage facilities, housing co-operatives). The German government did the same in the 1920s and 1930s, after World War II ("First German Self-Help Day", for instance, organized by the Standing Committee of Self-Help in September 1950) and in our days. Swedish dwellers in Stockholm and Göteborg have built over 20.000 houses with their own hands, stimulated by the municipal organization Småa. In Belgium do-it-yourself building is even an integrated aspect of the prevailing culture; it is so common that no sociological information on the subject is available (Nitsche, 1981; Neue Ansätze, 1981 and 1982; Harms, 1982; Kroes and IJmkers, 1982; Goossens, 1984).

Great differences can also be seen between the Dutch situation and that of countries which are no welfare states, such as the U.S.A. and Canada. A much more reserved role of the authorities in these countries implies that dwellers have, and utilize, considerable formal freedom in self-help housing. American dwellers buy a lot more building materials than professional builders in the U.S.A. and in Canada; among other things, over a thousand housing co-operatives, established by dwellers themselves, maintain some 50.000 houses (Kern, 1975; Kern, Kogon and Thallon, 1976; Toffler, 1980; Turner and Fichter, 1972; Woonkoöperatieven in Canada, 1985).

Finally, the even greater discrepances between the Dutch situation and that of the so-called "third-world countries" are familiar. In many Latin American, Asian and African countries the only opportunity for most people to get a shelter is self-help housing, using all kinds of material and often building on squatted land. Sometimes dwellers are stimulated to do so by the government in question, the United Nations or other organizations (site and services projects, for instance), in other cases self-help housing occurs in spite of or in the absence of governmental and professional intervention.

With respect to the historical development of the phenomenon of self-help in general, finally, it should be mentioned that this term, as far as I have been able to ascertain, was first used in Western Europe by Huber (1848). Its history goes back to the seventeenth century. Under the influence of puritan ethics of work, poverty was no longer considered a symbol of evangelical simplicity and a subject of Christian charity. From then on poverty was viewed as a moral scandal and an obstacle to progress. The voluntary and charitable care provided by others, the *caritas*, lost at least the central position which it had occupied until then. People were held responsible for all their deeds with the motto: "God helps those who help themselves" (Adriaansens and Zijderveld, 1981). The Enlightenment later served to secularize and radicalize this puritanic vision concerning the personal responsibility of man. Thus the English utilitarianism of the eighteenth and nineteenth centuries saw the development of the idea of a natural harmony between the interest of the individual and the collective interest of society; see, for instance, Samuel Smiles' *Self-Help* of 1860. In the words of Adriaansens and Zijderveld (1981) "the concept of self-help then becomes a corner-stone of the ideology of *laissez-faire*". With the rise of liberalism this ideology found response far beyond England.

Mention must be made, however, of the fact that contemporary self-help theoreticians such as Katz and Bender (1976) do not view liberalism as its historical source, but rather utopian socialism - with Saint-Simon, Fourier and Owen as the most important thinkers - and the later but related social-anarchistic analysis of mutual help by Kropotkin (1914, 1972).

This varying emphasis is not surprising since both liberalism and utopian socialism are mutually influenced products of the Enlightenment, gaining concrete form particularly at the time of the French Revolution. The term self-help indeed has its origin within the orbit of liberalism. But this mainly concerns the more individualistic variant. Collective forms, on the contrary, in the sense of voluntary cooperation and mutual help, arose especially within utopian socialism and, later, social anarchism.

With regard to the current self-help of dwellers, the more individualistic principles of liberalism can be recognized to a certain extent in contemporary do-it-yourself building. In other words, this is a form of self-help of dwellers on an individual level, in which dwellers care for themselves as much as possible, with only occasional help from outside.

The more collectivist principles of utopian socialism and Kropotkin's social anarchism can today be recognized to a certain extent in the many dweller organizations and in the squatters movement, for instance. In these cases we are concerned with self-help of dwellers on a collective level. The distinction between self-help on an individual level and on a collective level will again be referred to later.

A Framework for the Analysis of the Current Self-Help of Dwellers

It will be clear from what has been said that currently the self-help of dwellers in the Netherlands is hardly taken into account by the official governmental housing policy. We have also seen that self-help housing does occur outside this field (self-builders, self-help by tenants, and the squatters movement, for instance). In other words, there is mention of "Shadow-Housing".

In order to analyse the present relationship between the self-help of dwellers and the care of the authorities and other professional institutions for housing, an analytical framework has been developed. Based on the theoretical notions of Illich, Gorz and Turner a continuum has been created, ranging from absolute autonomy to absolute heteronomy, in which heteronomy is defined as "subjection to the rule of another person or power".

These two extremes will never occur as such in reality. They are ideal types, concepts of a certain phenomenon with an overemphasis on the essential characteristics. In this case the phenomenon concerns the presence or absence of the self-help of dwellers; the essential characteristic is formed by the degree of interference of authorities and other professionals in the housing activities of dwellers.

Since both extremes of the continuum can never be reached, the analysis of the phenomenon self-help can "only" serve to establish which extreme it is closest to. Relatively autonomous and relatively heteronomous housing zones can therefore be distinguished on the continuum. The more dwellers' activities can be placed in the autonomous housing zone, the more there is mention of self-help. A clear distinction between the two zones cannot be made. In this respect only relative differences can be perceived in our complicated and interdependent society. That is why I prefer to speak of "zones" rather than "systems", as Turner (1976) does, for instance. In comparison with the latter term the word zone does not imply an exclusive entirely to the same degree. The following diagram illustrates the continuum.

```
absolute autonomy              absolute heteronomy
X                                                X
-------------------------- - - - --------------------------
autonomous                            heteronomous
housing zone                          housing zone
```

Description and Analysis of the Current Self-Help of Dwellers

In the Netherlands, more or less outside the field of official governmental housing policy, the phenomenon of self-help of dwellers nowadays occurs on a large scale. Considering *self-help on an individual level*, more than half of the Dutch population can be regarded as self-builders. There are even some 600.000 people who are capable of tackling virtually any job and who can be qualified as experts or even "professionals" (Knulst, 1983).

As already mentioned, many self-building dwellers work without governmental subsidy and/or building permit, and therefore with a minimum of interference from the authorities. These persons hardly seem to be known to local authorities, although from my own survey of 1,153 customers of do-it-yourself shops it appeared that one out of three respondents was personally acquainted with this kind of self-builder, and that one out of five operated in this way himself (Turpijn, 1987).

Dwellers also practise self-help in finding a place to live. In 1984, for instance, about 10.000 houses were sold or bought without the assistance of an estate agent (Turpijn, 1987). Around 1980, 21,000 caravans and barracks, 10,000 houseboats and more than 3,500 houses built on allotments were more or less permanently inhabited (NIROV, 1986; Over volkstuinen, 1978). A considerable number of these were illegally occupied, i.e. without permission from the authorities concerned.

In addition, one should take into account some tens of thousands of squatters still estimated to be active in the Netherlands. Because of the collective element in squatting (the squatters movement) this phenomenon is considered as a form of *self-help housing on a collective level.* In the mid-1980s we also counted some 20,000 communes, between one and two-hundred so-called "central-living" groups (i.e. mostly large groups of independent households sharing certain facilities) and some 7,000 dweller organizations of various types (Knoope and Jansen, 1981; Turpijn, 1987).

With respect to the relationship in the Netherlands between self-help dwellers on the one hand and authorities and other professional institutions in the field of housing on the other, the following can be established. Under present (and future) regulations the autonomous zone seems to flourish as far as *self-help of dwellers on an individual level* is concerned. This goes both for self-help in finding somewhere to live and for self-help in building acitivities. As far as the latter is concerned, many do-it-yourself dwellers avoid contact with authorities and other professionals as far as possible because they are afraid that demands will be made which will increase costs, cause bureaucratic fuss and--partly because of this--delay.

The interference of authorities in do-it-yourself activities of dwellers seems to become even less than before. Though largely a question of economic cuts, a policy geared towards reducing government regulations (laws and ordinances) and responsibility (deregulation, decentralization, privatization, liberalization) has this effect in any case.

But with regard to the quality of do-it-yourself activities, for example, the question is whether a continuing reduction in the role of the authorities really is such a good thing. Lower income groups in particular will need stimulation by the government, both financial and other, if they are to be willing and able to conform to minimum safety standards in their do-it-yourself activities.

Structural problems remain in the relationship between do-it-yourself tenants and their owners/landlords. There is a clear desire among tenants to engage in do-it-yourself activities; but the opportunity to do so hardly exists, legally speaking. Formal recognition by the government of the value of do-it-yourself activities in the field of housing would at any rate offer a solution to this problem.

Finally, employers and employees in the building trade have sometimes felt threatened in recent years by do-it-yourself dwelling construction. There is no reason for such fears, however, since research has shown that self-help in building and improving dwellings in fact offers the professionals new opportunities of trade and work. Here we are concerned with activities which would probably never be undertaken without the phenomenon of self-help, while these same activities may now offer all sorts of positive secondary effects for the benefit of professionals. The professional participation which I have in mind would include the building of the basic structures of dwellings (the finishing being left to the dwellers), the supply services of larger building firms as well as consultation and other assistance against payment. The money saved by the government through such self-building efforts could perhaps be put to use in other professional building projects, for not every dweller wants to be a self-builder or has the necessary skills. These also present new opportunities of trade and work for professionals (Boekhorst, 1982; Baartmans, Meijer and Van Schaik, 1987).

The self-help of dwellers on a collective level presents a somewhat different situation. In the case of self-help on an individual level the contact with authorities and other professionals seems to be avoided as far as possible, this self-help occurring largely in the autonomous housing zone. In the case of the differentiated forms of self-help on a collective level there is more contact with these insitutions from the heteronomous housing zone. This is hardly surprising since discrepancy has to do with the specific problems on both levels.

Self-help on a collective level concerns in all cases a problem which a person cannot solve satisfactorily alone (on an individual level). With the help of companions this is usually easier. The best conditions, however, for solving the problem (policy, finances, organizational skill, legal qualifications, influence) can usually be supplied by the authorities. Even if this is not the case, it is at any rate often seen this way by the dwellers concerned. In this context it is more effective to approach the authorities collectively than individually.

For these reasons a certain amount of switching to and fro between the autonomous and heteronomous housing zones can be observed in all the differentiated forms of self-help on a collective level - communes, "central-living" groups, dweller organizations and squatters. Solutions are attempted in all cases through intervention of the authorities. If for some reason this is unsuccessful then a withdrawal from the influence of the authorities may occur for a longer or shorter period, a solution being sought in the autonomous housing zone. Together with other sorts of action this autonomous search for solutions may in itself pressurize the authority concerned to formulate as yet the desired policy.

Such oscillation between the autonomous and heteronomous housing zones may occur more frequently, depending on the period in question and the nature of the problem concerned. It is in fact a continuous interplay of action and reaction. In other words, the autonomous and heteronomous housing zones seem to expand and contract periodically at each other's expense; they can be compared with a pair of communicating vessels.

Analysis of current self-help by dwellers raises the question whether the thesis of Illich, Gorz and Turner concerning the growing dominance of the heteronomous zone should not be toned down. People do indeed experience a dominant heteronomy in many social fields. But in the field of housing at least they continually seem to find answers, seek new ways to live their own lives, or to effectuate an adequate reaction to their problems from the heteronomous zone.

At the moment, however, a certain aversion to authorities and other professionals seems to be evident in all the differentiated forms of self-help on a collective level. The heteronomous zone is apparently adapted insufficiently to the needs of communes, "central-living" groups, dweller organizations and squatters. In the latter case this quite regularly leads to violent escalations which are a cause of anxiety for the future.

Self-Help of Dwellers in the Future

The problem discussed in this last section, when summarized, is that at present in the Netherlands we are concerned on the one hand with considerable self-help of dwellers in various forms and with differing needs in terms of recognition and support from the authorities, while on the other hand these authorities have generally not been able or willing to respond. With a policy of deregulation, decentralization, privatization and liberalization the authorities rather seem to go along with the interest of professional institutions concerned with housing. The possible and already partially evident negative consequences of this antithesis have been described above. The question, therefore, is how this antithesis can be removed. In other words, how can the self-help of dwellers in Dutch society function in harmony with the authorities and other professional institutions in the field of housing?

In my opinion the answer to this question, in contrast to what seems to be happening in the Netherlands at present, is that housing should not primarily become the responsibility of all kinds of professionals if the authorities wish to withdraw from this sector to a certain extent. Even now the professional care for housing is not satisfactory for dwellers as the present function of self-help demonstrates.

It is of utmost importance that dwellers themselves have a reasonable grasp, recognized by all parties, on developments in and around their housing area. But dwellers will not manage on their own. By far not all of them will be able or willing to look after themselves through self-help. In this respect the care of the authorities and other professional institutions should form a complement to the care of dwellers in the form of self-help rather than substitute it.

In other words, what applies to other fields applies to housing as well: The welfare state may not simply be dismantled. It is not just a question of what Schuyt (1986) called the "decline of planning". It should rather be a question of a "planning of decline", the deliberate creation of new and better balanced relationships between authorities, other professional institutions and citizens. According to Schuyt both government and citizens will have to learn "to be content with less, to accept limitations and to work together in a fruitful and efficient manner". It would seem to me that the emphasis here should be on working together fruitfully, from which I would certainly not wish to exclude all (semi-) private professionals.

It is impossible to give a concrete and detailed description here of the form of the proposed complementary relationship between the care of authorities and other professional institutions and the self-help of dwellers. But an "ideal model" in the spirit of Illich, Gorz and Turner may provide some indication. According to this model, authorities and other professionals in the heteronomous housing zone offer a number of basic facilities, such as financial and technical support (money, skills and advice, tools, materials, land), which can be used by dwellers themselves, or under their direct supervision, in the autonomous housing zone. In this way maximum co-ordination between the heteronomous and autonomous housing zones can be achieved. In offering basic facilities, points of attention should be the problem of do-it-yourself tenants and lower income groups.

Generally speaking, in all forms of self-help both on individual and collective levels the rights of dwellers to have land and the buildings on it at their disposal play an all-important role. This has a crucial influence on the problems of do-it-yourself tenants and lower income groups, communes and "central-living" groups, numerous dweller organizations and squatters. As long as users' rights have no priority over owners' rights the opportunities for dwellers to give satisfactory form and content to their home situation remain too limited. For the Netherlands too the International Year of the Homeless in 1987 could have been an opportunity *par excellence* to recognize and effectuate that the right to dwell is of a higher order than the right to own land and the buildings on it. Unfortunately this did not happen.

It is doubtful whether such a maximal or even ideal relationship between autonomy and heteronomy will be a final phase. There is always the danger that, in the course of time, responsibilities given to dwellers will become strongly regulated, canalized and steered by the authorities or other professionals, therefore becoming inflexible. The heteronomous housing zone will then once again expand at the expense of the autonomous zone. Another reaction will undoubtedly emerge in the form of an expansion of the autonomous housing zone. In this respect self-help housing will always continue. For, as Céline said in the quotation with which the chapter began: all things that are of interest to man--the real history of man--take place in the shadow.

References

Adriaansens, H.P.M. and Zijderveld, A.C., 1981: *Vrijwillig Initiatief en de Verzorgingsstaat.* Deventer.

Baartmans, K., Meijer, F. and van Schaik, A., 1987: *Zelfwerk-zaamheid, Woningonderhoud en Bouwwerkgelegenheid.* Delft.

Boekhorst, F.W., 1982: Werkgelegenheid Gediend bij Zelfbouwprojecten. *Bouw* 12, 31-34.

Céline, L.F., 1952: *Voyage au Bout de la Nuit.* Paris.

Goossens, L., 1984: *Het Fenomeen van de Zelfwerkzaamheid in België.* Antwerpen.

Gorz, A., 1980: *Adieux au Prolétariat. Au Delà du Socialisme.* Paris.

Harms, H., 1982: Historical Perspectives on the Practice and Purpose of Self-Help Housing. In: P.M. Ward (ed.): *Self-Help Housing. A Critique.* pp. 17-53.

Huber, V.A., 1848: *Die Selbsthülfe der Arbeitenden Klassen durch Wirtschaftsvereine* und *Innere Ansiedelung.* Berlin.

Illich, I.I., 1971: *Deschooling Society.* New York.

----, 1972: *Tools for Conviviality.* New York.

----, 1981: *Shadow Work.* London.

Katz, A.H. and Bender, E.I., 1976: Self-Help Groups in Western Society; History and Prospects. *Journal of Applied Behavioral Science* 12, 265-282.

Kern, K., 1975 (1972): *The Owner Built Home.* New York.

---- , **Kogon, T. and Thallon, R.**, 1976: *The Owner Builder and the Code.* Oakhurst.

Knoope, R. and Jansen, H., 1981: *Woongroepen in Nederland. Deel I: Dataverzameling.* Rotterdam.

Knulst, W.P., 1983: Doe het Zelf; Wat Weten Wij Erover?. In: P. Groetelaers and H. Priemus (eds.): *Doe het Zelf; Inleidingen Konfrontatiekollege Volkshuisvesting.* Delft, pp. 5-22..

Kroes, J.H. and Ijmkers, F., 1982: *Buitenlandse Vormen van Woningbeheer.* Delft.

Kropotkin, P., 1972 (1902, 1904, 1914): *Mutual Aid, a Factor of Evolution.* New York.

Loo, H. van der, Snel, E. and van Steenbergen, B., 1984: *Een Wenkend Perspectief? Nieuwe Sociale Bewegingen en Kulturele Veranderingen.* Amersfoort.

Nelissen, N..J.M., 1980: Geïnstitutionaliseerde Beweging; De Verstening van de Participatie op het Terrein van de Ruimtelijke Ordening. In: J.M.G. Thurlings, O. Schreuder, J.A.P. van Hoof, N.J.M. Nelissen and J.A. Janssen, J.A. (eds.): *Institutie en Beweging.* Deventer, pp. 135-181.

Neue Ansätze im Wohnungsbau und Konzepte zur Wohnraumerhaltung: Beispiele - Experimente - Modelle 1981 und 1982. Band I: Lesebuch zum Kongress in Saarbrücken und Band II (J. Brech, ed.). Darmstadt.

NIROV (Nederlands Instituut voor Ruimtelijke Ordening en Volkshuisvesting), 1986: *Andere Woonvormen Goed Geregeld? Een Verkennende Studie.* Den Haag.

Nitsche, R. (ed.), 1981: *Häuserkämpfe 1872, 1920, 1945, 1982.* Berlin.

Over Volkstuinen...Nu, 1978: *Amsterdam: Stichting Recreatie i.s.m.* Algemeen Verbond van Volkstuindersverenigingen.

Schuyt, K., 1986: De Verzorgingsstaat met het Oog op Morgen. In: K. Schuyt and R. van der Veen (eds.): *De Verdeelde Samenleving*. Leiden-Antwerpen, pp. 229-234.

Smiles, S., 1860: *Self-Help; with Illustrations of Character and Conduct*. London.

Toffler, A., 1980: *The Third Wave*. New York.

Turner, J.F.C., 1976: *Housing by People. Towards Autonomy in Building Environments*. London.

---- **and Fichter, R.** (eds.), 1972: *Freedom to Build*. New York.

Turpijn, W., 1987: *In de Schaduw van de Volkshuisvesting. Een Studie over de Zelfwerkzaamheid van Bewoners*. Den Haag.

Woonkoöperatieven in Canada, 1985. Amsterdam

THE GOLDSTEIN PROJECT
TWO WAYS TO AFFORDABLE HOUSING IN THE 1920S

Dieter Andernacht

Introduction

In the period before World War I the migration of people from rural areas towards industrial and urban regions led to very uncomfortable housing conditions in German cities. It is understood that during the wartime itself and soon after, no construction activity took place. This is even true till the end of the inflation period in November 1923. Thus, with the beginning of the reconstruction period the housing problem was considered as a main issue of public activity. The living conditions had to be improved under the aspect of a better reproduction of the working force, including a healthier life. The slogan of these days was "sunlight, fresh air and green environments for everybody".

In urban policy, the main idea was the separation of the working sphere and the living sphere, and the construction of large housing estates. It is the time of the Bauhaus-movement which was not only a movement for a new style, but also a movement where the social aspect of housing was of great importance, too. The modern architects wanted to minimize the rents by standardization and industrialization of construction. The aim was the affordable housing even for the low-income groups. It finally led to the concept of housing for the so-called "minimum of existence" at the CIAM congress in 1929.

By the end of the 1920s, housing construction slowed down due to the world economic crisis. The resulting unemployment led to a change in public policy. Many authors see the end of the Bauhaus period with the beginning of the Nazi regime in 1933 which obliged numerous modern architects to emigrate from Germany. I will argue that housing policy had already changed some years ago, and to demostrate this, an important housing project in Frankfurt, the so-called "Goldstein" project is chosen as an example.

Mass Construction for a "New Frankfurt"

When the Weimar Republic was founded after World War I, the leading political parties had to cope with drastic social changes in the German society since the end of the 19th century. The pacification of social conflicts was of great importance for the consolidation

Affordable Housing and the Homeless

of the republic. The housing shortage had become such an urgent problem that the development of a strategy in housing provision got a fairly symbolic value.

The lack of capital was very important after the inflation period. Any funds could be raised for construction in the free market. The private housing construction came rather to an end and the public sector had to take charge of it. The government created a special tax on the existing stock of houses as a mean to raise funds for new construction. The local authorities were enabled to manage the allocation of mortgage loans to private and public constructors. The interest rate of these mortgages was fixed from 1% to 3 %. By taking over this task "the cities had to assume the main part in the struggle against housing shortage" (Landmann, 1925: 28).

Frankfurt is regarded as the city in Germany which was almost leading in the realization of this idea. From 1925 to 1930 about 15000 dwellings were constructed in Frankfurt by public non-profit societies. Nearly every 11th household moved into a new dwelling during this period.

In Frankfurt, the number of inhabitants had increased rapidly since the beginning of the century. The old city was overcrowded, many families did not have a dwelling of their own and lived in lodgings. The housing office registered about 15000 families in need for housing. So the struggle for better housing became the central point in urban policy. The Mayor, Ludwig Landmann, a far-seeing liberal thought that the industry needs "technically and mentally qualified workers....Under this aspect social politics aiming at the furtherance of the working class have to become preponderant in local economic policy" (Kuhn, 1986b: 21). An important part of the housing program was e.g. realized to favour the localization of the I.G. Farben (the major chemistry company) headquarters in Frankfurt in 1928.

As the City of Frankfurt was the main shareholder in several local non- profit housing companies, the local authorities could push the construction by their own activity. A far-seeing policy in acquisition of land gave them the opportunity to build on a large scale. Inside the local government a special branch, the "Siedlungsamt" (office for settlement) was created to realize the communal housing program. The famous architect Ernst May was engaged in 1925 as head of this department.

Ernst May was a modern architect and a follower of the garden-city movement. His first task was the elaboration of a concept for the construction of large housing areas. Among the settlements he proposed to construct in the following years, there was one outside the city borders. This area of about 500 acres is situated on the riverside of the Main at about 4 miles from the inner city. This area already belonged to a foundation under the control of the City of Frankfurt. So it seemed to be a good choice for the construction of a large housing area with cheap dwellings for the workers in the nearby industrial enterprises.

The Initial Project

The Goldstein area, situated between the city borders and the adjacent village of Schwanheim got its name from the Goldstein farm-house in the middle of the area. The surrounding acres belonged to the farm and were cultivated by a tenant. The first document indicating future activities at Goldstein area dates back to 1926.[1] The department responsible for the farming out of the Goldstein farm wrote a letter to the Mayor and wanted to know, whether it could farm out Goldstein for another year or not. In his answer the Mayor said that a pre-project already existed in the Siedlungsamt but had to be reviewed for different reasons. He announced a new plan for the so-called "Schwanheim Garden Suburb" to come in about four weeks time.

In the following months no sign of any activity can be found in the documents. Presumably, this was due to the complicated negotiation with the federal government concerning the incorporation of Schwanheim and other surrounding villages and small towns into the Frankfurt Urban Community. Only when the incorporation had been accomplished in April 1928 preparatory work for the Goldstein project started again. The settlement office was now very busy to advance its project. The aim was the construction of 6000 dwellings at Goldstein. In August 1928 the office announced the construction of 2000 dwellings each year in 1930, 1931 and 1932. For the realization of the project the settlement office proposed to create an independent construction society and wanted to start the development of the area in spring 1929.[2]

The size of the other great housing areas within the Frankfurt housing program had been or was planned to be between 1200 and 1600 dwellings. Thus, the Goldstein project was by far the most important one. There was also a certain opposition against the Frankfurt housing program. Some people thought that the activity of the local government was too wide- spread and the financial engagement too important. Generally, they deplored the regression of private activity in the construction. We should not be surprised to learn that the opponents of the housing program opposed the Goldstein project above all.

This project had to face stiff opposition inside and outside the city administration. Especially the department for underground engineering tried to hinder the project. So they argued against the dislocation of the sewerage plant advancing by the high costs that would generate from it. Following the plans of the settlement office a tramway to Goldstein should have been constructed. When the opponents got this tramway project cancelled in late 1928 it was their most important success. The construction society had been created in February 1929, but work on the site did not start in spring 1929 as planned

1. Letter of 20-11-26 in document T 877 of the Frankfurt municipal archives.

2. Letters of 9-8-28 and 8-9-28 in document T 877.

A New Plan

From 1928 to 1929 construction activity in Germany had declined. But at the same time the need of cheap dwellings increased. In consequence the settlement department had worked out a new plan during spring and summer 1929. In response to the new demand the plan had been reviewed in two aspects:

- the average size of the dwellings had been diminished and a higher density of population in the area was planned,

- due to financing problems, a lower annual rate of construction was projected.

The new plan proposed for the Goldstein area the construction of 8500 dwellings instead of 6000. 5020 of the 8500 appartments were planned as smallest dwellings (41 to 53 sq.m.), another 2380 dwellings of medium size (53 to 60 sq.m.) and only 1130 dwellings of larger size were planned. Most of the houses were suggested to be two-storey serial houses, only 2800 dwellings were provided in four-storey buildings.[1]

The construction of the serial houses was proposed to be done in long rows. Goldstein was to become the most abstract kind of housing area. The simple multiplication of homogenous elements stood at the end of the evolution of the modern architecture in Frankfurt. "The negation of all organic idea comes to its peak" (Uhlig, 1986: 96). But not only the standardization of the appearance should go on. The Goldstein project also played an important role in the industrialization of construction. As it had been done before in the Praunheim housing area, most of the houses were to be built up by fitting of slabs. The City of Frankfurt together with two private constructors had created a factory for the production of slabs. This factory started production in Oktober 1928. The communal housing societies were supposed to give orders continuously to the factory to make it run regularly. But the retardation in the construction program already forced the factory in 1929 to work below its capacity.

Due to financial problems the construction at Goldstein was now conceived to take five years instead of three as in the initial plan. This meant a lower annual rate, 1700 dwellings per year instead of 2000. The costs of the whole project were estimated to 118,4 million Marks. The City of Frankfurt had to invest 10% of this amount into shares of the new construction society to start the operation. The executive council of Frankfurt decided on the payment of the first part (five millions) on September 2, 1929.[2] The decision of the executive council indicates that its majority was still willing to go forward in the realization of the Goldstein garden city. The official map of the Frankfurt urban area edited in spring 1930 also shows the Goldstein garden city and the legend says that this area was "under construction"

1. See document 2073 II.

2. See document 1335 in document p. 159.

Retardations and Objections

From September 1929 onwards the city council had to decide on the Goldstein project following the propositions made by the executive council. On one hand the councellors required a multitude of social regards, e.g. they required that the rent for the smallest type of dwellings should not exceed 1.20 Marks (M) per sq.m[1] and that no bonds had to be signed by the future inhabitants.

The social aspect of housing seemed to be of great importance for them. On the other hand they made a lot of objections to the program as a whole and insisted e.g. on a new expert evidence on the ground water table. Obviously some of these objections were advanced to prohibit a positive decision on the project.

The election campaign for city council votes had started in autumn 1929 and the propaganda of the right wing parties against the republican majority and their housing policy had become more and more aggressive. Up to the elections which took place in November 1929 the majority was composed of the social-democratic party, the democratic party and the "Zentrum".[2] The elections gave more influence to the opposition. The social-democratic and the democratic party declined. The so-called "republican coalition" held only the relative majority. Only the "Zentrum" gained some votes, but the Zentrum had been the most critical in the republican coalition concerning the mass-construction of houses. The executive council had to recognize the results of this election as a public vote against his housing program, because it had played an important role in the political campaign. The social-democratic newspaper had commented the propaganda against the housing program as follows: "The defenders of capitalist interests have begun to fight against social housing in a frank way. They officially refused the construction of the garden city at Goldstein."[3]

But not only the pressure of the opposition became stronger. The more important obstacle to the realization of the project was the lack of financial means. From December 1929 onwards the settlement office had no hope that they could realize the Goldstein project. The office did not even deliver the necessary documents the city council had asked for. Several times the Mayor pushed the settlement office to respect the appointed terms.

1. In December 1928, the standard wage of a fully employed male worker was M 214.90 for skilled, and M 177.70 for an unskilled worker in the chemical industry; M 232.60 for skilled workmen and M 202.47 for unskilled workmen in printing; M 161.50 for skilled workmen and M 135.53 for unskilled workmen in textile industry.

2. The "Zentrum" ("Centre") was a catholic-republican party.

3. Volkszeitung of 20-9-29 in document of the city council No 439.

Finally in July 1930, Ernst May, the head of the settlement department, himself wrote a letter to the Mayor to tell him that his department had renounced to start construction at Goldstein in 1931 and that any work on the planning should be deferred until further notice. Thus the original Goldstein project which had been the most important project within the Frankfurt housing program was stopped and Ernst May who had been the major inspirer of this program left Frankfurt some weeks later for the Soviet Union where he tried to realize his ideas in the following years (until 1934).

The Government Wants to Create Suburban Settlements

Lacking financial ressources, German cities were not able to continue their own housing policy. This is also true for Frankfurt. Thus the central government could force the cities to follow its orientation by the mean of the financial allocations. At that time more than seven million people were unemployed in Germany. In view of this mass-unemployment the central government proposed a program for rural settlements. Included in this program and as a first step the government projected the creation of suburban settlements with allotments. The general directions for suburban settlements on which the government had decided in autumn 1931 were very strict. They forbid sewerage for these settlements and insisted on building roads in the cheapest manner possible.
For the near future, a decline in the standard of living was expected by the government and these measures were taken to "accustom the homecrofters with more primitive living conditions" (Naleppa and Karger, 1938: 17). Another very important aspect of the suburban settlements was the self-help activity of the future settlers. The self-help activity gave a unemployed persons a task and it was considered to be a preventive measure against social violence. For many distressed families the settlements became the only hope. This psychological effect was intended by the government. The comments of the Third Emergency Decree clearly underlined this point. The Minister of Labour said in 1932, that the most important aspect in provision of work was "to divert the minds" (Köhler, 1969: 290).

Frankfurt's city council doubted that someone could earn his living by gardening in such an allotment. But the majority thought that the only chance for unmployed people to start a new life was to be found in agricultural activities. Following the arguments of the conservative party the majority asked the executive council to elaborate a plan for a rural settlement in Frankfurt.

Towards a New Goldstein Project

Without an approval of the State Commissioner for the Rural Settlement the City of Frankfurt could not raise funds for a suburban settlement. The restrictions he made were so strict that he finally forced the city to choose the Goldstein area for the localization of a settlement. In February 1932, the executive council proposed to construct the first 380 settlements on the Goldstein area.

To prove its intention, the executive council underlined the social and economical importance of the suburban settlements: "The settlement will enable its occupant to get a part of his victuals by gardening. As the short-time work will be very important in the future, the settlement will become an important mean to facilitate the subsistence of its occupant. We will give to the settler the possibility to lease more land nearby; so he can increase his receipts if he wants to. The breeding of small cattle (especially rabbits) will bring casual emoluments and with a good evolution the settler will perhaps completely convert to this activity".[1] These arguments correspond to the commissioner‘s view.

The costs for the settler‘s house were 3000 Marks. The government provided 2500 Marks per settlement while the self-help of the future inhabitants had to bring the equivalent of 500 Marks. The allotment around the house was of 700 sq.m. (27 roods); the settler‘s house had two rooms and a great kitchen, a little stable for chicken, rabbits or goats and a hay-loft. The settlers had to construct the roads by themselves. A labour service, organized and payed by the Labour Office had to help them in this task. The municipality only paid the material for the roads.

If we compare the projected houses with projects already completed in the Frankfurt housing program there is no doubt that there was a regress in living standard. Councellor Rebholz from the social-democratic party was very sceptical: "Everyone who is interested in progress of living style has to characterize the suburban settlements as a regress....There will be no sanitation....The houses are as primitive as in the remotest villages and we should worry about the hygienic conditions".[2]

Rebholz still believed in the idea of progress on which the Frankfurt housing program was based in the years before. Therefore he argued against the emplacement of the suburban settlement at Goldstein refering to the costs which would incur from the clearing of the area once when the "real buildings" would be constructed. And he saw a further contradiction in the concept as a whole. It was neither an urban nor a rural settlement. The defenders of the suburban settlements themselves said in public that the existence of a second job would be the condition to the realization of such a project. The settlers would need a stable income besides their benefits from gardening. Rebholz saw the danger that further wage-cut could be aspired by that. The employers or the government could argue that the second job would help these persons to earn their living. Despite these objections the social-democratic party finally decided to follow the propositions of the executive council. In their view such a project seemed to be the only way to raise funds for housing construction at that time. The Zentrum party agreed as well to the planning. It only required the tightning of the basement and a third room under the roof-top.

1. See document M 258 (31) in document of the city council No 445.

2. See 213 in session of city council on 23-2-32, document of city council No 445.

The communists were the only party remaining opposed to the Goldstein settlement as actually planned. They refused "to build up a village at a place where a modern town should be."[1] They critized the fact that at the same time more than 1000 dwellings in Frankfurt remained inoccupied because of their high rent. A communist councellor said: "You cut the rental allowance, you are not willing to give a reduction on gaz, nor on water and electricity for the unemployed; but you force those people to move to these settlements".[2] But the successor of Ernst May at the head of the settlement office, councellor Niemeyer, did not accept these objections. He referred to the fact that among the aspirants waiting for an allotment at Goldstein were also many adherents of the communist party. Indeed, the intended psychological effect of the Third Emergency Decree was visible. Under this influence the social-democratic newspaper of the Frankfurt region wrote in April 1932 that "by the construction of the Goldstein settlement 380 families have already been delivered from dejection and despair, effects of a long-time unemployment".[3]

The choice of the future settlers was done by the welfare,centre in Frankfurt. Since January 1932, even before the official announcement of the project, about 400 applicants to settle at Goldstein were already inscribed on a waiting list. At that time the public assistance had to pay on an average 35 Marks per month as rental allowance. The welfare centre hoped to lower this allowance to 25 Marks per month once when the assisted people could move into the self-help houses at Goldstein. The applicants had to accept a personal contribution of at least 2700 hours of work on the site. The welfare centre gave priority to families with many children and to persons whose profession could be useful in the construction.

Construction at Goldstein started in April 1932. Twelve to twenty men joined to form a working team under the guidance of a foreman. The 380 houses had to be built before one knew which house would be his own one. Only when the construction had been accomplished they would cast lots for the attribution of the houses.

They got 0.20 Marks a day for additional support, but some of them even reinvested this small sum to permit additional works on the houses, e.g. the finishing of a third room under the roof-top. The municipality offered a cup of soup each day to all of them. Relatives often came to help them. A group of 300 volunteers, organized and payed by the Labour Office, came to carry out the construction of the roads in the area.

The future settlers worked from 8 a.m. to 5 p.m. They decided soon to start working earlier in the morning and also extended their working time until sunset. The first houses were finished in September 1932 and the first settlers could move in one month later.

1. Councellor Lang at the session of city council on 23-2-32.

2. Councellor Fischer at the session of city council on 5-4-32.

3. Volkszeitung, edition of 19-4-32.

The welfare centre had registered 900 aspirants at the beginning of the project. Another 500 families asked for a settlement before July 1932. So the city council decided on July 1, 1932 to build a second segment at Goldstein. To found this resolution the council pointed to the fact that illegal breeding of small cattle was spreading everywhere, even in normal dwellings.[1] A third segment of houses was built up at Goldstein from 1933 to 1935. Finally, the settlement became the home for 926 families. It was one of the most important suburban settlements which have been constructed in Germany at that period.

Discussion: Housing Supply or Provision of Work?

The modern architects thought that provision of work would not make sense in housing policy. They thought that only a maximum of efficiency could lead to affordable housing with high living standard. In the view of May, Wagner and their collegues, the provision of work to unqualified workers, the self-help activities and the labor service represented an enormous waste of labor force:

- while unqualified men work on the site, qualified workers go to the Labor Office;

- in spite of the fact that a cheaper construction can only be realized with a higher level of industrialization machines were not used.

Once a councellor of the Zentrum party had asked to start a public employment program by the settlement department. Ernst May said that this program would be much more expensive than applying modern machines and he asked him if he would be ready to pay the difference of the rent in that case. In May‘s view the planning of the housing program should only be guided by the search for a physiological and economical optimum. Following these ideas the plan for the Goldstein settlement became an original product of welfare state policy.

The Goldstein project always reflected the changing priorities in housing policy. The housing shortage for the low-income groups had led to a concept for a housing area with 8500 dwellings. But in spite of standardization and in spite of construction of smallest dwellings the rents remained too high. In the same time the need to attract labor force to urban regions had declined with the beginning of the economic crisis. So the majority of the city council gave priority to a program under the aspect of employment.

The reason for the creation of suburban settlements was not the housing shortage but the mass-unemployment. The housing shortage was not even mentioned to substantiate the project of a suburban settlement in Frankfurt. In a matter of fact, the new project brought a reduction from 8500 to 926 dwellings in the Goldstein area, and this cannot be regarded as an answer to housing shortage.

1. City council, session on 1-7-32.

A study on the economic value of the Goldstein settlement was made in 1938 at Frankfurt University. The study aimed especially at the benefits of gardening and breeding and thus at the indirect raise in income. The authors of the study, W. Karger and W. Naleppa, posit that the government hoped to lower the costs of assistance to the poor by this way. This confirms the objections made by councellor Rebholz in 1932.

The authors reach the following conclusion: "The main force that made the projects of suburban settlements work was only the fear of an instantaneous discharge of political tension. The measures applied aimed primarily at a psychological effect and less at an economic one. The unemployed should feel that there was at least an attempt made to alleviate their misery" (Karger and Naleppa, 1938: 16).

In my view, the final shape of the Goldstein settlement was a symbol for the termination of a policy aiming at housing supply. Hence, we should see the self-help activities primarily as an answer to unemployment and only in second rank as an instrument of housing policy.

The Crisis of Welfare State Policy

Nowadays many economists believe that we have to face a long stagnation period and that the mass-unemployment will last for a long time. More and more people cannot be integrated into the normal economy. That is one of the reasons for the interest in strategies of self-help in housing provision. A lot of experiences are made and much research is done nowadays in the field of informal economy. By introducing concepts of self-reliance we try to join informal economy and housing problems.

A retrospective view could be useful then. Around 1930 the subjacent idea of all the applied measures was the inevitable persistence of mass- unemployment. Housing policy became a mean to provide employment in informal economy. In a critical examination it is not important that at that time informal economy could only be imagined in the agricultural sector. The main ideas were the same and the problems were either the same.

The initial motivation was to turn away from the welfare state policy, the costs of which could no more be afforded by the society. Another element that reoccurs today is the sedentariness as one aspect of social pacification besides the employment. Everyone who is engaged in such projects should clearly point out the priority of the employment aspect on the housing problem - today as well as they did at that period.

References

Andernacht, D., 1985: *L'activité d'Ernst May à Francfort; un enjeu politique.* Grenoble: IUG.

---- **and Kuhn, G.**, 1986: Frankfurter Fordismus. In: R. Höpfner and V. Fischer (eds.): *Ernst May und das Neue Frankfurt 1925-1930.* Berlin.

Stadt Frankfurt, 1926-1932*: Bericht über die Verhandlungen der Stadtverordneten-versammlung der Stadt Frankfurt am Main.* Vols. 58-64. Frankfurt.

Karger, W. and Naleppa, W., 1938: *Die volkswirtschaftliche Leistung einer Kleinsiedlung.* Frankfurt.

Köhler, H., 1969: Arbeitsbeschaffung, Siedlung und Reparationen in der Schluaphase der Regierung Brüning. *Vierteljahreshefte für Zeitgeschichte*, No 3, 276-307.

Kuhn, G., 1986a: *Das Neue Bauen in Frankfurt in der Ära May.* Franfurt: University of Frankfurt, Department of History.

---, 1986b: Landmann, Asch, May. In: R. Höpfner and V. Fischer (eds.): *Ernst May und das Neue Frankfurt 1925-1930.* Berlin.

Landmann, L., 1925: Das Siedlungswesen. *Jahrbuch der Frankfurter Bürgerschaft.* Frankfurt.

Miller-Lane, B., 1968: *Architecture and Politics in Germany 1918-1945.* Cambridge, Mass.: Harvard University Press.

Mohr, C. and Müller, M., 1984: *Funktionalität und Moderne. Das Neue Frankfurt und seine Bauten 1925-1933.* Köln.

Prigge, W., 1986: Regulierung. In: R. Höpfner and V. Fischer (eds.): *Ernst May und das Neue Frankfurt 1925-1930.* Berlin.

Uhlig, G., 1986: Sozialräumliche Konzeption der Frankfurter Siedlung. In: R. Höpfner and V. Fischer (eds.): *Ernst May und das Neue Frankfurt 1925- 1930.* Berlin.

PART THREE:

THE NEW HOMELESSNESS

THE NEW HOMELESS IN BRITAIN

Alan Murie and Ray Forrest

Introduction

Unlike many countries the definition of homelessness in Britain has an official and legislative dimension. This is associated with a long tradition of direct state intervention in the housing market and the existence of a large public rental sector administered by local authorities with a range of statutory responsibilities. In Britain, popular images of the homeless family are far removed from the stereotypical vagrant or drifter and more closely associated with the impact of changes in personal and financial circumstances on working class households in general. Explanation and analysis of homelessness among families (but less so among single persons) is more likely to be in terms of shifts in the social and economic structure and to emphasize housing market processes and constraints rather than pathological factors. There is inevitably considerable debate regarding the extent and nature of homelessness in Britain, the adequacy of official definitions and policies and the avoidance of statutory responsibilities. Nevertheless, the existence of a clear homeless category does enable certain trends and developments to be analyzed.

In this chapter particular attention is given to two related contemporary features of an increasing level of homelessness - a greater awareness of homelessness as a consequence of economic and labor market change and the development of low standard of housing provision compatible with a strengthening of the definition of the homeless as an undeserving or powerless category. In this context discussion of the housing experiences of homeless households in contemporary Britain links to broader discussions of the downgrading and residualization of council housing in general (see, for example, Forrest and Murie, 1983, 1986).

What is new about the homeless and homelessness in Britain in the 1980s? Is it to do with numerical increase, the changing characteristics of homeless households or the transformed pattern of housing tenures and opportunities? All these factors are certainly evident. There has been an explosion of homelessness which has been most apparent in the major urban areas; young people and ethnic minorities are more heavily represented; and the mono-tenurial nature of recent housing policy with its preoccupation with the extension of home ownership has placed less emphasis on the provision of cheaper, easy access rental accommodation. Those in more vulnerable and insecure social and financial circumstances have faced an increasingly hostile housing environment. What is novel, however, is the changed context in which homelessness is increasing and becoming more diverse in nature and origin. There is recognition that homelessness is one symptom of multi-dimensional exclusion from the social consumption norms of the majority and that

Affordable Housing and the Homeless

whatever the housing policy response, those who become homeless (in both official and unofficial categories) are likely to experience much more intractable and long-term problems of social and economic disadvantage. Pessimistic scenarios abound of the widening and deep-seated divisions between the haves and have-nots. In the British context, Halsey (1987: 19) has referred to a new form of polarization in society and the emergence of:

> "a more unequal society as between a majority in secure attachment to a still prosperous country and a minority in marginal economic and social conditions, the former moving into the suburban locations of the newer economy of a "green and pleasant land", the latter tending to be trapped into the old provincial industrial cities and their displaced fragments of peripheral council housing estates".

In a similar vein Gamble (1987: 16) has asserted that the pressures:

> "to maintain public order in civil society and continuing prosperity has produced policies that have increased the freedom and mobility of private capital while strengthening the powers of the state against those groups excluded and marginalized".

Others have noted (e.g. Pahl, 1986) that the pursuance of majority politics whereby most households experience real economic gain and a minority real economic loss is contributing to a changed income structure. The privileged minority at the top progress on an ever upward wealth and income trajectory, the middle mass of the employed benefit from appreciating domestic property and rising real incomes (often in multiple earning households) and a diverse and expanding group of the socially, economically and electorally marginal represent the bottom part of this onion-shaped structure. Whilst the increase in social polarization is now widely accepted, it is recognised that the diversity and complexity of this process require more subtle and sensitive analysis. It is, for example, inappropriate to conflate the various forms of official and concealed homelessness, young black unemployed, marginal home owners, low paid workers and so forth into a general category thus implying common origins, destinations and consequences. Nevertheless, the common pattern is of divergence and bifurcation, of increasing disparities of wealth, income, lifestyle and life chances among different groups at different stages of the life cycle. In housing terms, in Britain, this polarization has apparently striking dimensions dividing the population into the home owning privatized majority and those dependent on the rental sectors. Transformations in patterns of employment, the impact of recession, the specific history of housing tenures and the recent phase of privatization has strengthened this division. As the majority are drawn into home ownership and public housing becomes the stigmatized tenure for the dispossessed and homeless this division becomes more evident. Over time, however, the penetration of home ownership down the income structure, the impact of government policy aimed at reviving private renting and the further rounds of privatization of public housing is likely to lead to a less clear tenure polarization.

Evidence on the re-emergence of mass poverty and growing social polarization is by no means confined to Britain. Ferge and Miller (1987) have pointed to a commonality of processes in Europe as a whole. And Dahrendorf (1987: 13) has commented on the growth of an underclass (and those balanced precariously on the edge) in all OECD countries:

> "For many people in the OECD world, there is today - and has been since the 1970s - a sense of downward movement, or at least of the precariousness of what has been achieved. This is not incompatible with the spectacular success of a few: on the contrary casino capitalism would seem a fitting concomitant of general decline. This negative propensity may well be one of the reasons why the underclass is so important. It represents, so to speak, the ultimate extrapolation of the fate of many. And indeed, it is growing in significance, if not always in size".

It is then this chronic and pervasive deprivation in the context of burgeoning affluence which gives rising homelessness a new and worrying dimension. It is a prospect of entrapment, containment and social and spatial immobility rather than temporary disruption which faces many households. The inner urban areas are gentrified and revalorized and the hi-tech architecture and exclusive waterside residences co-exist with low grade hostels for the homeless and displaced. It is a very different context from the homelessness of the 1960s with elements which parallel many of the characteristics of third world cities and the emergence of what Townsend (1987) has referred to as "market value" poverty with an emphasis on reduced public spending, the minimization of welfare assistance, and the acceptance of much higher levels of "natural" unemployment. It is this sort of perspective which has characterized recent policy responses to rising homelessness.

Background

The post-1945 history of policies towards the homeless is fully described elsewhere (Richards, 1981). War time measures including the provision of hutment camps and billeting were regarded as temporary emergency measures. The continuing responsibility for homelessness was laid down in the National Assistance Act 1948. This abolished the Poor Law and established local authority Welfare Departments. It was these departments which assumed responsibility, as successors to the Poor Law authorities, for care (including residential care) of the old, infirm and handicapped. The emphasis was placed on rehabilitation rather than institutional care and the duty (under Part III of the Act) in respect of homelessness was "to provide ... temporary accommodation for persons who are in urgent need thereof ... in circumstances which could not reasonably have been foreseen". Richards notes that the relevant Ministry of Health Circular (87/48) emphasized that the section was "primarily intended to cover persons temporarily without accommodation as a result of such circumstances as fire, flood or eviction" and *not* for "dealing with the inadequately housed". Temporary accommodation was provided for homeless *families* only and welfare departments had no statutory obligation to accept responsibility for single people who were below retirement age and not infirm. The only statutory provision for the single homeless was in reception centres provided by central government through the National Assistance Board. These reception centres were the successors to workhouse casual wards which had been provided on a deterrent basis under the Poor Law and were to be less punitive than their predecessors and to encourage "resettlement".

The Welfare Departments located at county council level were not also housing departments - and housing departments which in Britain developed an unusually important social housing role were often located in a different tier of local government. Welfare Departments operated under the general guidance of the Minister and as the successors to Poor Law authorities had access to former workhouses which could be used as hostels. Rather than this being a transitional arrangement it remained normal and there was a reluctance to build new units. Local authorities tended to interpret the Act as a hostel and casework service and to draw on the experience of previous administration (Glastonbury, 1971). This involved provision of communal facilities, limited stays (resulting in children being taken into care), sex segregation and restricted contact between husband and wife.

These and other deterrent aspects did not prevent numbers rising but did contribute to the increasing concern about the inadequacy of provision. This limited family based provision was always deficient. However, its shortcomings were made more apparent by the restructuring of the housing market in the subsequent period. The common lodging house, charitable provision and more generally the private rented sector underwent significant decline. Full employment in the post-war period and major investment in housing provision raised general housing standards but the supply of lower priced, easy access accommodation was being steadily eroded. Slum clearance and the decontrol of rents had specific repercussions. Watson (1986) refers to a changing climate in the 1960s in which homelessness reentered the public arena. Households were splitting into small units, marital breakdown was increasing, remarriage decreasing and the population was ageing. New legislation relating to the mentally ill emphasized care in the community - effectively competing for the declining supply of less secure private rented accommodation.

Rent decontrol did not increase the supply of private renting - indeed it speeded its decline - and insecurity of tenure and speculative sale and redevelopment had serious impacts. The decline in lodging houses, hostels and reception centres was dramatic as these forms of accommodation gave way to more profitable land use.

All of these changes led to a considerable growth in homelessness as measured by admittance to accommodation provided under the National Assistance Act 1948 (generally referred to as Part III Accommodation). The Milner Holland Report and more directly the TV play "Cathy Come Home" (1966) focused attention on housing stress and homelessness. Following "Cathy Come Home", five housing-aid organizations combined to launch a new national charitable organization, Shelter: The National Campaign for the Homeless. Shelter's success in attracting funds and public interest was very considerable. This campaign, the continuing growth of homelessness and the result of a series of enquiries into homelessness (Glastonbury, 1971; Greve, 1964; Greve et al., 1971) were of considerable importance. The recurrence of a squatting campaign which had not been apparent since the 1940s was an associated development. Watson (1986) has outlined the revival of interest in homelessness in the voluntary sector in the 1960s and concluded that the emphasis in these agencies and government funding was on the defiance of the homeless rather than on structural changes which generated homelessness. In the 1970s the emphasis clearly shifted towards problems in the housing market. In a full employment economy the problem was increasingly recognised as one of supply and access to housing - although it was sometimes acknowledged that differences in income were key factors - especially for single parents with children.

Evidence about the nature and causes of homelessness grew considerably after the development of public interest in the topic in the mid-1960s. The evictions and harassment that followed the Rent Act 1957 and the continued decline of rental accommodation are generally referred to in explaining the growth of homelessness in the 1960s and its continuation through the 1970s (Burke, 1981). In 1966, there were 2,558 households in temporary accommodation in England and Wales; in 1970, 4,926; in 1976, 10,270. In 1970, 6,544 families were accepted as homeless in England; in 1976, 33,720 and in 1978, 53,000.

The studies by Greve (1964) and Glastonbury (1971) indicated that the characteristics of homeless families in temporary accommodation were similar throughout the late 1950s and 1960s. In addition to low-paid wage earners and unskilled or semi-skilled manual workers, there were high proportions of unemployed men and fatherless families dependent on Supplementary Benefits. Young families and those sharing accommodation were particularly important. Most of those becoming homeless had previously been in privately rented accommodation (87% in London and 62% in South Wales and the West), while only 3% and 10% were owner occupiers. Greve et al. (1981) confirmed this general pattern but identified larger proportions of black households and larger families among the homeless. This study confirmed housing shortage as a major underlying cause of homelessness.

How far family dispute is a response to impossible living conditions arising from enforced sharing and overcrowding while waiting for council or other separate accommodation will vary from case to case. However, Greve et al. (1971: 256) were quite clear that the predominantly young households with larger than average families and lower than average incomes who become homeless were "ordinary decent Londoners". The households concerned were at considerable disadvantage in their housing, the majority living in overcrowded conditions in furnished tenancies where they were at a high risk of becoming homeless through landlord action. Their long-term dependence on the furnished sector derived from local housing shortages and their lack of power in competition for council or owner occupied housing. "Difficult" or "problem" families were a small minority among the homeless, and housing shortage rather than fecklessness was the major factor.

New Legislation

Increasing numbers, increasing concern, increasingly effective pressure group activity and increasing identification of homelessness as a housing problem led to a series of policy adjustments in the 1970s. In an environment in which local authorities were being exhorted to liberalize their housing policies and take a wider view of their responsibilities especially towards those who in the past would have been housed in the private rented sector some local housing departments began to take responsibility for the homeless. They were encouraged to do this in Ministerial Circulars which attempted to overcome the lack of co-operation between welfare and housing authorities. It is worth bearing in mind that some of this lack of co-operation derived from housing departments' concerns to favour the respectable working class and to see the homeless as the disreputable. Rehousing the homeless into the permanent stock was seen as penalizing others who waited their turn or were more responsible.

A Ministry of Health Circular in 1966 had broken new ground in emphasizing that losing ones home was a socially damaging experience in itself and in attempting to lay down minimum standards for hostels. But it had resisted recommending that permanent accommodation should be provided. By 1967 increased pressure and publicity led to joint action by the Ministries of Health and of Housing and Local Government. A joint circular emphasized that homeless families (sic) "have a legitimate claim on local authority housing...". But it was not until 1974 that a more substantial response was made to changing awareness and political pressure (especially through the Joint Charities Group made up of five lobbying organizations). This response in the form of another joint circular was the precursor for legislation which shifted responsibility for homelessness to housing departments. The Circular stated that the provision of accommodation for the homeless should be an integral part of the housing function and therefore that housing authorities should take over the responsibility. It identified priority categories, recommended standards and procedures and identified homelessness as "almost always the extreme form of housing need" rather than as a personal problem of inadequate people. The new circular coincided with local government reorganization in 1974 and did promote changes in local policy. The following period however was marked by evidence of authorities which were not responding positively to new advice and pressure for legislation to bring these authorities into line. The Housing (Homeless Persons) Act 1977 completed this process.

The Housing (Homeless Persons) Act was significantly amended in the process of legislation and never reflected the aspirations of pressure groups, especially in relation to definitions of priority needs and to the inclusion of "tests" of intentionality and a local connection. The Act imposed a duty on local authorities to provide housing for people who were "unintentionally homeless" if they were in "priority need" of accommodation and had a "local connection". The Act was primarily intended for those with dependent children. The notion of vulnerability which was applied to homeless single people served to marginalize their homelessness. The Act also emphasized the role of the voluntary organizations, as opposed to statutory ones, in providing accommodation for the single. Local authorities were empowered to give financial and other assistance to such bodies. Nevertheless, the Act shifted responsibility for housing the homeless from social services departments to housing departments and represented a recognition that homelessness was primarily a housing rather than a social problem.

Reflection on Legislation

Having noted that legislation relating to homelessness was flawed from the outset it is important to reflect upon the experience of it. Britain is unusual in explicitly acknowledging homelessness and treating it as a housing problem involving rights for homeless people which are enforceable in the courts. The numbers of people being accepted in the homelessness category have risen significantly (Table 1) and many local authorities in developing their housing service have redirected resources towards the homeless and others in the greatest housing need.

Table 1a: Homelessness Acceptances

Year	England	London
1979	56,750	16,600
1980	2,920	17,480
1981	70,010	18,470
1982	74,800	21,100
1983	78,240	24,050
1984	83,550	24,820
1985	93,980	27,390
1986	102,980	30,036

Source: Shelter Factsheets and Department of Environment.

However, this is by no means an indication of even qualified success. Four initial observations on the operation of legislation are relevant:

1. Many of those currently housed as homeless would previously have been housed through another route (say the waiting list).

2. Many local authorities use the legislation to minimize the number of households accepted as priority homeless.

3. Many local authorities have continued to use "deterrent" hostel and temporary accommodation for priority homeless households.

4. Homeless households commonly are given fewer offers and "worse" offers for accommodation than others being allocated permanent council housing.

Table 1b: Homeless Households as Percent New Local Authority Lettings, England and Wales

Year	All new tenants (000s)	% as homeless
1976	287	9
1978/79	303	13
1979/80	288	15
1980/81	291	15
1981/82	265	16
1982/83	271	17
1983/84	260	17
1984/85	255	19
1985/86	261	22

Source: CSO, Social Trends.

One view of this is that the development of homelessness legislation has not increased the supply of housing available to those in the most acute housing need and that "homelessness" has been absorbed into council housing management. It provides an "official" category which helps allocators and managers to categorize applicants and ensure that there are households desperate enough to accept and unable to refuse (if they refuse they can be seen as intentionally homeless and undeserving) those properties which other categories of applicants would not accept. This absorption of the homeless category so that it is of mixed benefit to those who are in it is not an inevitable consequence of legislation although the pre-occupation with abuse and intentionality does make this more likely. Nor do the attributes of the post-legislation homeless explain this.

Experience in respect of homeless since the passage of the Housing (Homeless Persons) Act 1977 has reinforced the view that those who become homeless are normal, local households affected by housing shortages. Some local authorities have gone to great lengths to minimize the number of households accepted as homeless and some have in particular interpreted intentions in respect of homelessness in a remarkable way. Nevertheless, over 90% of households accepted as homeless lived in the same borough, district or county as the borough of acceptance one month before acceptance and this applied to over 80% of cases one year before acceptance.

Table 1c: Homeless Households as Percent of New Local Authority Lettings by Region (England), 1983/84 and 1985/86

	1983/84		1985/86	
Region	All new tenants (000s)	% as homeless	All new tenants (000s)	% as homeless
North	24	11	24	11
Yorkshire and Humberside	33	14	36	15
East Midlands	22	10	22	15
East Anglia	8	11	8	20
South East	71	27	67	34
Greater London	37	36	34	47
Rest of South East	34	18	33	21
South West	15	20	15	27
West Midlands	30	17	32	27
North West	42	12	43	17

Sources: CSO, Regional Trends, HMSO, 1986; Housing Construction Statistics, 1976-86, HMSO, 1987.

Nor is the practice of local authorities best explained by scapegoating the manager. As Henderson and Karn (1987) argue in relation to racially discriminatory housing allocations "contrary to the prevailing view of racial discrimination ... discriminatory housing allocations are not primarily a consequence of a housing department having in its employ particular racially and socially prejudiced individuals ...". Rather the tasks and interests of officers predispose them to categorize both applicants and properties and to draw on a variety of positive and negative codes, images and stereotypes to make categorizations.

These considerations lead back to a focus on supply and demand. Rather than the legislation, the homeless themselves or the policy implementors being "at fault" it is acknowledged that the time *when* the legislation was introduced was not the most favourable. The housing market restructuring and decline of private renting which are widely recognised as generating the demand for legislation were not terminated by it. The decline has continued. Moreover, other factors have exacerbated the situation. Watson (1986) states:

"The most important point about the Act was the economic context in which it was passed. The Act was brought into force at a time when Britain was suffering severe effects of economic recession. By 1977 in Britain the gross domestic product was below the 1973-74 level in real terms; there had been successive cutbacks, in current spending on public housing since 1976, and capital expenditure (on new and renovated housing) in the public sector (including housing associations) had fallen in real terms every year since 1975. The crucial point, therefore, was that there was a wide gap between the intentions of the Act and the resources provided to meet its requirements. Inevitably the result of the situation was an increased hostility towards the homeless. They were seen to be "jumping the queue" of those people in "real housing need" on the waiting list, they were the new scroungers and rent evaders. The right wing elements of the media had a hey-day".

In the 1980s the decline of public renting has been added to the decline of private renting leading to a general contraction of rental opportunities. This is a new situation in the 1980s. At the same time economic recession and the end of the period of full employment have generated new demands for lower price accommodation. There are a growing number of failed owners and poorer households who are priced out of private renting in inner city areas. The increase in the size of the marginalized population has coincided with a decline in the supply of accommodation available to them. Various evidence is referred to to show a trend for the marginalized poor to funnel towards social rented housing (e.g., Forrest and Murie, 1983). However, in the 1980s the outlet from the funnel has been becoming more restricted.

As suggested earlier, it is this changing environment which involves some *new* elements in homelessness. There are important continuities in the class characteristics of households. However, in contrast to the 1960s, homelessness is less likely to result from landlord action and the households involved are less likely to be in employment.

The early studies of homelessness identified key causes as rent arrears, landlord requiring accommodation, unauthorized occupancy and family disputes. Landlord action and rent arrears have declined in importance and mortgage defaults grow - reflecting changes in the housing market. Violent and non-violent disputes with spouse or inability of parents, relatives or friends to accommodate account for some 60% of the reasons for homelessness in the 1980s compared with between 17% and 25% in London in 1959-61 (Greve, 1964), 34% in South Wales and the South West between 1963 and 1969 (Glastonbury, 1971) and 17% in London in 1970 (Greve et al., 1971). Differences in definitions, some of which emanate from the passing of the Housing (Homeless Persons) Act, 1977, create difficulties in comparing figures. Nevertheless, the growth of marital and family disputes as a cause of homelessness is undeniable. The problems facing women, especially battered wives, have become more apparent in recent years. Court orders to prevent molestation are unlikely to prevent recurrence of violence but many local authorities have been reluctant to accept claims of violence as grounds for rehousing, and the extent of this problem is not likely to be fully indicated by homelessness acceptances.

There is a further perspective on this view of "causes of homelessness". It is to seek to distinguish between immediate and underlying causes and argues that, for example, family disputes result from tensions created by problems of obtaining employment - especially for younger people.

The new homeless are more obviously affected by economic change and restructuring rather than housing market changes alone. The problem of homelessness is exacerbated by a closer fit between economic situation, income, employment and housing situation. In this sense the way the economy has developed and the increasing dominance of home ownership in the housing market have resulted in problems of negotiating access to housing being more dominated by affordability issues rather than questions of rent control, and bureaucratic management. One consequence is that the homeless include those most vulnerable to economic change and those who have not yet negotiated access to council housing or home ownership or whose economic vulnerability threatens their continuing occupation of current housing. This involves younger households and those in vulnerable economic groups, those with recent or substantial mortgages or affected by marital breakdown. The prominence of black households reflects both a historic underrepresentation in council housing and economic position. Recent research has shown that more Asians and West Indian tenants than white tenants are likely to have been housed because they were homeless; and the properties occupied by black people in the public sector are markedly inferior to those occupied by white people (Brown, 1984, P. 81). The decline in rented opportunities and discriminatory practice in relation to homelessness represent aspects of institutional racism. Women headed households form another group more heavily represented among the new homeless. The changing environment in which homelessness has developed includes a significant shift in policy towards housing. Especially since 1979 there has been an increase in the encouragement of home ownership and a shift of subsidy towards owner occupation. But this shift of subsidy has not directly addressed the affordability problem affecting rates of homelessness. Few of the new initiatives and special schemes to increase levels of home ownership have the capacity to draw in households with significantly lower incomes than first time buyers in general and the most significant measure - the sale of council dwellings - benefits those already well housed and results in a change in patterns of access which will over time reduce access for those who look to the rented sector.

Bed and Breakfast Homelessness

There is another dimension to the new homelessness in Britain. The significant growth of homelessness in recent years has been accompanied by an increasing use of temporary accommodation in bed and breakfast hotels. In 1980/81 there were 32,000 homeless households in temporary accommodation in England and Wales. By 1985/86 this figure had risen to 41,100. In 1985/86 some 17% of homeless households were initially housed in bed and breakfast accommodation and 20% in hostels (compared with 12% and 16% respectively in 1979/80). Although the homeless took up a larger proportion of local authority lettings (Table 1) the use of temporary accommodation also rose. The position was most striking in London (Table 1a, 1c and Table 2).

The experience of the new homeless is less likely to be of rapid permanent rehousing or of a short stay in temporary accommodation than was true in the past. Homelessness acceptances and the use of bed and breakfast accommodation in London is highest in some Inner London boroughs where high prices in the owner occupied and privately rented market pose particularly severe problems for lower income households (see Table 1c). In Brent, for example, there are currently 1,000 households in bed and breakfast accommodation. This compares with less than half that number in 1983 (Hansard, 21..10.1987, Vol 120, No 26: col 831).

Table 2: Homeless Households Placed by London Councils in Bed and Breakfast and Other Types of Temporary Aaccommodation

Year	Numbers in B & B	Numbers in other temporary accommodation
June 1981	890	3,760
June 1982	1,300	3,570
June 1983	1,807	3,280
June 1984	2,357	3,730
June 1985	3,251	4,140
June 1986	5,206	5,522
September 1986	6,142	5,901
September 1987	7,970	7,256

Sources: Shelter Fact Sheet and Surveys, 1986, and Association of London Authorities.

Perhaps the most effective way of illustrating the new position of the homeless is to refer to interview data for households in bed and breakfast accommodation (see Murie, 1987). Interviews completed in London do not present identical histories. There is a variation in the nature of accommodation, in previous experience and in encounters with officialdom. However, the variation is within a low standard sector. For families, cramped space, lack of privacy and absence of playspace is severe. While lack of privacy is most likely to be expressed by adults, children's awareness of their housing situation is evident in expressions about their lack of a home. All of these factors contribute to behavioural and psychological problems and to increasing stress in the family. These problems are made worse the longer the time spent in such accommodation. Moreover, they are complicated by the impact of this form of housing on ability to maintain or obtain work, by the lack of social service, health care and other facilities targeted on a "temporary" population and by the distancing from kinship and community networks.

A wider range of health and safety issues are directly linked with conditions in the hotel. The inadequacy of cooking, toilet facilities, problems of sharing and overuse, and inadequate cleaning are directly linked to bouts of sickness, weight loss and faster development of latent health conditions and are also linked to lack of fresh air and play space and dependence on takeaway food often with low nutritional value. The lack of kitchen, cooking and food storage facilities forces families to rely on what is an expensive as well as unhealthy coping strategy. Pressure on budgets also arises from lack of laundry and especially drying facilities for clothes. The facilities in hotels are not suitable for long stay residents in these and other ways. The status of the homeless has turned full circle - from households with individual and personal problems rather than housing problems, to households where the response to their housing needs generates health, work and other personal problems! Heating, electrical and other safety, the provision of hot water and facilities for visiting or telephoning all leave a lot to be desired. In late 1984 a fire in a hotel in Westminster resulted in the death of an Asian mother and two young children placed in the hotel by the London borough of Camden. Other fires and incidents have not led to any response which has reduced the use of bed and breakfast accommodation.

Even though the costs of hotels are higher than almost any alternative form of provision (Greve et al., 1986; Walker, 1987), the pressure for policy change has had almost no impact. The antagonism of central government to increased spending on municipal housing has not been affected by evidence of wasted expenditure or low standards. The lack of political power of the homeless has been evident from evictions by Tower Hamlets and is apparent in the actual histories of individuals. One explanation for the quality of service being delivered lies in the very powerlessness of the homeless, their lack of economic and political bargaining power and the ease with which the category "homeless" can be manipulated and associated with undeserving and undesirable categories. Hotels are expensive and although the accommodation is totally inadequate there is a confusion over how generous provision is. The families involved are aware that if they were able to use the same level of resources to obtain other accommodation they could establish more satisfactory homes for their families. They could also begin to increase their independence because it would be easier to find work. The benefit and "credibility" problems associated with working (usually in low paid jobs) while living in a hotel are generally regarded as insurmountable. And, in some cases, becoming homeless had led to loss of employment.

The response to this situation adds to depression and frustration. Some families retain a belief that they should wait patiently for rehousing - others make more vociferous demands. While a feeling of powerlessness pervades this should not be interpreted as resignation or apathy. The families involved develop active coping strategies to help children attend schools and to develop social contacts. Some adults (usually the men) can spend a lot of time away from the hotel and their family. Women and especially those with younger children and those most at risk of harassment are trapped all day long in hotels.

The disruption experienced by the bed and breakfast homeless has various dimensions. The location of hotels is in established hotelling areas - not the areas where families lived. Schooling and friendships have been disrupted and the neighbourhoods are more threatening. Distance from familiar neighbourhoods and communities involves a break in caring and friendship networks and less familiarity with available services and resources. General problems of poverty and low income are exacerbated by loss of possessions and loss of community support. The very fact of moving requires renegotiation with health and income maintenance services and "temporary" status means that this negotiation is often difficult. The experience of homeless families (which have moved house regularly) in these negotiations is more difficult than that of poor families in general although some have found real support from health visitors, social workers or voluntary organizations. The most directly involved local authority department - the housing department - often maintains sporadic contact and homeless families have no real appreciation of how long they will be in hotels or of how best they can negotiate permanent housing. Some of this reflects the general pressures placed on local authority housing but there is variation in response which reflects policy. The number and reasonableness of offers varies and in one case (Tower Hamlets) large numbers of homeless families have been evicted.

Many of these problems are equally experienced by homeless single people although issues of crowding and privacy are less apparent. Among both families and single homeless people issues of racism and racial harassment are important, given the disproportionate number of families from ethnic minority groups among the homeless. The households involved have a variety of employment and housing histories - including former owner occupiers. However, the largest group have worked in low skill service sector jobs which are essential to London but which are insecure and low paid. In the London housing market such essential workers are not in a strong position to obtain housing. They are generally dependent on the private rented sector and early housing histories are of moves as single people in bed and breakfast and insecure private rented homes. Marriage, family growth and the coming together of families previously living apart changes housing needs but does not change ability to obtain housing. It means eligibility to apply for and wait for the only low price adequate housing (which is in the social rented sector). Waiting involves moving between hotels and between rooms in hotels.

Other Dimensions

Most of this paper has referred to official homelessness and it has been argued that there are new elements in relation to this group. It is important to acknowledge (briefly) that these same new elements also affect other homeless households. The preceding discussion has referred to families in priority need and the groups of "vulnerable" persons accepted in official policies. Clearly these do not represent the full extent of homelessness. Representing the full extent raises questions of definition which have been widely discussed elsewhere. Watson (1986: 6) argues that it is useful to consider this question in terms of a continuum with sleeping rough at one end and absolute security of tenure at the other. She states:

> "There would be little disagreement with the notion of the former state as literally homeless and the latter as not. In between, however, lies an extensive grey area, ranging across hostels, hotels, temporary accommodation, sleeping on friends' floors, licenses, to insecure private rented accommodation, mortgaged accommodation and so on".

It is not intended to pursue this discussion here, but it is important to acknowledge that while in London in 1984/85 some 42,000 homeless households were placed in temporary accommodation and some 75,000 were accepted in official priority need homeless categories there were some 150,000 to 200,000 sharers, 80% of whom would prefer to live separately. On another estimate there were some 300,000 potential households, many of which could be regarded as potentially homeless, given their modest incomes and savings and poor prospects of rehousing in the rented sector. Moreover, it is also important to distinguish between the flow of new homeless households and the number in homeless categories at any time. All of these issues are concerned both with numbers and with the characteristics of the homeless - for example moving away from official definitions increases the importance of the single homeless.

Discussion

Legislative and public acknowledgment of homelessness as the extreme form of housing stress experienced by ordinary decent people has resulted in substantial rehousing of homeless people. In comparison with some countries and with the past this may imply increasing the bargaining power and access of the homeless. However, the change is not as dramatic as might be assumed. Flaws in the legislation, lack of resources to mobilize on behalf of the homeless and a changing economic housing and political environment have been reflected both in the nature and scale of homelessness and in responses to it. The homeless have in important ways been absorbed into housing allocation and management becoming a convenient category which has low esteem and low priority. In this sense official recognition does not alter the reality of being regarded as undeserving or less desirable. The realities of this process have been described in a variety of studies of housing allocations (e.g., Henderson and Karn, 1987; Phillips, 1986).

One important perspective on how this has arisen relates to ideas of bargaining power and to labor market position. The idea of bargaining power has been widely mobilized to explain differential outcomes from housing allocation processes in Britain. It is argued that those households in the most desperate housing circumstances and least able to wait for a better offer will accept the least desirable properties on offer. Those who obtain better quality rehousing are those with more bargaining power. This feature and the allocation practices which enable it to operate provide part of the explanation for the position of homeless households. However, as we outlined at the beginning of this chapter, there is a wider perspective on bargaining power which relates to economic and political marginalization and not solely to the housing process. The new homeless in the 1980s are not just those at the extreme of housing need. They are also those in the most marginalized sections of the labor market and with least political power. It may be argued that the form of service provided is both a demonstration of this and in turn exacerbates it. The most obvious conclusion from this discussion is that the experience of homelessness is critically affected by the economic and political position of the homeless and by the changing economic and housing environment in which homelessness emerges as well as - and to a greater extent than - by the development of formal policies.

References

Brown, C., 1984: *Black and White Britain: The Third PSI Survey.* London: Gower.

Burke, G., 1981: *Housing and Social Justice.* London: Longman.

Dahrendorf, R., 1987: The Erosion of Citizenship and its Consequences for us all. *New Statesman,* June 12, 1987.

Ferge, Z. and Miller, S.M., 1987: *The Dynamics of Deprivation: A Cross-National Study.* London: Gower.

Forrest, R. and Murie, A., 1983: Residualization and Council Housing: Aspects of the Changing Social Relations of Housing Tenure. *Journal of Social Policy* 12, 453-68.

----, 1986: Marginalization and Subsidized Individualism: the Sale of Council Houses in the Restructuring of the British Welfare State. *International Journal of Urban and Regional Research* 10, 46-65.

Gamble, A., 1987: The Great Divide. *Marxism Today*, March, 12-17.

Glastonberry, B., 1971: *Homeless Near a Thousand Homes.* London: Allen and Unwin.

Greve, J., 1964: *London's Homeless*. London: Bell and Sons.

---- **et al.**, 1971: *Homelessness in London.* Glasgow: Scottish Academic Press.

-----, 1976: *Homelessness in London.* Bristol: University of Bristol, School for Advanced Urban Studies.

Halsey, A.H., 1987: Social Trends Since World War Two. *Social Trends,* No. 17, 11-19.

Henderson, J. and Karn, V., 1987: *Race, Class and State Housing.* London: Gower.

Murie, A. (ed.), 1987: *Living in Bed and Breakfast: The Experience of Homelessness in London.* Bristol: University of Bristol, School for Advanced Urban Studies.

Pahl, R., 1986: *Social Polarization and the Economic Crisis*. Paper presented to Seminar organized by the Hungarian Academy of Sciences. Budapest (Mimeo).

Phillips, D., 1986: *What Price Equality*. London: GLC.

Richards, J., 1981: *The Making of the Housing (Homeless Persons) Act 1977*. Bristol: University of Bristol, School for Advanced Urban Studies.

Townsend, *P*., 1987: *Combatting Poverty*. Paper presented to the 35th Annual Summer School Conference, 1-6 August, Inchigeela, Co. Cork (Mimeo).

Walker, B., 1987: Public Sector Costs of Board and Lodging Accommodation for Homeless Households in London. *Housing Studies* 2, No. 4.

Watson, S., (with Austerberry, H.), 1986: *Housing and Homelessness*. London: Routledge and Kegan Paul.

HOMELESS IN FRANCE: PUBLIC AND PRIVATE POLICIES

Dan Ferrand-Bechmann

Poverty and Homeless: An Increasing Problem in a Rich Society

It is a strange paradox to write about poverty and homeless in France 1987, since there is a social policy. Yet, the problem exists. The reason is, like in many capitalist countries, that housing is more for profit than for social purposes. One of the symptoms of poverty, to be homeless, is visible and is taken in account by the media. Each of us can see these bag people or imply a caravan still occupied after the period of holidays. These facts that were formerly marginal or seldom are now occuring more frequently. It provokes each of us in our deepest phantasms and imagination and remains quite scandalous in our comfortable society.

If many authors admit there is a problem of poverty, they insist that people can answer of their primary needs (Milano, 1983). Few begin to claim that to be a dramatic new problem and the collectivity wakes up. But new solutions are created to maintain people in social lodging and to help them to pay for electricity, heating and gas, but fewer solutions are offered to help those without lodging. In fact, our social policy is quite sufficient to cover the needs of handicapped people, elderly, recently jobless and families with dependent children. But there are groups not having the qualifications to apply to special locations and thus remain in a deep misery. The media inform more about the public policy than about those who cannot apply especially because they cannot give an address. If they can obtain food they still remain homeless or do not have their own lodging being in collective institutions, such as welfare hotels, in emergency shelters or in the streets under the bridge or in the underground. All these homeless people are first poor and isolated and then homeless.

A recent statuary report indicates that the number of people homeless or in emergency lodging would be 200,000 or 400,000 (Wresinski, 1986). Among them are about 10,000 errants. The places offered in emergency shelters would be officially of 30,000 and 8,000 in hotels, providing a total of 500,000 nights. Statistics indicate officially in the census of 1982: 20,620 emergency dwellings and 120,700 people living in lodgings.

It is difficult to obtain the exact number of homeless, because our statistics are mainly built on the household and also on people that are qualified to ask for a social lodging. They are not done for the people who cannot apply for these lodging because they have not enough revenues, children or because the municipalities have asked that or that criterion to be admitted on a list. But by the admissions to emergency shelters and some

Affordable Housing and the Homeless

census made in the street, relatively precise data can be provided. Same remarks have been made by Marcuse (1987), but in the U.S. there are probably more people sleeping on the street (see, the article by Huttman in this book). There are also less statistics made in social centers and welfare hotels.

Local inquiries are better to know the real situation: among 323 persons asking for social housing, one third were really without lodging. They were with families or friends, in caravans or cars, or squattered. Among the same number of people asking to be admitted in an emergency shelter a quarter were living with families or friends, a quarter should be evicted, others were really homeless (sleeping in huts, cars or cellars or on streets), others were in prisons, hospitals.

Emergency shelters are more numerous because there are more applicants. The vagrants in Paris or elsewhere go to these centersto sleep when the winter is deep cold or are sent into them by the police. The freedom to sleep in the fresh air does not exist really and every citizen is guilty not to have a shelter or a home. Consequently, the local authorities have to provide a bed to anyone that needs one. In fact the possibilities are not every time sufficient and the conditions of living in these shelters quite unbearable for new poor. The famous Maison de Nanterre is not really very comfortable and new shelters built recently in Paris with four storied beds were not a perfect solution.

The municipality could have said in the media, there ere enough beds and despite it, many people were still on the streets. Did they really choose to be out in that cold January or did they could not accept to be lodged in inadequate conditions? Apart from this problem of cold, there is also violence and robbery; if these people could find a proper shelter they would accept it. Why were people to whom I talked, for instance, women begging in the stations, saying there are no more beds in Paris? It is sure that these persons were homeless and that beds in shelters were vacant.

Normally, all our legislations offers various forms of affordable housing, however, not for families with small revenues (Petrequin, 1986). Probably two million households with 75% of the minimum revenu exist in France and have urgent problems to pay their rents and housing expenses. Many efforts are made to resolve the problems of such persons before they could be evicted. Special collective social funds have been set up. Charitable efforts have been made to help people to pay their rents and housing expenses. Public legislations have been voted by the congress to give more rights to people as tenants during the socialist government, since then some of the laws have been abolished. Among the 20% poorest, a third have no comfort at all in their lodging. Private owners wishing to evict their tenants and sell their lands for profit, were able in Paris that winter to let fire empty their property quite easely and rapidly. Even with a strong legislation, informal procedures and pressures are such that the situation of families could be to sleep on the streets the next morning after a fire. Similar is the situation of those without revenues, that can give no guarantee to private owners or public institutions providing social housing. These people even with children are evicted and become homeless.

Lodging is a dominant problem for poor people. Many of the clients of social workers come to the services to ask for a help concerning lodging. The poverty programme's first goals appeared to be lodging.

What are the solutions? Emergency shelters, collective institutions with the aim of social reintegration, families and friends, welfare and normal cheap hotels, cars, caravans, bridges, huts, cellars, old buildings, undergrounds, prisons, hospitals and streets.

Who are the Homeless People?

Part of them are the tramps that tourists have seen and that could be one of the exotic charms of France. Some of them could have really choosen that situation and that freedom (Declerck, 1983). Part of them (10%?) sleep in the underground stations, others find spaces under the bridges and in old houses. It appears they are younger and younger and more and more numerous. Violence becomes more severe, and alcoholism still a huge problem. There is a real society of tramps with norms, solidarity, friendship, sex, violence, crimes and day to day life and pleasure. The police knows them because they are sent to the Maison of Nanterre or go there by themselves when it is too cold or too dangerous.

There are also young mothers with children around 27 years old, and hobos, male or female vagrants. People with drug problems or not, some mentally ill, others not. Probably less than 10% of women and 20% of foreign-born; a study in the north of France indicated that they are more often men. Women have their children and are given social housing or beds in special homes because of their children. Training and qualifications are low.

In many cases they wander from emergency shelters or collectives homes to another in a vagrant system. Those who were living with parents or friends are numerous, indicating the importance of this solidarity. Despite our welfare state, the role of the nuclear and extensive family and of the networks of friends still remains important. 16% of the jobless with no more allocations are living in other's flats or houses. More people are poor, even more ask for help from these networks and give it, as enquiries of A.T.D., a voluntary organization with its own social survey center, have shown. More and more families are obliged to lodge their children still living with a friend or a husband or wife. Surveys show that among homeless people 50% have no revenues at all. The others have a special allocation for single-parents with dependent children, or allocations for handicapped people. Few have jobs. More and more young people come to be homeless. On the contrary, elderly benefit of a good public policy and have no big problem but loneliness.

These people are without money, without job and homeless. They are not in that situation due to mentally illness, but due to the economic crisis and because of the gaps and holes of the public policies. Perhaps the fact that the commissions whose roles are to define who should have a special allocation for handicapped people are less generous. For years these allocations were one solution for people without revenues. They were said not to be able to work and could apply, for this allocation. That generous period is over and there are less and less solutions. Certain categories of people have no minimum revenues and are very poor indeed (Ferrand-Bechmann, 1987).

It appears that the present social programmes are not appropriate to cope with these new situations. The existing structures are neither sufficiently numerous, nor suited to the new jobless situations. The social problems are new in their dimensions and in their caracteristics. The new normal families structure are such that half of the families among poor people are with only one adult. This is one of the reasons, why the government was obliged to set up a new poverty programme in 1985.

The Poverty Programme

To cope with this emergency problem, French social institutions have established a special programme against poverty, of which mainly non-profit organizations are in charge. It runs during the winter, one of its aims is to alleviaftae the needs of the homeless. The organizations that running the programme are:

- Salvation Army,
- A.T.D. Quart Monde (Fourth World),
- Banques alimentaires (Food Bank),
- Emmaus,
- F.N.A.R.S.,
- Entraide Protestante,
- Federation des Equipes Saint-Vincent,
- Fonds Social Juif Unifie,
- OFIVAL,
- Petits Frères des Pauvres (Brothers of the Poor),
- Secours Catholique (Catholic Help),
- Secours Populaire Francais,
- Red Cross,
- Societe Saint-Vincent de Paul
- Union des Foyers de Jeunes Travailleurs.

They have different actions against poverty and homeless. 43,9% of their actions concern problems of lodging; 7,500 emergency beds have been added. Part of the financial aid assistis given to these organizations, part to the départements (90 in France), but the départments give it to these organizations at the local level, being in a way unable to organize that programme without the help of these private charitable organizations.

Part of these actions is just to assist such persons, part is to give them an emergency lodging with the aim of social reintegration or just for giving a shelter: in a normal lodging, in young workers housing, in a hotel. 500,000 nights have been apparently offered during the winter to 40,000 places, an average of ten nights. Where do the people sleep the others nights? Why the beds are empty some nights?

The organizations themselves give the equivalent of the amount given by the state and the départément, this money comes from the estates, real estates, gifts, works or benefits etc. These lodging are emergency or more permanent ones. Clients can be helped by a social action or social reinsertion or just with a bed and a soup. These shelters are more or less subsidized by the state. Some places offered in these charitable organizations are funded up to $ 100 a day. A quick calculation shows that the total sum given for a month could pay for a decent rent. But in many cases, these people could not pay regulary rents and could not apply for housing. Very few collective action or self-help groups have been organized neither by the organisations nor by the people themselves. What are the specific actions of these organizations mainly focussed on homeless? (cf. D.A.S., 1986).

Salvation Army

Different types of action are provided by the Salvation Army such as: lodging in hostels and emergency shelters, but also special funds to pay for the rents. This organization pays for more than 2,000 nights in hotels, 58,000 nights in shelters, 361 months of rents. The people who came to ask for help are normally without any money or say they are in such a situation, because it is the key of entrance in this organization. Mainly they are bachelors without family even when they had had one: they cannot support it anymore. Paris is the most important place for these homeless people and would be where the Salvation Army has the largest center. The hotels are the only solutions for families without lodging. Especially in Paris or in the big cities where there is no emergency other solutions for these people. This traditional organization has a very strong programme toward homeless since years but also because of the actual crisis and shortage of other possibilities for those homeless. The Salvation Army has an evangelical organization but welcomes everyone without money and if left without help forced to sleep on the pavement.

A.T.D. Quart Monde

This organization is one of the most radical one in France. It does not run any shelter but helps people to pay their rents and covers their housing expenses. More than half of its budget is devoted to it. It gives a guarantee to the owners even collectives ones or public ones, it has special collective funds managed with others institutions and struggles in the day to day life to help the people not to become homeless despite their lack of money. It has a community action and a political activity. On a larger scale, it gives a minimum revenue to very poor people and works with some local community. It acts with the people and not for them, living with people in need in their poor neighborhood.

Emmaus

This organization is very well known in France because of its famous leader l'Abbé Pierre. This extraordinary charismatic man had been a member of parliament after 1945 and began an anti-poverty campaign, and struggled with a dramatic faith to destroy the slums and to help the homeless families. He was able to collect sufficieent money to have his own social housing and to offer a home to vagrants and homeless people. But he claimed for the right to work and develop an industry of recycling. Many French give to that famous organization old furniture, electric equipment or clothes. The key to join these communities is to accept to work and to contribute to the expenses through work's products. The homeless people ecoming members of Emmaus communities repair and sell these objects, using all the rubbish of our consumption society. They live on the money provided by that industry of recuperation and recycling. With their benefits and the public help, but also the gifts and real estates they run emergency shelters and soup kitchens. The poor help the poorest!

They have two kinds of action toward homelessness, one is emergency shelters, especially in winter, in where homeless people can have a warm night and a soup, the other is the system of community. There are permanent communities, all around France, where people work and live for one or more years. Some are totally isolated from their families and friends and are unable to find a new autonomy, the Emmaus communities are their new families and communities. Facing dangerous situations in underground, vagrants and tramps prefer more and more to exchange their freedom for a home even with a compulsory work. Some have been isolated by illness, by war, by crime or delinquency or just after a family break or the lost of a job.

The Emmaus communities are all around France and well known, they are a safety belt. The poverty programme has helped them to settle more place in their emergency shelters. They also help families to pay for their housing expenses, rents and debts. In some cases they pay for hotels when families with children have no more solutions.

Fédération Nationale des Associations d'Accueil et de Réadaptation Sociale (FNARS)

This is a federation: a network of organizations whose main task is lodging but also social reintegration. By its special poverty programme, the federation has helped to create more than 600 new beds in the organizations, but also has given money to emergency shelters etc.. Part of the voluntary organizations linked to them are subsidized by the state and have a social action goals. The total amount of money they control, directly or indirectly, is quite large, including 150,000 places in permanent centers that are shelters for the homeless, isolated, and jobless, whose situation gives them access to these centers. But the places are fewer than the demand.

Fédération Nationale de l'Entraide Protestante

Their action is mainly toward persons who have just found a job or are in job programme. Like other organizations, they pay for special expenses or hotels or offer shelters. More specific is the way they give money for renewing and repairing collective housing. Their main organizations are near Montpelliers a famous calvinist city in the south of France and in Paris, where the needs are much more acute than in others big cities. It has also tried to organize a meeting place for homeless people in the north of France.

Fonds Social Juif Unifie

This organization does not run special shelters but tries to help financially the people who are homeless. They use more than the third of their funds for that type of problems. Their action is more important in Paris and Marseille where the jewish community is more numerous.

Les Petits Frères des Pauvres

This organization focusses on elderly persons. Though it has special actions to help them to pay for housing expenses and it help others age groups. They run a shelter. The following few statistical data characterize this group: single: 63%, married: 37%; French: 78%. After a period in that home, some obtain a retirement pension, only few a job.

Le Secours Catholique

This powerful organization was also obliged to face the new situation created by the increasing number of homeless people or people that cannot face the expenses of their housing and who would be evicted if they could be helped to pay their debts. It runs a large home near Paris where more than 10,000 nights have been offered to adults and children and also to families. It is a specific situation. But a quarter is women, and three quarter men. Half of the families are single parents families. It gives a good image of the different situations: men ithout families relatively young, women without families more jobless than the men, couples without children very young too, single parents families sometimes recently evicted despite young children. Since there is no other solution, families come to that organization that tries to indicates them social welfare institutions, but it seems that the actual difficult situation for families finds little solutions.

Red Cross

This large traditional organization is also involved in actions to help the homeless especially to run emergency shelters for families and vagrants. It has not more beds in Paris than in others cities.

Société Saint-Vincent de Paul

Like many others, this organization spends a large sum for shelters. It tries to welcome the people during a longer period to help them to find a solution and social help.

Union des Foyers de Jeunes Travailleurs

This organization generally has one aim: to give lodging to young workers. But in fact, because of the economic crisis, it is more and more obliged to have also a social programme and eventually to welcome young people that cannot pay their rents. They run about 500 centers, however, this association has had an important action in the poverty programme and could have welcome more people or give them a better help. Because the beneficiaries are young and mainly jobless, the action was not only toward a shelter but also a training.

Conclusion

The question of poverty and homeless are partly resolved by public policies, partly by private ones through a new collaboration between the voluntary associations organizing flexible actions and programmes, and the state on the national and the local level, providing supplementary additional money through the poverty programme. The state provides social affordable housing and homes for handicapped and elderly people, the voluntary organizations are concerned with the more urgent problems and provide especially emergency shelters during winter and after. The role of families and friends is still crucial and appears to be the one best or the last solution for many people when they are not isolated and could still benefit from this mutual help. The urban question has to include homeless question. Selection made for affordable housing applicants is probably too limited. People remain without qualification to apply and even to be counted by official statistics as people in need for housing. Homeless is no more the question of tramps or new immigrants, it becomes a social question that has to be studied by urban sociologists, political scientists and economists.

References

A.T.D., 1986: *Enquete sur Caen en 1986*. Caen: Ave. du Gal. Leclerc Pierreelaye 78. Coordination des associations du logement, 1985: Etude sur 79 familles en situation d'éxpulsion. Toulouse: 274 rte Seysses 31100.

C.R.E.D.O.C., 1986: *Pauvreté, Precarité, Tentatives de Mésure*. Paris: 142 rue du Chevaleret.

D.A.S., 1986: *Bilan du programme d'action contre la pauvréte et la precarité. July 1986*. Amiens: 123, rue Sadi Carnot Vanves 92.

Declerck, P., 1983: *Ethnographie des marginaux vivant dans le metro Parisien*. Paris: E.H.E.S.S.

Ferrand-Bechmann, D., 1987: Pauvres et tres Pauvres. *Revue Solidarité-Santé,* April (Paris: Edition Masson).

Lae, J.F. and Murard, N., 1986: *L'argent des Pauvres*. Editions Sociales.

Marcuse, P., 1987: *Isolating the Homeless*. New York. Columbia University

Milano, S., 1983: *La Pauvreté en France*. Paris: Syros.

Observatoire Regional de la Sante de Picardie, 1985: D.A.S *L'hébergement social des adultes en Picardie octobre 1985*. Amiens.

Wresinski, J., 1987: Grande Pauvrete et Precarite Economique et Sociale. *Journal Officiel* February 11-12, 1987. Paris: 26, rue Desaix.

HOMELESSNESS AS A HOUSING PROBLEM IN AN INNER CITY IN THE U.S.

Elizabeth Huttman

Homelessness is essentially a problem of lack of one's own permanent shelter, forcing one instead to resort to such temporary solutions as emergency shelters, use of one's car, tent or such, or sleeping in public places, or doubling up with relatives or friends. Homelessness is due to inability to find a private or public accommodation, usually because of inability to pay for such, but in some cases because of social problem characteristics such as substance abuse or mental illness that make landlords reluctant to rent to the person in a housing scarcity situation.

Focus of this Paper

Much of the literature on the homeless has focused on their characteristics including social problems, rather than the essential shelter problem stemming above all from lack of affordable housing (Baxter and Hopper, 1984; Campbell, 1987; Hensell, 1986; Wright et al., 1987). This paper concentrates on the latter. It gives evidence of the decreasing availability of affordable housing in one major American city, San Francisco, due to loss of stock, vacancy rate, rent level, and housing start situation, as well as availability of subsidized housing. It also mentions effect of rent control on decrease in the rental stock. The paper then discusses demand for low rent housing, and then homelessness and demand, and finally type of homeless and type of demand. It especially covers demand of the "new homeless" such as families, women with children, and singles, including aged without substance abuse problems.

This focus on the underlying housing cause of the homeless situation is partly stressed to point out that long-term permanent shelter accommodations are the end solution to the problem, rather than the present solution of short term emergency accommodations. (As Marcuse [1987] does.) As a San Francisco official has said, today we are using short-term solutions to a long-term problem. In San Francisco where it is estimated there are eight to ten thousand homeless (National Coalition for the Homeless Survey, 1986), over $9.8 million was spent in 1986 by the city for housing the homeless, with half going for use of 32 hotels for 2500, the rest to help the non-profit agency shelters that house another large group. A complaint about this short-term shelter approach has also been made by the New York Times editorial (June 2, 1987), criticizing the lack of focus on preventiveness

Affordable Housing and the Homeless

measures when the city, state, and federal agencies spend $125 million to house 4,800 New York homeless. Experts are saying, that with shelters across the country housing more than 111,000 (1985) each night (Hoch and Huth, forthcoming), there is a need for a more permanent housing solution. San Francisco community shelter workers (Goode, 1986) demanded, there is "a need to get the poorest of the poor off the low rent merry-go-round that keeps them moving from the streets to the dormitory-like shelters operated by non-profit foundations (for limited short stays), to the hotels and then back again." As Hoch and Huth emphasize, a variety of long-term types of housing for this diverse homeless population are needed, for the problem refused to go away. As a San Francisco city leader in 1986 said: we didn't realize in 1983 that the homeless were going to stay around" (Goode, 1986). But they have, partly due to the increased scarcity of affordable housing, as the below shows for San Francisco.

Loss of SROs and Apartments

Homelessness is due to inability to find shelter, whether an apartment, house or room. This is most likely to occur when one moves to a new area; returns from an institutional setting such as hospital; mental health facility; prison; moves out of a relative's home whether parents, spouse, or such; is displaced from the present unit due to property sale or conversion or demolition; or eviction from one's present unit. The hunt for alternative housing is not successful in the case of the homeless.

Lack of affordable apartments can be shown for San Francisco in terms of loss of cheap housing units in the city, especially single resident occupancy (SRO) hotels, number and proportion of units at cheap rents, vacancy rates, and lack of units qualifying as fair market rent units under Section 8, the American housing allowance program.

San Francisco traditionally has had a large stock of SRO units (Koch, 1987). But in the 1970s these were taken out of the stock in large numbers for use as tourist hotels or conversion to quality apartments. For example Hartman, Keating, and LeGates (1982) point out that between 1975 and 1979, 17% (5723 units) were lost of the 32,214 SRO units. Ovrebo et al. (1984) reported that around 1200 SRO units were lost on average each year between 1975 and 1984. The city, due to major protests and demonstrations on loss of these SROs, such as the International Hotel, had a moratorium on conversion from November 1979 to December 1980, but due to loopholes it is reported 2374 more units were lost and even after the city's permanent restrictions on conversion more were lost (Hartman, Keating and LeGates, 1982). Examples were conversion of ten Tenderloin SROs (1,192 units) to tourist hotels; and conversion of others to Section 8 rehabilitated units (Lincoln, 1980; Kasinitz, 1984). In New York City a similar large drop in SRO units occurred, from 50,454 in 1975 to 18,853 in 1981; here the city gave tax abatement incentives to upgrade SROs and this, Kasinitz (1984) reports, caused units to be removed from the cheap rental pool. Ironically, this government action, as with the San Francisco

Section 8 conversion, increased homelessness. And in addition the city of San Francisco program of using SROs (32 hotels housing 2500) for housing the homeless decreased the units available and in addition upped the rental price of the remaining SROs. The city in 1986 paid $7.50 to $14 a night for these contracted SRO units. (Goode, 1986; Weeden and Linehan, 1987).

This loss of SROs is a serious cause of homelessness since SROs are the most likely accommodation for those homeless or at risk of displacement; of Weeden and Linehan's San Francisco sample of those 60 and over, 42% in temporary shelters (or board and care or transitional mental health housing) had formerly been housed in SROs; a third of their "at risk of displacement" from housing (selected from social service agency information) were in SROs. In addition to the loss of SROs the decrease in board and care facilities in San Francisco also caused homelessness; in 1980 there were about 1100 such beds and by 1983 only 800 (Goode and Hsu, 1986). As did the earlier closing of mental hospitals in California.

Loss of Low Rent Housing in General

There are debates on how serious displacement is in U.S. cities (Palen, forthcoming) but in general the Annual Housing Survey (1981) shows 1.7 to 2.4 million persons displaced annually. Studies show this more serious in San Francisco than many other cities (Grier, 1980; U.S. HUD, 1981). The HUD (1981) study found, particularly for San Francisco of the six cities studied, those most affected in displacement were renters, short term residents (three years or less), those working part-time, poorer families, minorities - though not the elderly.

Condominium conversion is another reason for loss of units and this is major in San Francisco. While, as Kain (1983) argues, many such units are sold to the former renter, or returned to the rental market, and are mainly units occupied by the higher income person, some are low rent units. In many cities in the 1970's more than 5% of the rental stock was converted to condomiums (O'Connell, forthcoming); San Francisco was among the leaders. The pace however has now slowed, with less interest in condominium purchase. The HUD 1980 study of conversions show while more than half of the former residents were angry over the situation, the majority (90%) were satisfied with their new housing; yet among those who rented elsewhere (23% turned to ownership), 28% had to pay at least 25% more rent than they did in the pre-conversion building. O'Connell warns this HUD sample did not include what he calls the "invisible evictions" (also see Hartman, 1979) from threats, arson and other forms of harassment. He adds, "but the increasing numbers of homeless must make us look at the 'invisible evictions' that result in the turmoil that often precedes formal conversion".

Loss of rental units can also be attributed to the existence of strict rent control laws. The HUD 1980 condominium conversion study found rental control was not a major reason for conversions. However, Downs (1983) and others see the existence of rent control causing a disincentive for investors to be in the rental business. Certainly a number of apartment house owners moved out of the business in San Francisco, yet for others they benefited by the law that allowed 7% yearly rent increases that they had not before tried to obtain from ongoing good tenants. Second, the law allowed greater increases after remodeling. The rent control law actually hurt the mobile population and new renters, while for long-time renters keeping the rent increases within limits. These new renters of low income, often at risk for homelessness, were faced with any increase the landlord could make when a unit vacated. In San Francisco, in addition, new renters were faced with an increasingly high initial outlay as more and more landlords demanded first and last month rent and a large security deposit, often totalling $2,000-2,800 (see, Baar and Keating, forthcoming, for general discussion of rent control; also Huttman and Huttman, 1986).

An early source of overall loss of units in San Francisco, including SROs, should also be mentioned. In the 1960s San Francisco led the country in urban renewal and some of this was in areas of low cost housing such as Western Addition, the black ghetto area. In the U.S., as the Fainsteins point out, this federal spending peaked in 1969 and then decreased. In San Francisco as elsewhere, due to neighborhood protests and shift in governments in Washington, rehabilitation/conservation of neighborhoods became more popular. This rehabilitation again caused the loss of low rent units, as has the considerable private gentrification in many San Francisco neighborhoods, including in the gay community in the Castro area and Duboce Park area. Victorian houses have been rescued from their run-down apartment and boarding house condition in these areas, Cow Hollow, Russian Hill area and other city neighborhoods. A recent last cause of loss of low rent units is the converison of such to office buildings, especially in the Chinatown and North Beach areas bordering on the financial district, where new buildings have very high square foot costs.

Vacancy Rate

These rates are usually used as an indicator of the supply of housing; however, they may be misleading as they do not distinguish between high rent units and low rent ones. It also can be misleading as a number of vacant units are not available for general rental. For example, in the Bureau of Census data on vacant housing units, it includes those held off the housing market (3.6 million of the 10.3 million vacant units, 1986) and even those "in the housing market" include those for sale (1.0) million): "rented or sold, not yet occupied" (0.6 milliion), as well as the 2.7 million "for rent". The Federal Home Loan Bank Housing Vacancy Survey includes *all* vacant units, as identified by postal workers.

According to the latter source, San Francisco multi-family vacancy rate doubled in the 1985 period, from 0.8% September 1985 to a tight 1.5% in September 1986. In adjacent counties it was somewhat higher, but actually declining: San Mateo county declined from 2.4% to 2.2% and 2.5% to 2.3% in Marin county (Bay Area Housing Briefs, 1987f). This is much worse than the national picture where rental vacancy rates have actually risen in 1986 (7.7% in April, 1987) and were very high in the South (10.3%); however, with a slump in apartment house building from late 1986 onward these are likely to go down (Business Week, May 4, 1987).

Starts

In San Francisco the multi-family housing starts went up in 1986, from 1217 in 1985 to 1898 in 1986. However this situation is unlikely to last because the changes in the tax laws, especially the change in the depreciation time period, have had a very negative impact on multi-unit builders' future plans, as three fourths of such Business Week surveyed builders said (40% said very negative effect). This is already shown nationally in the drop of starts, averaging only 464,000 annual rate during the first quarter of 1987, compared to a high of 1,100,000 multi-family units in late 1985 (the earlier 1980s had also had some drop in multi-unit construction). Since some experts believe multi-family unit starts should be between one million and one and a half million a year to meet demand this is low. In San Francisco it is estimated 1500 units are needed annually according to the San Francisco Residential Housing Element (1984) but in 1980-82 less than a 1000 units were started [Weeden and Linehan, 1987].

Even with somewhat higher vacancy rates in San Francisco (though still very low at 1.5%) and multi-unit starts somewhat higher, this does not effect the low rent market. As Cook in the Bay Area Housing Briefs (1987f) reports, "while the rental construction boom has increased vacancy rates (in the Bay Area) and resulted in stable advertised rents, much of the new rental housing coming on the market is unaffordable to most rental households". In other words, this building distorts the vacancy rate statistics as these new units remain empty while there is a scarcity of cheap units; the more construction, the possibility of more distortion if the new additions are not subsidized units. Cook, to back this up, states that "the Consumer Price Index surveys reveal that high levels of production may not have had much effect upon improving the affordability picture for renters in older, less expensive units. Rent levels measured across a wider spectrum of rental units show a continued, though lessened, rate of increase during the past two years. The demand for low-priced units remains undersupplied despite increased levels of rental housing" (Bay Area Housing Briefs, 1987d). (See Figure 1.)

This statement indicates the lack of "trickle down" or "filtering" process at work. While San Francisco rents have not increased in the last year, and for medium to high rent units there has been some decrease (limited by landlords' worry over inability to pull the rent back up under rent control), this has not effected the low rent market. Because rent unit operating costs have risen at a fast rate (50% faster than renter incomes in the

1976-83 period) and construction costs also risen faster (Downs, 1983) apartment house owners have been limited on how much they can reduce rents. They abandon the units first--not a common occurrence in San Francisco but certainly in Detroit, New York and elsewhere (see, Lawson, 1984).

Figure 1: Bay Area Median Rent* for Two-Bedroom Apartments

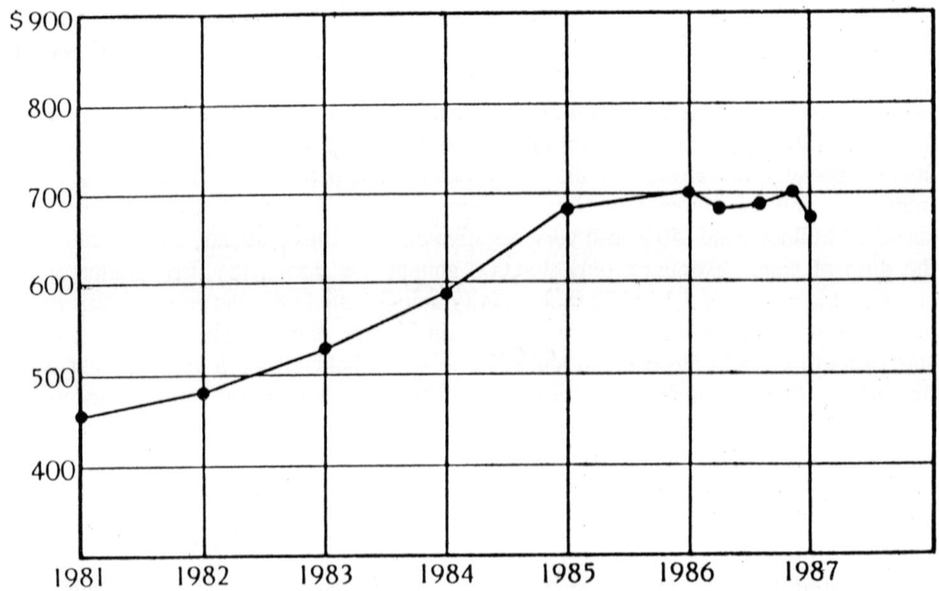

* Annual Figures are for January of each year. Sample size averaged 309 for 1981 through October 1986. 449 in January 1987. Based on sampling of rents advertised for two-bedroom unfurnished apartments in the Saturday and/or Sunday classified sections of six Bay Area newspapers: San Francisco Chronicle and Examiner, San Jose Mercury News, The Tribune, Marin Independent Journal, Contra Costa Times, and Peninsula Times-Tribune. Rents reflect the cost of renting an available apartment--not what all current renters of two-bedroom apartments are paying.

Rents and Affordability

The high cost of the new units is shown by the Bureau of Census (1984) statistic that median gross rent of units added to the stock between 1970 and 1983 was 20% higher than overall median rents, and the median income of those who occupied these units was about 25% higher. The median rent for a two bedroom apartment was $850 in San Francisco in January 1987, down from $900 in October 1986. This rent is among the highest outside of New York City. Advertised rents in the Bay Area increased 75% from 1980 to 1986 (while household incomes only increased 40%). In 1984, Bay Area rents skyrocketed 16.8%. The Census shows 41% of Bay Area renters pay over 30% of income for rent; in San Francisco it is worst. In San Francisco, the typical renter household with a 1986 median household income of $17,948 would need to pay 60% of its income to rent the median rent apartment. For Oakland/South Alameda County it was 44% and for central San Mateo County, 39% (Bay Area Housing Briefs, 1986, using U. S. Census and Urban Decision Systems data; see Table 1).

Table 1: 1986 Bay Area Rental Housing Affordability

Sub-Region	Median Household Income ($)* All HHs	Renter HHs	Percent of Income Needed for Rent (Renter HH)
San Francisco	22,435	17,948	60
Oakland/So. Alameda Co.	26,002	16,901	44
Central San Mateo Co.	32,483	23,063	39
Central Contra Costa Co.	32,322	19,176	39
Palo Alto Area	33,206	22,192	38
Marin County	36,182	24,242	37
Santa Rosa Area	25,034	17,274	36
San Jose Area	33,206	22,912	34
Regional Average	*28,810*	*19,303*	*44*

* Median renter household income is based on percent of total household income as estimated by 1980 U.,S. Census, applied to county estimates of 1986 median househoild income.

Sources: Urban Decision Systems; U.S. Census; Bay Area Council.

Nationally rent burden was high for those with low family incomes (0-50% of gross annual median family income). According to a GAO study (1985), of this poverty group only 22% paid 30% or less of their income for rent, while 49% (almost six million households) paid over half their income for rent. In fact, almost a third of this poor population (0-50% of median family income) paid over 70% of their income for rent (3.7 million households). (See Table 2.)

Nation-wide, Zigas, of the National Low Income Housing Coalition, has stated that "there is absolutely less housing renting at prices affordable for low income households than there was five years ago; about half of the 8.1 million renter households that earned less than $7,300 in 1985 paid more than 30% of their income in rent" (San Francisco Examiner, April 19, 1987). The number of units renting for less than $250 per month in 1983 nationally fell to 8.8 million from 10.8 million in 1974, while the number of households with income below $10,000 (in 1983 dollars) increased from 8.9 million in 1974 to 11.9 million in 1983 (Carliner, 1987).

Table 2: Rent Burden of Households With Incomes 0-50 Percent of Area Median Family Income

	1975		1983	
Rent Burden*	Housing Units (000s)	Percent of Total	Housing Units (000s)	Percent of Total
30% or less	2,777	29	2,695	22
Over 30% to 40%	1,670	18	1,897	15
Over 40%to 50%	1,309	14	1,635	13
Over 50% to 60%	982	10	1,339	11
ver 60% to 70%	589	7	935	8
Over 70%	1,995	21	3,681	30
Total **	*9,321*	*99*	*12,182*	*99*

* Rent burden, or rent-to-income ratio, equals gross annual household rent divided by gross annual household income.

** Figures do not add due to rounding.

Source: U.S. General Accounting Office (1983).

The lack of such cheap units in San Francisco is verified by the situation of Section 8 eligible households. A very large proportion (60%) eligible (in possession of a certificate) have not been able to find housing units at rents (fair market rents) allowed for San Francisco by the federal government for Section 8 housing. (San Francisco Housing Authority, June 29, 1987; cf. McLeod, 1987). Section 8 hunters can only pay $765 (1987) for a two-bedroom by HUD regulations, and cannot find anything available.

Low Income of San Francisco Households

Part of the housing affordability problem as shown above is that incomes have not risen as much as rents, even though the CPI (Consumer Price Index, Bureau of Labor Statistics) shows rents rising at a slower rate than utilities and maintenance costs, and one could add construction and operating costs (Downs, 1983). (Figure 2.) In San Francisco (1985) 21.6% of the population was below the very low poverty level ($11,000 annual income for a family of four).

Figure 2: Homeowners' (a) and Renters' (b) Costs and Incomes, USA, 1973-1980

a)Homeowners

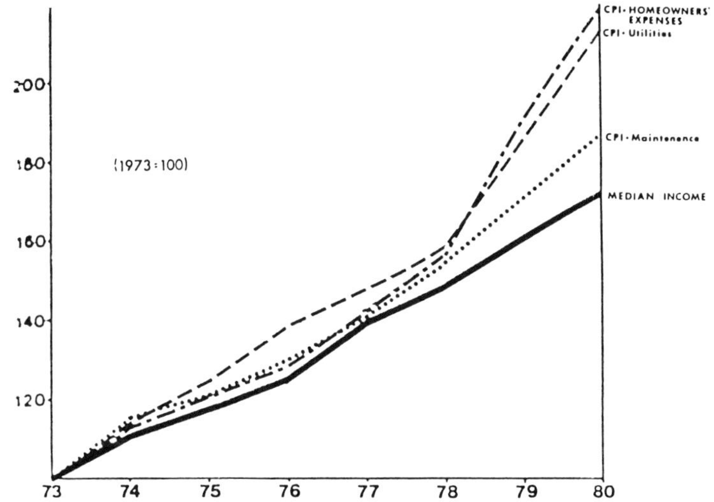

b) Renters

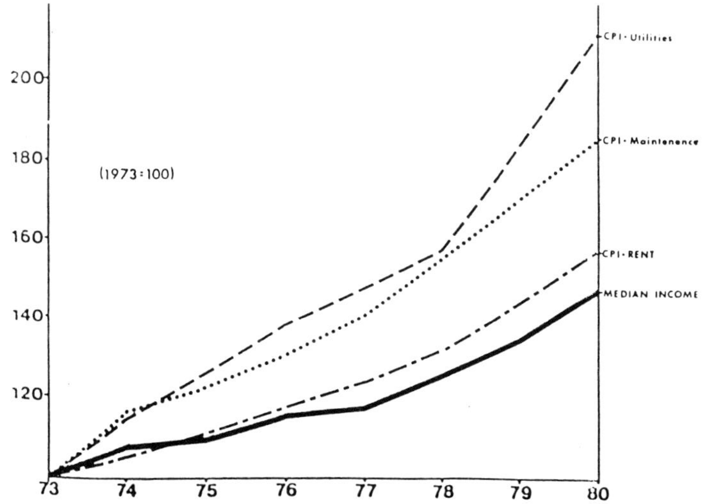

Sources: Bureau of Labor Statistics; CPI Detailed Reports.

In San Francisco, 159,840 (1985) lived below the poverty line; 8-10,000 were homeless; and 41,195 receiving food stamps (San Francisco Chronicle, November 27, 1986). For those elderly homeless or "at risk of displacement" in San Francisco, Weeden and Linehan found incomes low--46 percent on SSI ($533 a month for a single person).

Unemployment was above that of surrounding counties, especially for minorities, and wages were depressed by the influx of immigrants to work in the large service sector. Murtagh of the Ecumenical Association for Housing points out for the Bay Area (1986) a bank clerk's starting salara was only $12,000 and thus he should only pay a maximum rent (30% of income) of $300; a school secretary's was $18,000 and a school teachers $20,000, so they should pay $450 and $500 respectively, and a county sheriff (policeman) a high of $22,800 should pay $570; much more, over $30,000, was needed to afford San Francisco's median rent for a two bedroom (or a working wife was needed, as true for the large majority of home purchases in the Bay Area).

Rental Supply Increased by Home Purchase

This was true to some minor degree in1986 in San Francisco due to heavy home purchase by pent-up buyers who had long waited for interest rates to go down to the below-10 percent level they did in spring and summer 1986. Some of these were first-time buyers, baby boomers now having their own children, but many were previous homeowners upgrading. First-time buyers, with the salaries mentioned above, found it hard to enter the buying market even when the wife's income was included. With an average $166,011 sales price on San Francisco homes, one needed almost $40,000 for a down payment and closing costs, and an income of $58,003. Monthly payments on a 9.5%, 25 year mortgage would then be around $1500 a month, plus $150-200 a month property tax.

This keeps many would-be owners as San Francisco renters and they compete for the available rental units, as they do elsewhere (Harloe, 1985; Huttman, 1985). It thus makes less likely the filtering down process - in fact in San Francisco with these young families unable to buy new housing, we have the filtering-up, that is upgrading of Victorian houses. The rental supply is also not opened up as fast as in the past because the city's considerable elderly population are living longer, thus occupying units longer (Huttman, fothcoming).

Affordable Housing Supply Increased by Subsidized Housing

Low income in San Francisco in the past have benefited from various housing subsidy programs, whether public housing, Sections 236, 221(d)(3), 202, Section 8 new or substantially rehabilitated or tax exempt bond programs. Nationally, 22% of eligible low income are in units under housing subsidy programs (Carliner, 1987); one of the "at risk" groups, female headed households, is even more likely to be in subsidized units (two out of three such households live in such according to Sullivan and Damroch, 1987). A large proportion of elderly are likewise in subsidized housing (Huttman, 1975). In total three million renters were in such, over half (1.8 million) in private rental units (Harloe, forthcoming).

Figure 3: Subsidized Housing Production, USA, 1969-1984

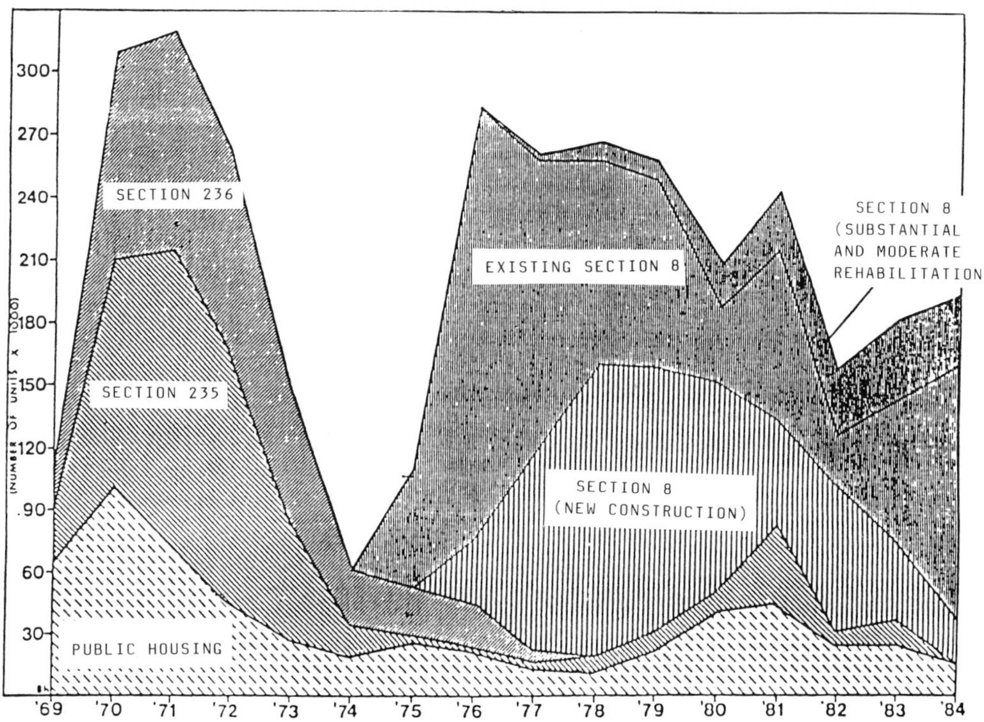

Sources: Pre-1975 data from HUD, 1979 Yearbook; post-1975 data compiled by National Low Income Housing Coalition from HUD sources.

Little new subsidized housing is being built, however, as that Figure 3 shows, from 1980 onward Section 8 new construction dropped way down as did public housing. And in 1987 Congress authorized almost no new public housing at the same time some public housing units were sold. Section 8 new and rehabilitated housing starts have fallen, from about 132,000 annually in 1980 to 15,500 in 1986 (Harloe, forthcoming; Low Income Housing Information Service, 1985). Other programs were also cut back, and the federal new budget authority (1985) a third of that in 1980; and in 1986 far below that for housing (Harloe, forthcoming).

As Pit and Van Vliet (forthcoming) point out, from 1981 on the Reagan Administration determined that housing assistance consumed too much of the federal budget. Of course, as Carliner (1987) states, outside of public housing to a minor degree, and some Section 8, these programs were not aimed at the population, mainly singles and transients, at risk of becoming homeless. In fact only these two programs were aimed at the real low income.

In addition to little new subsidized housing, some of the present units are likely to be pulled out of the market, not only by sale of public housing units, but through arrangements made with investors in the contractual agreements for their investing in and building low rent housing under Section 8 new and rehabilitation programs, Section 236 and Section 221(d)(3). The investors received below market interest rates, with the provision of having the rents of the units at levels affordable to low and moderate income households (usually moderate income) or in Section 8, to 30% of their income. To encourage private sector participation, and to reduce long-term budget expenses, project owners were given the option of ending their participation at a future date, such as prepaying their 40 year mortgage after 20 years, for Sec. 236 and 221 (d)(3). For Section 8 project owners pre-1979 contracts were for five years, and after 1979 for a minimum of 15 to 20 years (Bay Area Housing Briefs, 1987e; Huttman, forthcoming). HUD data shows for San Francisco this means 2950 units can face early prepayment or contract opt-out, many in the next five years.

Another program, the locally-issued mortgage revenue bond housing, a major source of new units in San Francisco for low income, is also being cut back under the federal tax reform law. In 1985, in San Francisco 3789 units were produced under this program and 27 of these units were for low income. Under federal regulations at least 20% must be for low income (Bay Area Housing Briefs, 1987b).

In reality the number of affordable units is not large, as also true under other programs for affordable housing heralded by the City of San Francisco government such as the hotel tax contribution ($2.8 million a year) for low income senior housing or the funds given by developers of high-rise buildings in return for permission to build (Bay Area Housing Briefs, 1987b). A little more significant may be the inclusion of low and moderate income housing (after protests by concerned groups) in several new San Francisco large developments, for example the 300 acre Mission Bay area, with 7,700 housing units, with a goal of 30 percent affordable (now judged at around $650 monthly rent) (Bay Area Housing Briefs, 1987c). It is doubtful that much of this housing will find its way to the low income "at risk of displacement" or presently homeless.

Demand for Affordable Housing in San Francisco

As the above indicates, demand is high as rents go up. San Francisco has had a major upturn in immigration in the 1980s, first from the Vietnamese refugees who made it one of their major relocation destinations, then Central American refugees, and the increasing group of Mexican immigrants; in addition it has had a heavy influx of Filipinos, of Hong Kong residents leaving before Hong Kong's British rule terminates, of Korean and Taiwanese, and earlier, of Iranian refugees. All of this has added to housing demand. The Tenderloin, the traditional location of low income singles, has been inundated by Vietnamese and other Asian families. Chinatown has continued to be very densely populated.

Demand has also come from the many baby boomers forming their own households. Likewise it has come due to the continuing high divorce rate whereby one household turns into two. Until the Aids epidemic, demand came from gays from all over the country who were seeking a more comfortable urban environment. It came from runaways who considered it a haven from their family. Even from battered women demand developed, due to shelter and counseling programs.

This high demand for affordable housing is attested to by the long waiting lists for public housing and other subsidized housing; in San Francisco these waiting lists have run as high as 5000. Another indicator of demand is the degree of doubling up, with experts saying this has greatly increased (New York Times, April 5, 1987).

The Homeless and "At Risk" Group and Housing Demand

The size of the homeless population, and the increasing number of families and non-traditional homeless in this population, indicates that demand for low rent housing can not be met in San Francisco, where it is estimated that 8-10,000 are homeless (San Francisco Mayor's Taskforce on the Homeless Survey, 1986). Most homeless are without shelter because they can not afford the rent for the unit and/or the initial housing outlay, and/or they have been evicted from their housing. In the San Francisco Weeden and Linehan study (1987) they found that of elderly homeless and the "at risk of displacement" group, the main reason for housing need was financial. The 1986 National Coalition of the Homeless in its many city study found the same. In the San Francisco study a number said they ran out of money before the end of the month, with too many bills to pay. For a number their money was decreased by medical expenses as about two-thirds of them were physical disabled (though under MediCaid and MediCare in many cases). Those who ran out of money before the end of the month. A large proportion (46% had only an SSI check of $533 and some had less than that) were likely to spend part of a month in a SRO or apartment and part homeless in shelters, or on the street. (San Francisco shelters often must turn several hundred a night away.)

For those homeless with a job, three out of five still had financial problems that brought them to shelters. This is found for women, especially those with children, and for large families. In San Francisco while those in shelters are likely male (88.8% in Mayor's Survey, 1986) and white (55.1%) and between 20 and 44, an increasing number are families and female headed households. In some areas the latter group make up half the population. Witty (1986), in her study of San Francisco homeless women over 50, found a large number; she found a non-uniform pattern of alcohol consumption with some never drinking. The National Coalition of the Homeless reports that in several states such as Illinois and Massachusetts, homeless families by 1986 made up the majority of the homeless population. They also found in their 21 city survey that the homeless population had jumped 25% from 1985 to 1986.

Homeless women and especially families are often not in the shelter statistics because the shelter does not have facilities for them. McChesney (1986) found that "during 1985 and 1986 Los Angeles County had no county, state or federally funded shelters for homeless families"; five privately funded shelters were used. They were unable to accommodate the number of families seeking shelter, and second, were quickly discharged back on the street. Some shelters did use apartments (McChesney, 1986). Some shelters, of course, are only for battered women. Besides financial reasons, a reason for being homeless is because one has left a home where one is abused, or where divorce is in process; it may even be due to financial abuse as with elderly living with relatives (Weeden and Linehan, 1987).

As mentioned earlier, homelessness may be due to discharge from a mental health facility, board and care, or from a hospital. Weeden and Linehan (1987) found this true for their elderly homeless sample. And in New York City the Project Future survey found 9% of the homeless elders could not find an apartment after hospitalization or institutional discharge, 25% were no longer welcome in shared housing, and 59% were homeless due to eviction. In the San Francisco survey by Weeden and Linehan eviction was again a major reason. At the same time they found 9.3% of their homeless had been in board and care facilities and 6.1% in medical facilities.

While affordability was the main cause of housing need of those evicted, another cause of eviction and inability to relocate in another unit was the fact of high alcohol or drug use or mental illness or other disabilities. In every study this group makes up a large part of the total population. A number of these in the Weeden and Linehan study were no longer acceptable in the family home, where there was a family. In their study 41% were in contact with a mental health provider; 41% had substance use; 35% in shelters were confused; and again over 60% had a physical impairment. This was hardly a group that could even search for its own housing or face applying for subsidized units. But it was also a group that had a 40-50% portion who might not be the type of tenant desired by landlords, thus have a hard time getting in a tight housing market.

Conclusion:. Thus, the solution to the housing of this group can not be just regular subsidized apartments; there is need for renovated SROs; for some type of mental health facility for some; and alcohol abuse programs and special housing settings.

References

Bay Area Housing Data, 1986: Bay Area Housing Data: Rent Levels. *Bay Area Housing Briefs*, December.

----, 1987a: Bay Area Housing Data: Mortgage Revenue Bonds. From Production to Affordability. *Bay Area Housing Briefs*, January.

----, 1987b: Trends and Information. *Bay Area Housing Briefs*, January, pp. 1, 3.

----, 1987c: San Francisco/The Peninsual. (Draft Ordinance on Establishing SRO Standards.) *Bay Area Housing Briefs*. February, p. 3.

----, 1987d: Bay Area Housing Data: Rent Levels. *Bay Area Housing Briefs,* March.

----, 1987e: Special Issue: Potential Loss of Substandardized Housing. *Bay Area Housing Briefs*, April, pp. 1-3.

----, 1987f: Bay Area Housing Data: Building Permits. *Bay Area Housing Briefs*, May.

----, 1987g: Trends and Information. *Bay Area Housing Briefs*, May, p. 1-2.

Baar, K. and Keating, D., forthcoming: Rent Control in the U.S. In: E. Huttman and W. Van Vliet-- (eds.): *Handbook on Housing and the Built Environment.* Westport, CT: Greenwood.

Baxter, E. and Hopper, K., 1984: Troubled on the Streets. In: J. Talbott (ed.): *The Chronic Mental Patient*. New York: Greene and Stratton.

Bingham, R., Green, R.E. and White, S.B. (eds.), 1987: *The Homeless in Contemporary Society*. Newbury Park, CA.: Sage.

Business Week, 1987: Tax Reform Hurts Apartment Building. *Business Week*, May 4, p. 28.

Campbell, K.E., 1987: *Work Experience of the Homeless*. Paper presented at the Society for the Study of Social Problems. Chicago.

Carliner, M.S., 1987: Homelessness: A Housing Problem? In: R. Bingham, R.E. Green and S.B. White (eds.): *The Homeless in Contemporary Society*. Newbury Park, CA: Sage.

Downs, A., 1983: *Rental Housing in the 1980s*. Washington: The Brookings Institution.

Fainstein, N. and Fainstein, S.S., forthcoming: Urban Renewal. In: E. Huttman, E. and W. Van Vliet-- (eds.): *Handbook on Housing and the Built Environment.* Westport, CT: Greenwood.

Garland, S. and Reilly, J., 1987: Nowhere to Go: Dilemma of the Poor in America. *San Francisco Sunday Examiner and Chronicle*, April 19, pp. 1-8.

Goode, E., 1986: Hotel Owner Ousts Homeless - Mayor Gets Him to Relent. *San Francisco Chronicle*, October 11.

----, 1986: The Filthy Hotels for the Homeless. *San Francisco Chronicle,* October 10, p. 1.

----, 1986: Why S.F. Program for the Homeless Failed to Work. *San Francisco Chronicle,* October 13, p. 6.

---- **and Hsu, E.**, 1986: San Francisco Can't Handle the Homeless. *San Francisco Chronicle*, October 15, p. 6.

Harloe, M., forthcoming: Private Rental Housing. In: E. Huttman and W. Van Vliet-- (eds): *Handbook on Housing and the Built Environment.* Westport, CT: Greenwood.

----, 1985: *Private Rental Housing in the United States and Europe.* London: Croom Helm.

Hartman, C., forthcoming: Housing Affordability. In: E. Huttman and W. Van Vliet-- (eds.): *Handbook on Housing and the Built Environment.* Westport, CT: Greenwood.

----, **Keating, D. and LeGates, R.**, 1982: *Displacement - How to Fight It.* Berkeley: Legal Services Anti-Displacement Project.

Henslin, J., 1985: *Today's Homeless.* Paper presented at the Society for the Study of Social Problems Meeting. Washington, D.C. August.

Hoch, C.., 1986: Homeless in the United States. *Housing Studies* 1, 228-240.

---- **and Huth, M.J.**, forthcoming: The Problem of Homelessness in the United States. In: E. Huttman and W. Van Vliet--, W. (eds.): *Handbook on Housing and the Built Environment.* Westport, CT: Greenwood.

Huttman, E., 1985: Transnational Housing Policy. In: I. Attman and C. Werner (eds.): *Home Environment.* New York: Plenum.

-----, 1985: *Private Rental Housing Crisis.* Paper presented at the International Ad Hoc Committee on Housing and Built Environment Conference. Amsterdam. June.

----, 1985: Policy Approaches to Social Housing Problems in Northern and Western Europe. In: W. Van Vliet--, E. Huttman and S.F. Fava (eds.): *Housing Needs and Policy Approaches in Thirteen Countries.* Durham, NC: Duke University Press.

----, forthcoming: The Elderly and Housing. In: E. Huttman and W. Van Vliet-- (eds.): *Handbook on Housing and the Built Environment.* Westport, CT: Greenwood.

---- **and Huttman, J.**, 1986: *An Economic and Social Analysis of the International Private Rental Housing Crisis.* Paper presented at the International Housing Policy conference. Swedish National Institute of Building Research. Gaevle. June.

Kain, J., 1983: America's Persistant Housing Crises: Errors in Analysis and Policy. *Annals of the American Academy of Political and Social Science* 465, 136-149.

Kasinitz, P., 1984: Gentrification and Homelessness: The Single Room Occupant and the Inner City Revival. *Urban and Social Change Review* 17, 9-14.

Koch, J.Q., 1987: The Federal Role in Aiding the Homeless. In: R.D. Bingham, R.G. Green and S.B. White (eds.): *The Homeless in Contemporary Society.* Newbury Park, CA: Sage.

Lawson, R., 1984: *Owners of Last Resort.* New York: New York City Housing Preservation Department.

Marcuse, P., 1987: Isolating the Homeless. *The Nation*, April.

McChesney, K.Y., 1986: *Homeless Women and Their Children.* Unpublished report of Ford Foundation-funded project.

McLeod, R., 1987: Rent Subsidies for S.F. Poor Often Can't Be Used. *San Francisco Chronicle*, June 29, p. 8.

Murtagh, M., 1987: Government Housing Policy: The PEA Shooter Approach. Keys to Housing. *Eucumenical Association for Housing, San Raphael, CA., Newsletter* 11, p. 2.

National Association of Home Builders, 1986: *Low and Moderate Income Housing: Process, Problems, and Prospects.* Washington, D.C.: NAHB.

National Coalition for the Homeless, 1986a: *New Survey Shows Increase in Homelessness Since 1985.* Press Relase. New York.

----, 1986b: *Suit Filed Against HHS Seeks Relief for Families.* Press Release. New York.

New York Times, 1987: Stop Homelessness Before It Starts. *New York Times*, June 2, p. 34.

O'Connell, B., forthcoming: Cooperative and Condominium Conversions. In: E. Huttman and W. Van Vliet-- (eds.): *Handbook on Housing and the Built Environment.* Westport, CT: Greenwood.

Palen, J., forthcoming: Gentrification, Revitalization, and Displacement. In: E. Huttman and W. Van Vliet-- (eds): *Handbook on Housing and the Built Environment.* Westport, CT: Greenwood.

Pit, F. and W. Van Vliet--, W., forthcoming: Public Housing in the U.S. In: E. Huttman and W. Van Vliet-- (eds.): *Handbook on Housing and the Built Environment.* Westport, CT: Greenwood.

Project FUTURE, 1986: *Project Future: Focusing, Understanding, Targeting, and Utilizing Resources for the Homeless Mentally Ill.* New York: City Human Resources Administration.

----, no date: *Senior Center Survey of Elderly Homeless.* New York: Human Services Administration (Unpublished).

San Francisco Chronicle, 1986: Survey Tells Who Is Homeless in San Francisco. *San Francisco Chronicle.* October 13, p. 7.

San Francisco Housing Authority, 1987: Phone Interview. June 29.

San Francisco Mayor's Task Force on the Homeless, 1986: *One Night Survey of Homeless Shelters.* August (Unpublished).

San Francisco Residence Element, 1984: *The Residence Element of the Comprehensive Plan of the City and County of San Francisco.* Draft for Citizens' Review. San Francisco: Department of City Planning.

Stoner, M.R., 1984: An Analysis of Public and Private Sector Provisions for Homeless People. *Urban and Social Change Review* 17, 1, 3-8.

Snow, D., Baker, S.G., Anderson, L. and Michael, M., 1986: The Myth of Pervasive Mental Illness among the Homeless. *Social Problems* 33, 402-423.

Sullivan, P. and Damroch, S., 1987: Homeless Women and Children. In: R.D. Bingham, R.E. Green and S.B. White (eds.): *The Homeless in Contemporary Society.* Newbury Park, CA: Sage.

U.S. Bureau of the Census: *Annual Housing Survey. 1981 and 1984.* Washington, D.C.: GPO.

U.S. Census, 1987: *10.3 Million Vacant Housing Units.* Press Release. March 22.

U.S. Congressional Budget Office, 1981: *The Tax Treatment of Homeownership: Issues and Options.* Washington, D.C.: GPO.

U.S. General Accounting Office, 1983: *Changes in Rent Burdens and Housing Conditions of Lower Income Households.* GAO/RCED-85-108, April 23. Washington, DC.: GPO.

----, *1985: Changes in Rent Burdens and Housing Conditions of Lower Income Households.* GAO/RCED-85-108, April 25. Washington, D.C.: GPO.

----, 1979: *Rental Housing: A National Problem that Needs Immediate Attention.* Washington, D.C.: GPO.

U.S. Conference of Mayors, 1984: *Report to the Secretary on the Homeless and Emergency Shelters.* Washington, D.C.: U.S. Department of Housing and Urban Development.

----, 1985: *The Growth of Hunger, Homelessness, and Poverty in America's Cities in 1985: A 25 City Survey.* Washington, D.C.: U.S. Department of Housing and Urban Development. Office of Policy Development and Research

Weeden, J. and Linedan, M., 1987: *Elders and Housing Displacement.* San Francisco: University of California Institute for Health and Aging.

Witty, C., 1986: *Homeless Women: Recent Research Findings.* Unpublished Abstract of research at U.C. San Francisco.

Wright, J.D., Rossi, P.H. et al., 1987: Homelessness and Health: The Effects of Life Style on Physical Well-Being among Homeless People in New York City. *Research in Social Problems and Public Policy* 4, Spring.

PATHS IN HOMELESSNESS: A VIEW FROM THE STREET

Dennis Culhane and Marc Fried

Home is the place we belong to, the place which belongs to us. As the stationary sphere of our most private and personal thoughts and feelings, it provides a sense of stability and security as we move about in the environment. It is a precious resource for human well-being.

To be deprived of a home, to be homeless, is to confront the overwhelming sense of being cast out and outcast, to be naked and deserted in the most profoundly social sense. Given the extraordinary human capacity for tolerating the intolerable, for coping with depletion and destitution, even this experience is sometimes moderated, albeit at the expense of many human potentials. The initial realization, however, the dawning recognition that one is homeless is a terrifying experience for many homeless people. Listen to Manny: "When I began to realize that I was actually homeless, I had no place to go, it was a shock that you could never experience without going through ... I was riding the subway back and forth, trying to figure out who was I going to see, what friend of mine was going to be up that time of the night, that time of the morning. Where was I going to get my next meal at. I wasn't used to at that time walking around two or three days without a shower. I wasn't used to looking for a place to eat. I wasn't used to wearing the same clothes. These things, when I began to smell myself, these things told me something about society. These things told me that society says, "You are now unprotected. You are now no good to us". That's what it really told me. I was so hurt, I was so damned angry, and afraid to admit that I was homeless."

Manny has been homeless in a large mid-Western city for nearly two years. As he indicates in his interview, he did not want to admit his homelessness. To admit to himself that he was homeless was to feel, as another homeless man put it, "that you are unloved, unwanted, and that no one gives a crap about you". Estimates of those who are homeless in America vary greatly and, in fact, the actual numbers may vary considerably over time. But the millions who do find themselves without a home encounter a painful experience that is often obscured in analyses, statistics, or charitable agency plans. All too often, reports focus on manifest malfunctioning as a cause or consequence of homelessness, and without adequate attention to the disastrous conditions of life on the streets. A brief review of the literature reveals this clearly.

The last five years have seen a surge in research on and observations about homelessness. Many reports have appeared in the media and have figured prominently in public debate. The image of homelessness which has been popularized in the press

Affordable Housing and the Homeless

(Newsweek, January 6, 1986, p. 1), and encouraged by psychiatric research (see Arce, Tadlock, Vergare and Shapiro, 1985; Bachrack, 1984; Bassuk, 1984, 1986; Bassuk, Rubin and Lauriat, 1984; Jones, 1983; Lamb, 1984; Lipton, Sabatini and Katz, 1983) has characterized the homeless as mentally disabled, disorganized persons, many of whom are castoffs of mental health systems (deinstitutionalization). While it is generally acknowledged that psychological disabilities and inadequate aftercare for mental patients account for some part of the problem of homelessness, the extent to which homelessness is primarily a mental health problem has been vigorously debated (Landers, 1987). Mental health advocates and government officials have been accused of over-stating and over-emphasizing disabilities among the homeless, or "blaming the victims", while housing advocates have been accused of ignoring the fact that the homeless "need more than homes", i.e., health services, education, domestic skills, institutional care.

But the primary focus of existing psychological and psychiatric research has been to explain homelessness by characteristics of the homeless themselves. Whether it is alcoholism (Garret, 1986), chronic psychoses (Bassuk, 1984), personality disorders (Arce et al., 1983), criminal histories (Bassuk, 1984), or abusive tendencies (Bassuk, 1986), homelessness is depicted as a consequence of the problems of homeless people. However, reported prevalence rates of mental illness vary from 20% to 91% (Crystal and Goldstein, 1983; Bassuk et al., 1984) and reports of previous psychiatric hospitalization vary from 10% to 35% (Crane, 1984; Arce et al., 1983): Such *widely* discrepant estimates raise questions about the validity of these research findings and their traditional, diagnostic focus.

Existing studies are problematic for the following methodological and theoretical reasons. (1) Sampling procedures have generally relied upon emergency shelters for men for subjects; shelters, at best, represent only a portion of the homeless population and may introduce their own bias. (2) The class bias and other diagnostic problems of professional psychiatry make the accuracy of diagnosis questionable. Yet, no studies have measured the inter-judge reliability of the diagnoses of homeless people. (3) In these reports it is widely assumed on the basis of correlational data that mental illness causes homelessness, but the hypotheses that homelessness leads to mental illness or is an intervening factor are equally plausible. (4) The deepening problem of homelessness in America among families and working people raises serious questions about the utility of formulating the homelessness debate within a professional discourse such as psychiatry which almost entirely overlooks, not only the social and economic context generally, but quite specifically the enormous costs of housing and the continuing decline of affordable housing in the United States (Even the most sympathetic of these reports, which steer clear of blaming the victim, nonetheless fail to appreciate the potent problem of affordable housing as a major determinant of homelessness). These problems not only suggest alternate avenues for epidemeological research but reveal the need for a deeper understanding of the issues involved. One critical source of information stems from the effort to enable and empower the voices of those who are themselves homeless. And it is our purpose here to allow the homeless to speak for themselves, to present their stories, so we can begin to unravel the complex paths into homelessness. Interviews have been conducted with homeless men and women who are leaders of the National Union of the Homeless, and are quoted here to create a space for the voices of those who are themselves the victims of this serious, worldwide problem.

Disruption and Loss

The literature on stress has familiarized us with the fact that the traumatic events and conditions, the undermining experiences that are encompassed within the term stress, often involve a lag-time before their effects become manifest. And in the intervening stages, many different economic, social, and psychological changes may take place which lead down the path of destitution and the loss of a home. Indeed, more than half the people we interviewed began their stories with the fact that they no longer had a home but were unable to confront the devastating reality of homelessness.

For Jim, a middle-aged man who lived in a metropolitan area in the South, "a bad divorce" began his search for a new life. "I foolishly quit my job. I had $1,500.00 with me, and I went to Miami and I figured I'd easily get a job 'cause I can type. I've done a number of jobs in my life, and I figured it would be very easy." Only able to find sporadic employment through temporary labor pools, Jim's money ran out, and he could no longer afford a week's rent for a room. All of the eight people interviewed have similar stories of a life disruption, followed by living with friends, relatives, in a car, or in cheap rented rooms, until finally money runs out. The initial disruptions were as varied as a business failure, divorce, domestic abuse, layoffs, eviction, or escaping a living situation embroiled with drugs. And, despite intense economic and personal stress, despite many courageous and many desperate efforts to keep things together, to maintain a modicum of stability, all of these men and women were swept into the streets sooner or later.

As with other stress experiences and consequences, the road to homelessness is usually a slow transformation. As one man describes it: "It was a gradual thing ... spending some period of time with friends, and really very rapidly, very quickly wearing out my welcome there. So that was a slow process, and all the time money was very swiftly moving away from me. I was spending and nothing was coming in. Looking for jobs and job interviews, and food, and trying to maintain my clothes, and plus a car."

Roger's realization of his being homeless came after months of struggling to recover from a business failure: "My business went bankrupt and my whole life fell apart. I guess there was no question, even though I started sleeping in the car, and on very cold nights staying in the Third Street shelter in New York City, I still didn't consider myself homeless until the car was vandalized, my clothes were stolen, and I was completely broke. In fact it was just such a shock that the moment that I realized that I was homeless without clothes, without any material things at all, and that I was just absolutely naked in the world ..., I ended up in Bellevue Hospital, in the psych ward there."

Another man, Richard, worked for sixteen years with a company that began farming out work to cheaper overseas labor. Consequently, Richard lost his job and became homeless. Yet, as he and the others were quick to detail, the conditions which one finds for the homeless are inadequate at best, and often cruel and damaging in their own right. Shocked by his own homelessness, now Richard faces a world of temporary labor pools, emergency shelters, long food lines, and harassment from police, thugs, and thieves. But that first, forced recognition of the very *fact* of his homelessness was most demoralizing. After working a long day on temporary labor, Richard sat down one evening in the subway to catch some sleep. "I was awakened about 2:00 in the morning", he reports, "by four policemen and two German Shepherd dogs. And I just sat down there and I said to myself, you know I did everything I was supposed to do. I went to school, I was mischievous as a child, but not a violent child. I went in the service. I came out of service. I worked. I took care of my children. Why? Why is this happening to me? And I started blaming myself for it, you know, and I felt my sanity sort of slipping away from me, because at that moment I wanted to attack the policemen and the dogs".

Initial Stresses

For most of the homeless people we interviewed, the shock of the recognition of their homelessness was so stark and sudden because they were totally unprepared for this situation on the basis of childhood or adult experience. And, in fact, the combination of events and chance occurrences could rarely have been anticipated. Manny tells about his tragic experience: "First of all, I have to say I worked from the time I knew what work was up until the time I got laid off. I used to work for a food distributor ... Two days before Thanksgiving in 1984 I was laid off. The impact ... I really hate to think about that. It was a situation that Thanksgiving time, two days away, you're all hyped up and then someone snatches the rug out from under you. I had an apartment. I was paying $400 a month rent, I had a telephone ... and a house full of furniture, a car, and I mean I had what society says makes you wealthy. And I worked hard to get it ... And when I was told that I was laid off, my American dream went down the stream. When I got back out there, in the rat race, applying for a job and putting in applications and, at the same time, trying to figure out what am I going to do with my stuff, my personal belongings. I had a ten year stamp collection. And when I seen that stamp collection disappear, I just said fuck it ...".

Richard, whose job loss we previously described when his factory declined under foreign competition, tells a similar story. "I have worked all my teenage and adult life", he says. "I never was out of work longer than a week at any time in my life". He was one of the last three people to be kept on in the factory where he worked. "And", he goes on, "at that particular time jobs just weren't there, or .. the type of jobs that was there I had no training for, even though I had a high school education. So after my employment compensation exhausted, I had to give up the apartment ... because surely welfare wasn't enough at that time ... So I went out there into Southern New Jersey ... and worked out there on the farms ... picking peaches, and then when the apple season came, I went out there picking apples. They pay you minimum wage ... You worked nine hours if you were lucky ... You have to get up 3:00 in the morning ... We'd all meet at this one place in order to catch the bus. And there you ran into a problem also ... There's one bus, and there's about 150-200 people who want to try to get on that bus. And the bus only takes between 40 and 45 people. So if you made it then, all right, so then you go to work. If you worked there nine hours, then you made thirty dollars and fifteen cents. Now if you are homeless and don't have anywhere to go, the next morning you're lucky if you got $10 or $15 still in your pocket. Why? Because you spend more money being homeless in the street. You go into a restaurant and eat and pay five or six dollars on a meal ... You cannot go in, being homeless, you can't go and buy enough food, then cook it, and what you don't eat you put away...".

And then there is Darlene. She says: "My story surrounds low-income, affordable housing and in the fact of being in an abusive situation. In 1985 I was pregnant, five months pregnant. I was ill at the time and had to be hospitalized. As she indicates later, this was due to a beating and a kick in the stomach from her batterer. "The doctors stated", she goes on, "that they didn't want me to work ... so I had to stop working ... I could no longer afford my apartment and from the hospital I went straight into a shelter ... They placed me in a battered women's shelter, which I ended up staying in ... for a total of 13 months. My son was born during that time, and I just felt so lost, so alone ... I spent six years in the army, and I've always had an excellent work history. I attended college, I was a student majoring in sociology ... I am a cosmetologist but there was nothing ... there weren't any jobs, and there wasn't any daycare in the shelter ... My son was a newborn infant, and I couldn't even afford milk, so I had to breastfeed my son".

Generally, the tragic histories have a great deal in common. In only one of these instances do we have a situation involving drugs, a pattern that may represent a sub-group quite different from those homeless people we interviewed. But even Josh's situation reflected his getting caught up in circumstances he could no longer control and finding himself gradually becoming homeless. "The guy I was sharing an apartment with", he tells us, "was always into cocaine, smoking, even before we got the apartment together. But I figured, you know, I didn't and that I could continue to not deal with drugs and cocaine. Living under them conditions I was wrong. Him, his lady, a couple of friends would come over, they would have smoke parties ... and that leads on after you get high, the fun, the activity, the women. It tends to draw you in and make you want to be a part of that. So eventually I got into it, and ... cocaine isn't something to get into because if you get into it, you'll like it ...". Homelessness, in Josh's case, was inevitable because, as he says, "Every bit of money you make is going towards getting drugs, staying high, you know, just getting high every day. You work, you live to get high tomorrow".

Life on the Streets

Living on the streets as a homeless person means spending your days - and nights - in dark, forbidding, and unforgiving passages. The initial stresses that precipitate or implement the misfortunes of homelessness are further compounded by unremitting bruises and barriers. Daytime has its massive problems. Nighttime has its terrors. For the majority who are not able to get a bed in an emergency shelter, they must develop their own means for making it through the night.

First, of course, there is the necessity of sleeping, to be capable of searching for a job or an apartment. One of the men describes sleeping on the subway. "When you get to the end of the line there's always another train waiting to go back on the other side. Go back north or south. I seen pickpockets work on the L. You pull into every station and you open up one eye because you don't want nobody picking your pocket. You ain't got nothing, it's just a thing that you would normally do. Sense of security for yourself. I've slept in the back of cars, also slept in abandoned buildings, not thinking of the danger of the roof collapsing, the dangers of the rat bite, the danger of just the walls collapsing. You know you're tired, who cares about that shit when you're tired. You just want to go in and lay down. Basically on the street sleeping in those conditions, you don't get a good two hours straight sleep. You're always waking up, you know, noise on the street, noise within the building".

Another man, Jim, describes it this way, "You're not able to sleep because wherever you sleep you're, someone is going to challenge you, even when you stay in Charity Hospital. The guard will come around and say, are you a patient here, and somehow, they'll kick you out ... You sleep in an abandoned house, you don't know if the police are going to come in and arrest you, or if some crook or robber is going to come in and hurt you while you're asleep. At least three homeless men since I've been in New Orleans have been found dead, beaten to death, in these abandoned buildings".

Richard explains that he sometimes avoids shelters, "I was opposed to going into a shelter because I had heard about shelters in the city, and I know how it's run, and I knew there was no way in hell I was going to endure that abusive treatment, inhumane treatment, that exists in these shelters ... and I couldn't see my life being dependent on someone ... So you get varied (sleep) because you sleep with fear. See, a lot of the times we are victims of being mugged ourselves because we are very vulnerable. Why are we vulnerable? Because number one we are deprived of food, we don't get the proper rest. So therefore we are weakened to whoever decides they want to mug us, or rob us, or anything. They usually hang around the welfare offices, and watch whoever comes and goes, and then they walk down a street, a dark alley at night, sometimes we ourselves are robbed ... You're living in fear of your life also, as well as your health".

But it is not only the difficulties of finding a place and a way to sleep. The same problems attend every aspect of life: eating, shelter from the elements, going to the toilet, taking a shower, finding a way to look respectable in seeking a job, and trying to get medical help.

Manny talks about trying to use the bathrooms in a local college. "We used to sneak in through the side doors. ... It's a public building but they don't want people in there who's not going to school. But ... my tax dollars helped to build that school. ... Some of us who like to clean ourselves carry some soap and a rag or something. When you get around some hot water that's the first thing you want to use. For those of them who do want to shave, they got a razor, just use the McDonald's up there. ... You can't keep yourself up, make yourself presentable even when you do go looking for jobs; you still look like a bum...".

And Richard talks about the humiliation of trying to get medical treatment. As he talks, other sources of his anger and sense of maltreatment begin to well up. "When you go to the hospital and tell them that number one, you don't have a medical card, they'll just band-aid you, give you a pill and send you back out there on the streets because, I mean, you're nothing to them ... And that's the people that turn and call us drunks. That's not really so. Sometimes people buy drinks, or buy a bottle of wine. It might be cold out there. This is the way that they get warm. They just get drunk, and there's heat in there, or just because all day long they had, all the shit they had to go through. All the elements of eating, of sleeping, just merely surviving".

It is evident that, certainly for many of the homeless, the path to functioning effectively, to getting back to a decent way of living, is fraught with myriad and often wholly unreasonable impediments. Darlene finds this to be so up to the very last. After many struggles, she finally was able to obtain a 707 housing subsidy certificate (allows people to rent housing in the private market and receive some part of their rental cost from the federal government). As she says, "... with that certificate you have to still, you have to run around the whole city and try to find some realtor or some landlord that will accept the certificate ... So I moved into (an) apartment after thirteen months of being homeless, and it was a rat infested, sleazy, rundown place. So I'm still homeless. Right now I'm homeless. I cannot accept this as being home. I'm still trying to get on my feet. I need, I don't even have forks. ... you find a place to live, then you have to find a way to survive in that empty shell of a house ... So you're still depressed at each and every angle. Where's the way out?"

Finally, Jim describes an encounter with the police which shows how the homeless continue to be exploited for cheap or free labor, subject to the whims of the police. "A van will come around and we hear the officers in the van joking that they need so many people, and this is why we're around today, and they sometimes they ask you if you have any medical problems like once I was sleeping underneath a bridge, and they came around, and they hadn't been around, I understand they hadn't been around in weeks or months, and they said, we need a lot of people to work. We need a lot of prisoners. And they ask you your medical history, whether you have any problems, and I told them I had a heart problem, but they realized I was bullshitting ... The people who seemed in good shape, they piled them in the van and took them to jail, and after that they started working

... They come up with these amazing charges and every time you see a homeless person he pulls out his arrest sheet says look what they got me on this time and everybody has a big laugh about it, but it's really frustrating and makes you just feel angry".

The threat of arrest, and the subsequent problems which that causes, such as loss of a job, or a potential criminal record, these are used as forces to continue taming the homeless, as well as fulfilling the need in the society to have certain public, menial labor done, which no one wants to do. These are among the forces that shape the social construction of the homeless and their homelessness. The very agencies that are designed to ameliorate the most urgent features of the problems of the homeless, the shelters, mainly serve to sustain the sense of degradation and powerlessness. The threat of losing a bed, and the struggle to obtain entrance to the shelters, and the dangers of victimization, help to keep the homeless docile in this site which only exacerbates their helplessness.

The Shelter System

Superficially women and families receive more consideration in their efforts to stay within shelters than do single men but, more often than not, they all share the shocking and obscene life of the temporary shelters. A phenomenon hailed as a solution by many government officials indeed is one of the cruelest forms of bureaucratic dehumanization.

Darlene, whose situation we described in earlier sections, was battered by her husband, and found herself in need of emergency shelter. Actually giving birth to her son in a shelter, without childcare available she was forced to take her newborn son with her everywhere, searching for a job, for an apartment, and spending hours in the burger King to keep warm and to breastfeed her baby. "I wasn't getting the proper care, the healthcare, or anything that I needed. The counselors, in fact, they would speak about things right in front of our faces as though we ... weren't comprehending what they would say. There was a particular incident that happened at one of the shelters, the battered women's shelters ... where the staff actually was stealing the food. Me and the other women in the household had to sneak down in the cellars after midnight and the freezers were bound with chains and we had to try to lift up that freezer to get food for that week and to feed our families that were in the shelter. The shelter providers were taking our necessities, our basic necessities, for surviving in there; they were taking our toilet tissue, our soaps, I mean everything, our deodorants, I mean you know, it's unfair. It's unfair".

The shelter system serves to ameliorate the guilt of society by its appearance of harboring the down and out, the homeless. In fact it only serves to keep people alive and communicates its message o the homeless, that keeping alive is all that can be done for them. As institutions of social control, the shelters tend to confirm people's self-blame, to increase their feelings of helplessness, and to perpetuate their powerlessness by denying virtually all opportunities to allow people to control their own lives. In the rituals of obtaining food and shelter, the homeless are forced to be utterly dependent and without a voice, often denied even the minimal chances to improve their situations.

Roger provides a graphic picture of what one can expect to see if one becomes homeless and must rely on an emergency shelter. Turned away by his brother for a place to stay, Roger tells us, "I walked to the center of the city, and met a policeman, and told him I was stranded overnight ... and was there someplace I could spend the night, because I was without funds. And he directed me to the city-run Drop In Center. And I went around and they rang the bell, and they sent me around to the back. And in the back alley, in the back of the shelter, there were about 200 people in all states, some drinking. People huddled around a can, a 55-gallon can with dropped wood fire in it. Some people at the steam vents. I mean I just couldn't believe the whole amount of people. And at some point the back door opened and a kind of man came out. He was a counselor and announced that women came in first and all the women went in and when the women went in, it was just a free-for-all. People fighting, men fighting their way in. And I went through that for three days and three nights and I just never got in ... For two nights I said I'm not going to go through this bullshit, I'm not going to be fighting no one to get inside. I also said look, they're like animals, they're fighting like animals. I'm not going through this shit, ... I won't dignify this kind of bullshit by engaging in it. But on the third night I was completely exhausted, and just decided that I was going to fight my way in. And they said women in, and after the women went in I fought my way in and went in. What I fought to get in was a basement where they had fifty chairs and as you go down the steps there's a counselor at the head of the steps that gives you a peanut butter and jelly sandwich. And you go downstairs, and at that time there was some coffee there, and they let in men and women. And there were fifty hard back chairs that you sat in all night 'til six o'clock in the morning and then they'd turn you out at six o'clock in the morning".

Tired, full of anger and shame, the homeless are pitted against one another to get even a chair in a basement on which to rest. Roger continues, "After I got a nice rest, my thing with the counselor was where can I go look for a job at, could I use this place as a reference, can I use a typewriter to type a resume, can I use the telephone, can I go out, you know during the daytime, and look for some work, and then come in at night. And people looked at me like I was some kind of weird animal from a strange planet. Absolutely not, that everything that I said was against the policies of that organization, that once I was in there I had to stay for the three days, and then be released on the third day, and then wait a week, and then I could come back again for three more days ... And that's it. People laid around for those three days, watched television, played cards, and that was essentially it".

The shelters exist as a private-public partnership, and in every city, the number of people far outnumbers existing beds. The shelters function on implicit assumptions that create invalids among those who are disabled, and downgrade the needs of those who are not disabled, but in need of assistance to locate jobs, job training and housing. By derogating and downgrading, shelter providers are exonerated from any responsibilities except those of keeping some homeless alive. But the shelter providers are merely low-level proxies for societal attitudes. In a Southern city, Jim tells us that "At the Salvation Army (they have) 200 beds, and at Baptist Mission about 300. So they've got roughly 600 beds for 4,000 homeless people." Unlike other cities, the only existing shelters actually charge people $5-$8 per night. Manny explains the role of shelters this way, "The shelter system was established to help keep you in that binding condition. *You* are there. *They're* getting paid. They don't want to see you leave. All they want is a head count ... They don't even care if that's my name ... Suppose I'm supposed to be taking medication. They should know that. Suppose I've got relatives in the south, and suppose I die. They should know that. They don't take this kind of information. All they take is a body count ... They ought to know how to identify people for what they are, and not for what they think they are ... Once there were times when I had to get up in the morning to go apply for a job and I tell them they had to wake me up at 5:00 in the morning. He oversleeps. I oversleep, and therefore I can't leave the shelter system. So then therefore I'm totally dependent on them again, as long as I keep coming to them, as long as homeless people keep going to the shelters, and as long as the shelters keep saying 'well, what else can we do?' They don't -- the shelter system do not consult homeless people for what they know their needs are. The shelter system sits there and dictates what they think the homeless people's needs are. The homeless people don't have any input, as to the rules of the shelter, what is needed in the shelter, how do we view the shelter".

Silenced, excluded, and left to fight for survival, this is the outcome of perceptions of the homeless which make them undeserving, and in characteristic fashion result in blaming the victims. In this way, the shelters and the labor market together encourage dependency upon a Band-Aid system of temporary and emergency services.

Conclusion

During the past year and even more recently than that, increased attention to the homeless has modified, without entirely altering, the stigmatization of the homeless. In focusing mainly on the language, observation, and thoughts of the homeless themselves, we have tried to fill in some large lacunae and to compensate for other reports. Frequently, the discussions by psychiatrists, social scientists, and public officials try to explain the conditions of the homeless in terms of characteristics of the homeless themselves. Much of this discussion virtually ignores the economic, social, and cultural contexts in which homelessness occurs and opts for an individualistic psychologism. The homeless and the conditions of homelessness are presented as caricatures, frozen in a space which silences them, makes them into outlandish images of tramps, bums, alcoholics and psychotics. Some meager factors that may, indeed, provide a partial accounting for some small proportion of the homeless population, are generalized beyond all warrant. Even the sympathetic discussions often view the homeless as unfortunate failures without adequately evaluating the ways in which our society facilitates the process of skidding economically, socially, psychologically. Thus, the discussion is wrapped around the homeless, to cloak them in a pseudo-explanatory otherness which ends up controlling them *and* our understanding of them.

For these reasons we have felt it essential to tell of the suffering, the anguish, and the painful realization which accompanies the paths to homelessness. In this sense, we have tried to provide a place for homeless people to contest the naming and stigmatization which silences them and to challenge the formulation of homelessness which relegate them to an undignified, dehumanized space.

Not only are the realities of homelessness graphic statements about advanced capitalist society, perhaps about all mass societies, but they point to ways in which such abuse and inhumanity is sustained. Primary among these staying forces is the language which keeps homeless people in powerless positions, which isolates them from access to gaining stability and control in their lives. Throughout the interviews there are stories of strategies used by people to survive. But time and time again, the homeless are met with the most absurd of circumstances. Trying to locate a bathroom, a place to shower, waiting four hours in line for soup and a stale sandwich: these are some of the countless examples of ways in which society encourages the demeaning and degradation of a whole mass of people who are already suffering from inadequate resources. Moreover, the care systems that society has established serve more of a function of sustaining dependency and powerlessness, than of mobilizing people for real change. Without attempting a detailed examination of the options for coping with the problems of homelessness, a brief example may help to point to one important direction.

As was stated earlier, the people interviewed for this paper are members of the National Union of the Homeless. The National Union was founded in Philadelphia in October, 1985, by homeless people, for the collective empowerment of the homeless, socially and politically. The strategy of the organization has been to disrupt service agencies, governmental forums, construction projects, and tourist districts, to call attention to the anger and militancy of homeless people. Chris Sprowal, himself homeless, and a former labor organizer, led 6,000 of Philadelphia's homeless in winning voting rights, the right to shelter, better pay and fairness from the temporary labor pools, and better access to employment training and education. After three years of sit-ins, blockades, building take-overs, and protests, Mayor Wilson Goode of Philadelphia agreed in March to give the Philadelphia Union 200 units of housing and $7.2 million.

The Union of the Homeless has now organized in 10 cities across the U.S., and claims a membership in 1987 of some 20,000 people. In each city, common themes emerge, and common political struggles. A popular tactic with the homeless has been the take-over of emergency shelters, a tactic unpopular with service providers and many homeless advocates. But the locals have maintained that the seizure of power at the shelters represents the unfettering of the population, and makes possible the movement of empowerment and social change among the homeless. In fact, two locals now run shelters, and have used them as organizing and leadership training centers. These shelters are entirely staffed by homeless people, and each offers literacy programs, job-placement programs, and community organizing classes. The Union of the Homeless is just one example of how involving victims in the challenge of their own circumstances helps to enlighten research and policy, but more importantly, it helps people to re-capture the dignity which they lose in the face of narrowly defined services and degrading living conditions.

Roger, in a deeply philosophical vein closes the issue for us: "We cannot continue to live where we have 'haves' and 'have-nots' in the wealthiest nation in the world. And we cannot continue to talk about millions of dollars going to dictatorships in other countries and building things like Star Wars and upping the arms race. We have people who live in poverty who go to bed hungry at night being born in shelters; born homeless in the richest country in the world. I don't think that we have any other choice but to be out there organizing, but to be galvanizing, but to be saying that we have to look for something that's going to work for us, we have to take government back and get it going. We have to run it on a fair and equal basis, not on your ability to have money and the whole question that we're a commodity. Homeless people have become a commodity in this country. In fact, we have become a growth industry. That alone tells me how sinister this kind of system is, that we can make a profit off the misery of homeless and poor people, and we have to change it".

References

Arce, A., Tadloc, M. Vergare, M. and Shapiro, O. S., 1983: A Psychiatric Profile of Street People Admitted to an Emergency Shelter. *Hospital and Community Psychiatry* 34, 812-817.

Backrack, L., 1984: Interpreting Research on the Homeless Mentally Ill: Some Caveats. *Hospital and Community Psychiatry* 34, 914-916.

Bassuk, E., 1984: The Homelessness Problem. *Scientific American* 251, 40-45.

----, 1986: *Characteristics of Massachusetts Sheltered Homeless Families*. Paper presented at Homelessness Conference, Harvard Medical School. Cambridge, MA.

----, **Rubin, L. and Lauriat**, A., 1984: Is Homelessness a Mental Health Problem? *American Journal of Psychiatry* 141, 1546-1550.

Crane, S., 1984: *Rhode Island MH-HR Department Reports on the Homeless Mentally Ill*. State Report, National Association of State Mental Health Program Directors. Washington, DC.

Crystal, S. and Goldstein, M., 1983: *New Arrivals: First-Time Shelter Clients*. New York: Human Resources Administration.

Garret, G., 1986: *Alcoholism and the Homeless*. Paper presented at the Homelessness Conference, Harvard Medical School. Cambridge, MA.

Jones, R., 1983: Street People and Psychiatry: An Introduction. *Hospital and Community Psychiatry* 34, 807-811.

Lamb, H., 1984: Deinstitutionalization and the Homeless Mentally Ill. *Hospital and Community Psychiatry* 35 (a), 899-907.

Landers, S., 1987: Homeless Families: Roots of Crisis Debated. *The APA Monitor* 18a, 4-5.

Lipton, F., Sabatini, A. and Katz, S., 1983: Down and Out in the City: The Homeless Mentally Ill. *Hospital and Community Psychiatry* 34, 817-821.

Newsweek, 1986: Abandoned: They are America's Castoffs - Turned Away from Mental Institutions and Into the Streets. Who Will Care for Them? *Newsweek*, January 6, 1986, p.1.

ABOUT THE AUTHORS

Dennis Culhane is currently doctoral candidate in Psychology at Boston College, Chestnut Hill, MA, U.S.A. He does research on social inequality and its psychological effects. He has worked with the National Union of the Homelessness for the past two years, most recently serving as the National Director of Technical Assistance and Organizing.

Jane Darke is currently a lecturer in housing, administration and policy at Sheffield City Polytechnic. She has researched, taught and written extensively on housing including an introductory text *Who Needs Housing* 1979 Macmillan (with Roy Darke) and a doctoral thesis *The Design of Public Housing: Architects' Intentions and Users Reactions* (1983). From 1983 to 1987 she worked in housing management in local authority area teams in Sheffield and Haringey, London.

Roy Darke is Director of Urban Studies, University of Sheffield. He has researched and written in the areas of housing, local government, public participation, town planning, planning theory and policy-making. His current interests in housing in the developing world was fired by recent visits to Central America and India. Recent action research undertaken includes work as principal consultant to Sheffield City Council on public participation in the central area plan and running an advisory service for community organisations seeking help with building and environmental projects.

Dan Ferrand-Bechman is Maitre des Conférences at the University of Grenoble and deputeee at the Department of Social Affairs and Employment in Paris. Her major interest is in housing problems and participation of dwellers in cities of Western Europe. She has contributed chapters to several French and English scholarly publications..

Marc Fried is currently Professor of Psychology and research professor of Human Sciences at Boston College, Chestnut Hill, MA, U.S.A. He has studied the role of the neighborhood, community life and the determinants of residential, community and life satisfactions. Along with his long-term studies of stress and malfunctioning, he has more recently become involved with the study of adult developmental changes and the social factors associated with mental disorder. He also has been examining homelessness and the dynamics of victimization.

Jürgen Friedrichs is Professor of Sociology in the Department of Sociology, University of Hamburg, and Director of the Center for Comparative Urban Sociology. He is a Senior Fellow of the Metro Center of the Johns Hopkins University, Baltimore. He has done extensive studies on urban structure and change of cities in Western and Eastern Europe, downtown development, urban unemployment (with John D. Kasarda), social ecology, and urban theory. Among the more recent publications are: *The Changing Downtown* (1987) and Large Cities in Eastern Europe (In: *The Metropolis Era*, Vol. 1, edited by M. Dogan and J.D. Kasarda, 1988). He has edited and co-authored *Urban Development in Western and Eastern Europe* (1985) and *Cities in the 1980s* (1985) He is currently working on problems of spatial effects of new technologies.

Ray Forrest, is teaching at the School for Advanced Urban Studies at the University of Bristol, Bristol, U.K. His major interest is in housing problems and housing policy. On these topics he has published several articles in international scholarly journals.

Elizabeth Huttman is Professor of Sociology at California State University, Hayward, and was formerly professor at the University of British Columbia and Visiting Scholar at the University of California Berkeley. She is co-editor of *Housing Needs and Policy Approaches: Trends in Thirteen Countries* (1985); author of *Housing and Social Services for the Elderly* (1977); *Handbook of Housing* (1988), and *Introduction to Social Policy* (1981). She has written chapters on housing in many books. She is co-organizer of the International Sociological Association Committee on Housing and the Built Environment. Her special interests are comparative housing policy and housing affordability.

Arne Karyd, master of economics and political science, is affiliated to the University of Gothenburg and the consulting organization GSU. Earlier reports and papers cover mainly various issues within the construction and housing sectors, energy conservation and planning, railway economy, and democracy within the planning process. Present work deals with the forrest industry and the cost structure in domestic air traffic.

Antonin Kerner is Professor of Economics at the Charles University in Prague, CSSR. His major fields of interest and publication are the changes in the economic structure and the role of the service sector in socialist countries, urban change, and housing policies. Among his more recent publications are *The Scientific-Technological Revolution and the Development of Services* (1975), and *Perspectives of the Service Sector* (1982).

Alan Murie is Senior Lecturer at the School for Advanced Urban Studies at the University of Bristol, Bristol, U.K. He has recently edited *Living in Bed and Breakfast: The Experience of Homelessness in London* (1987).

David C. Thorns is Professor of Sociology and Head of the Department of Sociology of the University of Canterbury, Cristchurch, New Zealand. He has done reasearch on suburbanization, urban change, and housing problems and policies in Australia and New Zealand. He has published books and written articles in several international scholarly journals. Among his recent publications is Owner Occupation, the State, and Class Relations in New Zealand (in *In the Public Interest*, edited by C. Wilkes and I. Shirley, 1983).

Wouter Turpijn is Associate Professor in urban studies, University of Utrecht, The Netherlands, Department of Urban and Industrial Studies. He is the author of books and articles on sociological and interdisciplinary reserach on urban development, renewal and maintenance; dwellers' participation and self-help housing, including e.g., self-building by dwellers and the actions of communes, dweller-organizations and squatters.

Willem van Vliet-- is an urban and environmental sociologist at the University of Colorado, Boulder, U.S.A. His research interests concern international housing, neighborhood and community planning, and the environmental requirements of women, children, and the elderly. He has contributed widely to anthologies and journals in urban studies, planning, and environment-behavior studies and is editor or co-editor of seven *books, including Housing Markets and Policies under Fiscal Authority (1987), Women, Housing and Community* (in press), and the *International Handbook of Housing Policies and Practices* (forthcoming).